THE POLICE SMELLED A RAT

Albert Snyder's body was in his bed under a pile of covers, two gashes on his head and a wire tourniquet twisted so tightly around his neck that the wire almost couldn't be seen beneath the flesh. His hands were bound with wire, also, and his feet with a necktie. Pieces of chloroform-saturated cotton were stuffed into his mouth and nose. A loaded revolver, broken open at the breach, was lying next to him. His wife, Ruth, said she had been knocked out by a rough-looking Italian man and left tied up in the hallway.

But, the whole crime scene didn't add up.

The doctor could find no injuries on Ruth Snyder, neither to her head nor where the ropes had loosely bound her. The pearls she claimed were missing were found under her mattress, the fur coat in the back of the closet. There was no sign of forced entry and all the windows were still locked. And what thief would leave a loaded gun and a scrap of paper from an Italian newspaper behind?

It was only the tip of the iceberg. Police were quick to find a canceled check made out to H. Judd Gray—Ruth's illicit lover . . . and the $45,000 insurance policy with the double-indemnity clause were Albert to die a violent death.

Murder One was the only conclusion—and Ruth Snyder was the prime suspect!

BOOK YOUR PLACE ON OUR WEBSITE AND MAKE THE READING CONNECTION!

We've created a customized website just for our very special readers, where you can get the inside scoop on everything that's going on with Zebra, Pinnacle and Kensington books.

When you come online, you'll have the exciting opportunity to:

- View covers of upcoming books
- Read sample chapters
- Learn about our future publishing schedule (listed by publication month *and author*)
- Find out when your favorite authors will be visiting a city near you
- Search for and order backlist books from our online catalog
- Check out author bios and background information
- Send e-mail to your favorite authors
- Meet the Kensington staff online
- Join us in weekly chats with authors, readers and other guests
- Get writing guidelines
- AND MUCH MORE!

Visit our website at
http://www.pinnaclebooks.com

MURDERESS!

LESLIE MARGOLIN

Pinnacle Books
Kensington Publishing Corp.
http://www.pinnaclebooks.com

PINNACLE BOOKS are published by

Kensington Publishing Corp.
850 Third Avenue
New York, NY 10022

First Printing: December, 1999
10 9 8 7 6 5 4 3 2 1

Printed in the United States of America

For Linda

"This woman, this peculiar, venomous species of humanity, was abnormal, possessed of an all-consuming, all-absorbing sexual passion, animal lust, which seemingly was never satisfied."

—From the trial of Ruth Snyder and Judd Gray

"When I walked I listened for my step—no sound seemed to follow."

—Judd Gray

"I couldn't hear my footsteps. It was the walk of a dead man."

—Walter Neff in *Double Indemnity*,
script by Raymond Chandler and Billy Wilder
from the novel by James M. Cain

Contents

Part I   The Crime, the Confessions, the Dramatis Personae

1.	Strangled	11
2.	Ruth Snyder Confesses	25
3.	Judd Gray Confesses	41
4.	The Murderee	59
5.	Mother Love	73

Part II   The Trial

6.	Queens County Courthouse	93
7.	Ruth Snyder's Defense	116
8.	Judd Gray's Defense	135
9.	She Takes the Stand: "Judd Did It."	140
10.	She Holds Her Own—then Crumbles	159
11.	He Takes the Stand: "Ruth Did It."	185
12.	Murder Night: "Help me, Momie!"	208
13.	Saint Judd	218
14.	Fair Ruth	234
15.	The Verdict	239

Part III   The Aftermath

16.	Parade to Death House	253
17.	Death Watch	267
18.	*Dead!*	274
19.	Resurrection	279

PART I

*The Crime, the Confessions,
the Dramatis Personae*

1

Strangled

On the morning of March 20, 1927, New Yorkers were thinking winter was officially over. The sun was glorious. Sea birds floated majestically in the bright blue skies and children were outside, playing stickball in short-sleeve shirts.

No place in the City looked more tranquil than the two-and-a-half-story frame home of Albert Snyder, age forty-six, his wife, Ruth, thirty-two, and their nine-year-old daughter, Lorraine. Located in Queens Village, just across the East River from Manhattan, it was set back about four feet from the sidewalk, providing just room enough for a suspicion of lawn and two half-grown maples. Except for a few architectural touches—a large white colonial door, a vine-covered trellis, and a homemade bird fountain in the backyard—the house looked almost as if it were a mimeograph copy of the others on the block.

It was ridiculous that this house could be the scene of a murder, but slowly, unmistakably, some signs emerged.

At seven-thirty A.M., Lorraine Snyder was awakened by an urgent tapping near her bedroom door. She was slow to respond because she had been out past two A.M. with her mother and father at a neighbor's party. She sprang out of bed finally when she heard her mother's voice call her name in a weak, barely audible whisper—"Lorraine, Lorraine."

When she opened her door, she found her mother, a fairly stout woman with a milky white complexion, stretched out in the hallway, her feet bound with clothesline. Some cheesecloth was tied across her mouth and a rope wound loosely around her wrists.

"Mother, what's happened?" cried Lorraine.

Her mother did not answer at first, but tugged awkwardly with her tied-up hands at the cheesecloth. Then, speaking through the ineffectual gag, she ordered her daughter to get help. Not stopping to untie her mother, Lorraine ran across the street to their neighbors, Louis and Harriet Mulhauser.

In a matter of minutes, Harriet Mulhauser was in the Snyder home, where she found Ruth Snyder still trussed on the floor. The one change was that Mrs. Snyder was now able to talk freely. She had somehow managed to remove the cheesecloth gag on her own. It lay beside her, on the floor. She babbled hysterically—something about two Italian thugs who whacked her over the head.

Mrs. Mulhauser told Lorraine to call the police and fetch Mr. Mulhauser, her husband. When Mr. Mulhauser got there, his wife urged him to go into Albert Snyder's bedroom to see if he was all right.

Mulhauser opened the bedroom door. The covers on one of the Snyders' twin beds were piled in a heap, with two or three bloodstains visible on the sheets. Mulhauser looked under the pile of covers and found the body of Albert Snyder. There were two great gashes on his head, and a picture-wire tourniquet looped around his throat. A metal pencil had been inserted into the tourniquet's eye and twisted so tightly that most of the picture wire couldn't be seen, buried beneath the folds of Snyder's flesh. His hands were bound with a bit of the same wire, and his feet tied with a necktie. Pieces of chloroform-saturated cotton waste were stuffed into his nose and mouth, and tear marks were visible on his neck. A loaded revolver, broken open at the breach, was lying next to the body on the sheet.

When the police arrived, Ruth Snyder was barely coherent. She fainted and screamed frequently. It was hard to question her, but the police managed to put together her story.

She and her husband and their daughter, Lorraine, had returned to their home at two A.M. from a bridge party at a friend's house. Her husband let her and Lorraine out of the car at the curb, then put the car away in the garage. Her husband, she said, went to bed at once, as did Lorraine. Mrs. Snyder said she was partially undressed when she heard footsteps in the hallway of the second floor. She was under the impression that they belonged to her daughter, believing that Lorraine was ill from something she had eaten at the party that night. She rose from her dressing table and went into the hallway to see if Lorraine was all right. She proceeded as far as the entrance to a room usually occupied by her mother, a practical nurse who was on duty that night, when a big, rough-looking individual with a black mustache seized her around the body and threw her into her mother's room. Then he hit her over the head. That was all she remembered.

The police asked her if she made any outcry, and she said no.

"In view of the fact that you knew that your husband had a revolver under his pillow, why didn't you try to warn him?" one of the policemen asked.

"I don't quite see what you're getting at, Officer," she replied.

"I'm saying that your silence is hard to understand."

Indeed, as the situation evolved, nothing she told the police made very much sense. Most glaring of her inconsistencies was the story she gave of being hit over the head. The physician who examined her could find no bump on her head or other external injuries to account for her long period of unconsciousness, nor were her wrists or ankles lacerated by ropes. She had made little effort to free herself though she had not been tied very tightly.

Ruth Snyder was asked if she could possibly explain why she was assaulted, and answered that she sometimes wore a necklace that looked quite expensive. She also had an expensive-looking fur coat. The burglars may have spotted her and perpetrated the crime to get at her pearls and coat, she suggested.

The police thought this very unlikely since the necklace was an imitation, worth only a few dollars, and the expensive-looking fur coat was not mink but muskrat. It was hard to imagine a professional burglar lured by such will-o'-the-wisps.

What the police found even more most suspicious was the discovery under Ruth Snyder's mattress of the very necklace which she reported missing. She said she was so upset by everything that she had forgotten that she had hidden the pearls there! The muskrat coat, which she had also assumed to be stolen, had a similar fate. It was found in the back of her closet, neatly wrapped in paper. She had forgotten about that, too.

The only property that appeared to have been stolen was $110 from Albert Snyder's wallet. Police wondered, if that was all the thieves wanted, wouldn't they have tackled Snyder when he was putting the car away, when he was alone?

The house looked like a tornado had gone through it. Drawers were flung across the rooms, coverlets torn from shelves, seat cushions tossed about. Cutlery and utensils were strewn about the kitchen floor from drawers turned upside down. Police could not understand why professional thieves would search an ordinary house so frantically, yet pass up valuables that were in plain sight. There were several articles of sterling silver still on the round center table in the living room. Albert Snyder's gold watch lay in the middle of his bedroom floor, easily seen from any angle, and valuable linens had been left untouched, carefully stacked on the dining room chairs.

The police could see that the burglary scene was a fake. It simply did not feel like a professional job. When Ruth Snyder was told this, her first reaction was indignation.

"What do you mean?" she demanded.

"Just that it doesn't look right," said one of the detectives.

"How can you tell?"

"We see lots of burglaries. They aren't done this way."

The absurdity of this exchange almost brought a giggle out of the police who witnessed it. It was astonishing that such a thing as laughter could surface during a murder investigation, but there it was, rising in their throats. Barely managing to suppress their smiles, they asked her to consider the curious fact that the burglars, if they were burglars, had no difficulty gaining entry into the house. There were no signs of jimmied windows or forced entry. In fact, all the windows were locked and, according to what Ruth Snyder had told them earlier, the front door had been locked shut after the family returned home.

Mrs. Snyder prodded the police to take into account the brief interval during which the burglars could have sneaked in. That occurred when she and Lorraine first entered the house while her husband drove the car into the garage, she said. The front door was open while Albert Snyder was in the garage, so the thieves might have entered the house and concealed themselves before her husband came in and locked the front door.

A full glass of whiskey found on the dining room table was another curiosity. Beside it was a whiskey bottle a little less than full. This suggested that a fresh bottle had been opened and that the person who poured the drink was either disturbed about something or changed his mind and left it untouched.

There was also the whole matter of how Albert Snyder had been killed: three wounds on his head, cotton waste stuck into his mouth and nose, and picture wire wound around his throat. It was unclear why professional thieves would use so many different methods. There was nothing to be gained by striking, strangling, and administering chloroform. It would have been easier to kill Albert Snyder by simply knocking him over the head a few more times.

It was also unclear why a loaded revolver was left lying on the bed. Professional thieves would not leave a gun where it could be picked up and used on them by someone coming into the house as they, the thieves, were fleeing. Thieves show more caution than this.

On Snyder's bed was a blue bandanna handkerchief and a piece of newsprint, a corner torn from an Italian newspaper, which Mrs. Snyder suggested

was left by the Italian thieves who committed the
crime. (This was just after the trial of Sacco and Vanzetti.) The police thought this an odd juxtaposition
of evidence. It seemed inconceivable that professional thieves would leave behind a scrap of Italian
newspaper to announce their national identity. But
even supposing that the killers were Italian, Italians
were not known to resort to such Byzantine murder
methods. They were known to prefer single murder
implements, either a knife or sawed-off shotgun.

The bandanna was yet another curiosity. Italians
did not usually commit crimes wearing bandannas—
except in the movies.

The police smelled a rat. By the time Deputy Inspector Arthur A. Carey began questioning Ruth Snyder in the late afternoon, it was pretty clear to him
that she was in on it.

According to Carey's biography, *Memoirs of a Murder Man,* the first thing he did on entering Ruth Snyder's room was to study her face. She was lying on
her side, moaning softly, but he noticed that "her
soft blue eyes, squinting out of their corners," were
observing his movements.

"How are you feeling, madam?" he asked her, pulling up a straight-back chair.

Ruth moaned, her eyes taking him in.

Carey was a big, red-faced man. He was wearing a
tie, but no jacket, his sleeves rolled up past the meaty
curve of his elbows. "Why don't you tell me what
happened?"

She related the same story that she had told the
police, about how a stockily built thug and his partner
grabbed her. She said she fainted and fell to the floor,
but could not remember what happened after that.

"You fainted, madam?" Carey asked.

She nodded.

"About what time did you faint?"

"When they first came in. About two-thirty in the morning."

"And you were found by your daughter about seven-thirty A.M.? Is that right?"

"Yes."

"Then you lay on the floor insensible from two-thirty until about seven-thirty A.M. in a dead faint?"

"Yes."

"That couldn't possibly have happened," Carey said. "You couldn't have lain five hours in a faint."

"I did," she insisted.

Inspector Carey explained to her that "it is an established fact that in fainting, the blood leaves the head for only a short period. If the body lies flat, consciousness returns within minutes."

But Ruth Snyder would not budge. She continued to claim that she was unconscious during the five-hour period.

Carey decided to change the topic. He asked her about her history. She brightened as she recalled her girlhood and marriage. Carey got her to the point where she was sharing about her household budget and how much money her husband gave her out of his weekly salary. According to Carey, "she was quite chipper in supplying answers to these questions."

"And you carry insurance on your husband's life?" he asked casually.

"Oh, yes," she answered, sitting upright on the bed. "A thousand dollars." Then in a low voice she added, "It was a thousand dollars."

"Not what it was, madam, but what is it now?"

"Now?" she asked. "Oh, it's twenty-five thousand dollars now."

"What kind of policy is it?" Carey asked.

"Accident and death."

"How long has the policy to run?'

"Three years."

"And it's paid up for—?"

"A year."

He asked her to tell him a little bit more about the insurance policy. Were there provisions, say, for accidental death occurring under unusual circumstances?

When Carey heard the answer, he was totally satisfied as to the motivation for the crime. The Italian thugs passed completely out of his mind. He learned that she had three insurance policies on her husband's life, one for $1,000, and another for $5,000, and still another for $45,000 and that the latter contained a double indemnity clause if his death was caused by violence. She acknowledged she would gain $96,000 if it was determined that Albert Snyder had been killed by burglars!

Carey knew that when a woman takes out an insurance policy that's worth $96,000 if her husband is killed in a bizarre way, and then, shortly thereafter, he *is* killed in a bizarre way, it's not on the up-and-up. It can't be. If there was a clear reason why some burglars needed to kill him—say, because he resisted or put up a fight—it might be, but even then it would be a very suspicious coincidence. A *very* suspicious coincidence.

A second, more intensive search of the house was undertaken. No picture wire of the type found around Albert Snyder's throat was found, but a five-pound window weight (the concealed long lead counterweights that make it easier to move windows up and down) was discovered in the basement tool chest. It was speckled with blood, and it was brand new, obviously purchased expressly for the Snyder break-in. The perpetrators, whoever they were, were not preparing to grab the loot and quietly slip away. They came equipped for murder.

One of the detectives found that the metal pencil used to twist the picture wire around Snyder's neck was initialed J.G. When asked about this, Ruth Snyder deftly claimed that it belonged to her husband, and that J.G. stood for Jessie Guishard, her husband's first love and fiancée. She had died of pneumonia before she and Snyder could be married.

Among the canceled checks signed by Mrs. Snyder, Carey found one made out to H. Judd Gray for $200 and endorsed by him in a masculine-appearing script. Judd Gray's name was also found on the back of a calendar. Another detective supplemented the mounting evidence by finding in Ruth Snyder's bureau drawer an address book containing the names of twenty-eight men, including the name of Judd Gray.

The police immediately suspected Gray was in on it—that he was her accomplice. That might explain the opened bottle of whiskey sitting on the table, since the Mulhausers, who had first seen Ruth Snyder in the morning, said that her breath did not smell of whiskey, and that she did not appear at all intoxicated. Judd Gray may have been the one who had drunk from the bottle and filled the glass to the brim.

The detectives decided to improvise a lie-detector test for Mrs. Snyder. They read to her the name of every male in her address book, asking her to explain who each person was and waited to see if her voice changed when she came to the name of Judd Gray.

They observed that she could not suppress a slight tremor when she came to Gray's name.

"You know Judd Gray pretty well, huh, Mrs. Snyder?"

"No, not really."

She was shown the canceled check made out to him. "Two hundred dollars is quite a lot to loan a man you don't know very well."

"I—I don't know what you're—"

"Come on, Mrs. Snyder, who is this Judd Gray character?"

Every question that followed was about Judd Gray. When had she last seen him? Where? For how long? What was his age? Where did he work? Where was he now? Had her husband known him? Was she intimate with him? Had she opened the door for him so that he could kill her husband? Judd Gray's name was used on her like a battering ram.

She flushed and her eyes rolled. She clenched and unclenched her fists. She wept and refused to answer, writhing to and fro on the bed where she lay supposedly recuperating from the blow on her head. She held herself forth as a sick, abused woman and demanded a lawyer.

The detectives decided to trap her by telling her that Judd Gray, who was actually still at liberty, had already confessed everything. They would spring it on her at the station house.

When told she was to be taken to the Jamaica Jail, she simply refused.

"I can't go."

"You must."

"I'm too sick, I tell you."

What Ruth Snyder did next made the police suck in their breaths. She flung off her covers, stepped quickly out of bed, and began dressing in the open: this fleshy housewife and mother, skin the color of flour, hair wild from tossing on her pillow, body exposed to all. She was not actually naked, but the negligee she was wearing was so meager her cleavage showed, as did the mole just above her rib cage.

"Clad only in a single, abbreviated slip, she tossed her pretty head defiantly," wrote a reporter for the *Daily Mirror,* "displaying among other things, a towering rage, though no embarrassment."

Her audience gaped. In silence, they just stood there, their eyes flicking nervously from her body to the floor, filling the room with a discomfiture so primitive and intense, it seemed to charge the very air.

"Cover yourself, Mrs. Snyder," a detective said at last. "For God's sake."

Mrs. Snyder did not reply, only raised her hand, a signal to be patient, and stepped into her stockings. Then she pulled a dress from her closet and held it in front of her, arms outstretched, as if trying to decide whether to wear it. She was selecting her outfit more slowly and carefully than if she were alone. She was taunting the police, ignoring their presence, as if refusing to acknowledge their power over her. As the *New York Times* put it, she was "bent on making a sensational scene in order to express her resentment at their insistence on her leaving the house."

At the station house, a new line of questioning was used on her. One of the members of the bridge party Ruth Snyder had attended with her husband the night of his murder mentioned that she had recently gone away on an automobile trip for longer than a week.

When asked about this, Mrs. Snyder insisted she made the trip with a "Mr. and Mrs. Kehoe," but she could not give any information about them or say where they could be found. She admitted they were all registered under assumed names, but it was a while ago, and she could not remember what they were.

"We know there was another man with you on that

trip and there was a man whom you know, in your house the night of the murder," Police Commissioner McLaughlin told Mrs. Snyder.

"I can't understand why you say that," was her icy reply.

"We also know that when you were in a faint, you were downstairs in your house," countered the police commissioner.

"Did I come downstairs? Did Lorraine say I came downstairs?" Things weren't going right; everything was coming out wrong. Instead of the police sympathizing with her for her loss, as they were supposed to, they were treating her as though she was the guilty party. Why couldn't she make the police *like* her?

"Never mind who told us," said the commissioner, who then ordered Mrs. Snyder placed in a small office in the police station while he questioned others. Among them was a portly, red-faced detective, with slicked-back hair named Peter Trumfeller. According to rumor, he knew Ruth Snyder on a personal basis. People said they had gone driving together a couple of times.

While Mrs. Snyder was sitting in the small office, still denying any knowledge of who had murdered her husband, Trumfeller peered in.

"Why, hello, Ruth." He grinned.

"Oh, are you—?" she blurted, a look of exquisite, impenetrable astonishment widening her eyes.

He came closer, and whispered something. What he said was not disclosed, but the effect was obvious. She sat as rigid as a bird before a copperhead's approach. All trace of her former stolidity vanished. Then she rose, dabbing at her eyes with a handkerchief, and approached the office where the commissioner was. She apologized for keeping everyone there all these hours. Then she said she couldn't keep up with the questioning any longer and wanted to tell the truth.

"What do you think they would do with me if I told everything?" she asked.

"Ruth," the commissioner said, "your story is getting all balled up. It doesn't fit. Why don't you tell the truth and get it off your chest?"

He handed her a piece of paper with Judd Gray's name on it. "Was that the man who killed your husband?"

Her breath came in great, silent sobs. "He's the one," she said. "Has he confessed?"

When told that he had, the announcement had the desired effect. A stenographer was invited in and Mrs. Snyder told the story of how she and Judd Gray murdered her husband. She spoke unevenly at first. Every two or three words were broken by a long pause, but it came out, bit by bit.

2

Ruth Snyder Confesses

"My name is Ruth May Snyder, and I want to make a full and truthful statement about the death of my husband, Albert Snyder, and I understand that anything I say may be used against me . . ."

"I was born at Morningside Avenue and 125th Street, New York City." It was a neat and respectable four-room apartment, but also cramped and dull, and completely without luxuries.

Her father, a carpenter, kept food on the table, but there were so many things young Ruth wanted but couldn't have: a flaxen-haired doll from a neighborhood toy shop, a Shetland pony, a monogrammed wristwatch, mulberry drapes for the parlor, picnics, trips to theaters, good times.

To magnify her malcontent, she was often sick. At the age of six she had an operation on her intestines, and a few years later a bungled appendectomy left her with permanent internal disorders. She suffered from congenital epilepsy, which she said was behind her frequent fainting spells.

Ruth Snyder attended Methodist Episcopal Church with her parents and older brother, and although she was active in Sunday School and prayed each night before going to bed, she was hardly religious. "I didn't believe in my inner heart [God] existed," she said, "but I went through the motions in case I was wrong."

After graduating from public school at the age of thirteen, she worked as a night relief telephone operator at $15 a week. She took a bookkeeping and stenography course from a business school. Her next position was as bookkeeper for a Bronx realtor. Different jobs followed: salesgirl, typist, switchboard operator. "The last permanent position I had before I was married was with M. Rusling Wood Co., Beaver Street, New York City, where I was employed as a stenographer. I met my husband, Albert Snyder, while I was employed with *Cosmopolitan* magazine, which was the position I held before the one with M. Rusling Wood."

The year was 1914. She was working as a switchboard operator. One day her boss asked her to dial a number for him. She did as she was told but instead of getting the manufacturing concern her boss wanted, she made the wrong connection and caught a busy, irritated art editor at a bad time. He let her know what he thought of absentminded telephone operators. She apologized. He called her back a half hour later to say that he was the one who should apologize. They met. Six months later they married.

He was nice at first. There were dates at expensive night clubs, restaurants, and theaters. He bought her a box of chocolates which contained, hidden beneath the candy, a solitaire diamond. "I think it (the diamond) had as much as any one thing to do with my consenting. I wouldn't have given that ring up for anything once I had it in my hand." She took Albert

Snyder up on his proposal. She was nineteen and he was thirty-three.

As might have been expected with such an age difference, she began having difficulty with Albert Snyder almost immediately after the marriage. "I was apparently too giddy for his years; while he was only thirty-three at the time he was like a man of fifty to me."

True, she conceded, Albert Snyder always took good care of her and their daughter, Lorraine, from a financial standpoint. His position as art editor for *Motor Boating* magazine brought in about $115 a week, and he earned some extra money with the freelance sketching he did occasionally. Their seven-passenger Buick was very nice, too. "But," said Mrs. Snyder, wearily, resentfully, "he never paid any attention to me."

If he had ever taken her out dancing, maybe, or just once told her she was pretty . . .

If he had ever been kind in some way, ever said or done anything the least bit complimentary, maybe she wouldn't have sought the company of other men.

But he didn't. So she did.

In June 1925, Ruth Snyder made a shopping trip to Manhattan with one of her married friends, Karin Kaufman, to buy some summer clothes. Kaufman suggested they have lunch at Henry's, a small Swedish restaurant noted for its inexpensive but plentiful smorgasbord. At Henry's, Karin excused herself, then returned a few moments later with a man she introduced as Harry Folsom. They chatted for a while. He explained that he was a traveling salesman in silks and hosiery.

A few days later, Folsom invited Snyder and her friend to lunch again at Henry's. After the three of them were seated, a small but impeccably groomed man approached. Except for his deeply cleft chin and a large, troubled forehead, he was well-proportioned. He wore great, owl-eyed spectacles.

"My name is Judd Gray," the man gasped, then shifted uneasily, explaining that he worked for Bien Jolie Corset Company as a traveling salesman.

"Charming to meet you," Ruth trilled. His eyes held hers in a peculiarly sustained way, she thought.

Gray called to the waiter to bring him a whiskey and soda, but his eyes hardly shifted from her. She could not explain why he was scrutinizing her so intensely, but she liked it.

Ruth Snyder ordered some items through Mr. Gray, which gave them an excuse to meet again. The next time they met, they again had dinner and drinks at Henry's, then stopped by his office to get his supplies. He rummaged among his stock, and reappeared carrying what he called a "corselet." He asked if she'd accept it as a gift. Yes, she said. And would she let him help her try it on? Yes, again. He drew her tenderly to him. Their cheeks touched, and then their lips, and she claimed his kindness moved her to tears.

Gray spread his jacket on the floor and they lay together, holding each other, running their hands lightly over each other's body. "Of course, my husband knew nothing of my relations with Mr. Gray," she told the police. "I had sexual intercourse with him on a number of occasions. We got a room as Mr. and Mrs. Henry Judd Gray.

"The first time that I occupied a room with Mr. Gray was at the Imperial Hotel in New York City, which was sometime during the month of September 1925. And from that time on, on numerous occasions, Mr. Gray got a room at the Waldorf Astoria. We always registered under the name of Mr. and Mrs. Gray."

Ruth Snyder and Judd Gray stayed at the Waldorf so frequently that they kept a small tan suitcase checked there on a permanent basis. After Mrs. Snyder shared this bit of information with the police, the police decided it was imperative to immediately see the suitcase. The reason for the rush: the suitcase was supposed to contain some photographs of Judd Gray. The police needed a picture of him as soon as possible because he was still at large. Mrs. Snyder and several policemen therefore arrived at the hotel at 2:45 A.M., March 21, 1927, and secured the bag. They went over its contents, item by item:

A gentleman's bathrobe
A lady's bathrobe
A set of gentleman's brushes
A set of gentleman's pajamas
A set of lady's pajamas
A napkin
Two brushes
A hair-curling iron and attachments
A rubber douche
A package containing Kotex
A comb
A pair of slippers
A deck of playing cards
A washrag
A Christmas card
A catalogue of Van Ordray, 1926
Two theater programs
A book, *Gentlemen Prefer Blondes*
A bottle containing an amber-colored liquid
A bottle containing a white-colored liquid
A bottle containing suppositories
A bottle containing a white liquid paste
A box marked DAY DREAM POWDER

Two bottles of bicarbonate of soda
A box marked TALCUM POWDER
A box marked MAVIS TALCUM POWDER
A box marked NAIL ENAMEL
A box marked AMOLIN POWDER
A box of Sapolin
A jar of cold cream
A jar marked DAY DREAM CREAM
A nail whitener
A pearl-handled nail file
A pearl-handled buttonhook
A pearl-handled scraper
A box containing needles and thread
Six pieces of soap
A small mirror
A brown leather valise
A shoe horn marked HOTEL ALLEN
A tube of lubricating jelly
A box containing rouge
A powder puff
Tweezers
Lipstick
A blue eye pencil and brush
A syringe
A tube of Colgate's Rapid Shaving Cream
A bottle of sodium bromide
Three toothbrushes
A box marked MIDAS TABLETS
A bottle marked DELICIA BREW
One tissue-paper package of condoms
A photograph of Judd Gray and child
A photograph of Judd Gray and Ruth Snyder

Part of the allure of such a list—why the police and later the newspapers made such a big deal about it— was the sense that it provided of the culprits' evilness.

Here was a moral grandiloquence comparable to Greek drama and Spanish bullfights. The douche, condoms, and lubricating jelly were signs of lusts, cravings, and uncurbed appetites. These items provided total knowledge of Ruth Snyder's and Judd Gray's depravity.

Oddly, though, just as people were lured into condemning them, they found themselves identifying with them, too. They found themselves angry and forgiving, revolted and sympathetic simultaneously. The itemization of all these creams, powders, and liquids made people feel they were getting a chance to glimpse backstage during a meticulously produced spectacle. Without this long list, Snyder's and Gray's melodramatic lines and grotesque actions would have left everyone squirming with impatience, ready to reject them outright. But because people could see all their perspiring preparations, all the props that supported their excessive performances, they were partly anxious for them to succeed.

People were sympathetic also because the items on this list seemed to domesticate Snyder's and Gray's crime, making it appear part of everyday experience. Such articles as suppositories and Kotex made it clear that Snyder's and Gray's world, just like everyone else's, was defined by the requirements of ordinary existence. They used Colgate's Rapid Shave, too, and tweezers and scrapers, and bromides and bicarbonate of soda.

In keeping with this redundant banality, when Ruth Snyder and the police returned to the station house, and her interrogation resumed, she could only explain why she killed her husband by stringing one domestic indignity after another. She claimed she and her husband "quarreled quite frequently about the accounting for the money he gave me," and "I was constantly being belittled . . . he was constantly picking and nagging at me and I had gotten to that stage where I would take any means to get out of it all."

He drove her to it, she said. He made her so miserable she couldn't have taken it any longer, not another year, not a week, not even an hour.

"Mr. Gray was the only one who would listen to my troubles," she asserted. For hours, she would talk and he would listen, about Albert Snyder's pettiness, his thickness, coldness, detachment, and insensitivity, never dreaming that unburdening herself in this way could bring such utter, contrite, prostrate relief. The unbearable part was knowing that talking to her lover always came to an end, her golden carriage changing back to a pumpkin, as Gray had to return to his spouse, and she to hers.

She could have gotten a divorce, she admitted, but that was all she would have gotten. No money; no seven-passenger Buick; no two-and-a-half story, white-frame house in Queens Village; and no satisfaction. Nothing to make up for all the years Albert Snyder had slowly tortured her.

Then one day, she forgot who introduced the idea, a permanent solution was proposed—Why not "get rid of him?" Why not just get rid of him?

The following letter, written right after Ruth Snyder and Judd Gray began formulating the plan to murder Albert Snyder (it was postmarked February 24, 1927), conveyed Ruth Snyder's antic joy at the prospect of actually carrying it off—of putting out "this blaze what's so much bother to me."

My Own Lover Boy—
   Gee, but I'm happy. Oh, ain't I happy. Tomorrow's my lucky day.

I'm so very happy, dear, I can't sit still enough to write what I'm thinking of.

You'll excuse it this time too, won't you, hon?

Went down to the movies in Q's and saw Johnny *get your hair cut. Jackie [Jackie Coogan] is certainly a sweet kid and a marvelous actor, I think. Wouldn't be a bad idea if I had me a haircut—it's beginning to luka-lika da wop. Wassa guda writin—huh? All I keep thinking of is U. A. & you, you darn little cuss. I could eatcha all up. Could I get lit & put out this blaze what's so much bother to me? Ah yes, hon, let's get good and "plastered"; ain't that a nice word? Beginning to think I'm already that way on nothing.*

Hurry home, darling, Ill be waiting for you.

All my love.
Your Momie.

Here again was the most conventional-sounding communication—a letter with which almost anyone could identify. Her language was filled with so many ordinary references—a popular movie, her need to get a haircut, all those clichés: "Tomorrow's my lucky day," "I could eatcha all up," "Let's get good and 'plastered' "—yet she was only three weeks away from murdering her husband. She was "so very happy" because she had just made up her mind to kill him.

Her decision to murder Albert Snyder was finalized, she said with great seriousness, when he promised, after an argument, "to blow my [her] brains out." She was afraid for her life, she told the police. After all, Albert Snyder had an awful temper.

Ruth Snyder said that her husband's threat to kill her startled Gray, snapping him to his senses like the rule of a game he was struggling to comprehend. "Mr. Gray wrote back to me in a code which only we

two understand, that it was better for Mr. Gray and I
to get him (my husband) before he got me."

It had to be done, he said. It was a matter of self-
defense.

All that remained was to figure out how to carry it
off. Chloroform was discussed, but it didn't seem sufficient. You can't chloroform somebody who's thrash-
ing about and resisting, and Albert Snyder was a
rock-solid man, far bigger and much more powerful
than Judd Gray. Thus, it would make sense to knock
him out first. One of them—Ruth Snyder was sure it
was Gray—came up with the idea of hitting him over
the head with a hammer or metal bar, something like
a window weight. Gray proposed strangling him, too,
just to be on the safe side.

These preliminary issues resolved, the plan was
complete. In a very short while, the "Governor," as
Ruth Snyder and her lover called him, would be
dead; he and his crude remarks, his stinginess, all his
dullness and callousness would be gone forever.

They picked a night early in March to finish him
off. Ruth Snyder recalled it was hailing that night.
The time was eleven o'clock when Judd Gray arrived
at her home. "It was understood between Mr. Gray
and myself on that night that he was to hit my husband on the head with this window weight and stun
him after he had gotten to sleep and then administer
chloroform to him, but Mr. Gray and I both got cold
feet that night and the two of us cried like babies,
and I said to him, 'Go on home, you're not going to
do it.' "

Judd Gray obeyed and went home.

She told the police, "The next day I got a letter
from Mr. Gray from Buffalo, saying he was glad I sent
him home."

On Saturday, March 12, Ruth Snyder had another

quarrel with her husband in which he told her that she could "either get the hell out or [he] would blow [her] brains out." She described this quarrel in a letter to Judd Gray, who wrote back asking if she thought her husband would actually do it. She said yes, that he would do anything in a fit of temper.

That sealed the matter. Judd Gray's resolve to do the deed was rekindled and stronger than ever. He wrote his mistress stating he was "going to deliver the goods on Saturday," which meant, according to their code, that they were going to "get rid of him" on Saturday, March 19.

One of the great benefits of doing the job on the 19th was that Josephine Brown, Ruth Snyder's mother, would not be home. She was a practical nurse, and was scheduled to take care of an old man in a private residence that night.

Another benefit was that Mrs. Snyder and her husband and daughter were to go to a friend's home to play cards and drink. This meant that Gray could sneak in without being noticed.

Before going to the party, Ruth Snyder made sure the cellar door and the kitchen door were left unlocked, so Judd Gray could let himself in. She also left a quart of whiskey for him to drink while he waited.

The Snyder family returned home from the party about two A.M. that Sunday. The husband left his wife and daughter out on the sidewalk, in front of the house. The two females entered the front door together. Then Mrs. Snyder walked Lorraine upstairs to her bedroom.

"As I was passing the baby's room, I saw Mr. Gray in my mother's room," said Mrs. Snyder. After she kissed Lorraine good night, she visited him there. They embraced. Her body pressed against the window weight that was now concealed inside his jacket, and she shivered with anticipation.

She asked, "You get away from Syracuse all right? No one saw you come here?"

"No one."

"Good. I'll see you in a little while."

"How long?" asked Gray. Frowning anxiously, he looked over her shoulder into the hall.

"I'll come back to get you as soon as he's asleep." They embraced again. "Very soon now, it will all be over," she said, and brushed her lips across his cheek, and walked slowly out of the room.

Ruth Snyder undressed and slipped into bed beside her husband. About a half hour later, she raised herself on one elbow to see if he was asleep. He was lying on his left side, completely out. That was the side with his "good ear," thus ensuring that her husband, who was deaf in his other ear, would not be awakened by the murder preparations.

"Albert," Ruth tested, her voice a hoarse whisper, her mouth almost touching his ear. He didn't budge.

Mrs. Snyder then rose and stepped backward into the hall. Light shone through the window from the street, coating the polished wooden floor with a white glaze. She saw her mother's room, the door opened a crack, with Judd Gray crooking his head into the opening.

Judd Gray was gripping the bedpost, his legs appearing to buckle. She hugged him once again, trying to firm him up. "I told him it was either my husband going or my going, that when a thing started it had to be finished, one way or another." Stroking his hand, she told him to imagine what it would be like after, how happy they'd be, with no more lies, no need to hide or sneak about, no need to pretend. They could be together all the time.

She again checked that Gray had the window weight. She also checked to see that he had the bottle of chloroform, the cheesecloth and cotton waste, and she made sure he had the blue cotton kerchief on which he was to pour the chloroform. The original wrapping that was on the window weight when they first got it, she noted, was still attached.

She told the police, "After we had all the details arranged, he kissed me and walked into my husband's room."

The room in which Albert Snyder lay sleeping was not completely dark. As Ruth Snyder described it, she "could see Mr. Gray raise his arm, holding what I believed to be the weight in his hand, and in the darkness the white paper around the weight stood out. I saw this weight in Mr. Gray's hand start to travel and immediately heard a thud, and my husband groaned twice after I heard the thud.

"I saw Mr. Gray tie my husband's hands behind his back. I was able to see in the dark because there is a street arc light on the opposite side of the street from our house, which at all times during the night lights up my room so that you can see objects in it.

"When Mr. Gray struck my husband, he was lying on his left side. He tied his hands behind his back and put the blue handkerchief and the waste with the chloroform on it on the pillow, and then turned my husband facedown on the pillow so that the waste and blue handkerchief with the chloroform on it would cover his nose and mouth.

"He then covered his head with the blankets to make sure of suffocation. He then tied his feet."

She said, "I'm quite sure that Mr. Gray then came out of the room and said to me, 'I guess that's it.'"

After that they went downstairs. Gray took off the pair of rubber gloves which he had purchased to avoid leaving any fingerprints and washed his hands in the bathroom. While in the bathroom, he discovered that he had quite a few bloodstains on his shirt. Ruth Snyder went back into her husband's room to get one of his new blue shirts—it had a silk stripe on it—and Gray changed into it in Snyder's mother's room.

They took the weight and the shirt and the bloodstained paper down to the cellar and burned the shirt and paper in the furnace. They sprinkled ashes onto the window weight and put it in the toolbox.

Moments later, they were sitting in the living room when, according to Ruth Snyder, Gray introduced the idea of binding Albert Snyder's neck with the wire "to make sure of everything."

"He took this wire from his pocket," Snyder explained. "He had two pieces of wire when he came in. One was intended, I think, for the hands and the other for the feet. In the shuffle, one piece of wire had gotten lost, so he took the piece he had left and went upstairs and I went with him, and he put it around his throat to make sure of everything. He tightened it up with his fingers."

At this point, all thoughts of her future happiness had vanished from Ruth Snyder's mind. Her single goal was survival—how to get away with the crime. "While Mr. Gray and I were in my mother's room, before he went into my husband's room, we had planned that in order to avoid detection—to upset the house and throw the stuff in the house around so that it would look like a burglary or robbery, and we had planned that I was to tell the police that it was a robbery. After we had disposed of the shirt and the paper around the weight, we then went back upstairs and emptied out all the drawers in all the rooms except my daughter's room." Then they went downstairs and upset everything there, and she took the wallet out of her husband's pants pocket, giving the contents to her lover.

She told him to tie her up, and he did so, winding the rope around her ankles and wrists.

Then she told him to hit her.

"Don't you think it's enough that you're tied up?" Gray said.

"No, you have to hit me, too."

"Why?"

"To make it look like a robbery. If you killed my husband without hitting me, too, it just wouldn't look right." She squeezed her eyes shut and pursed her lips.

"I can't do it. I've never hit a woman before."

"Judd!"

He did as he was told, not hitting her hard, but enough to satisfy her, then laid her down on her mother's bed.

At daybreak, Judd Gray left and took a train to Syracuse, and shortly thereafter Ruth Snyder got out of bed and crawled to Lorraine's door and woke her up.

Ruth Snyder said, "Mrs. Mulhauser came over first and the baby called Mr. Mulhauser and he came over and the police were notified for the second time. I told Mrs. Mulhauser and the police that I was attacked by a man coming out of my mother's room and fainted with fright. That was not the truth. I was asked about an Italian newspaper. That was part of the plan so as to make it appear that they were Italians who had come in and killed my husband and bound and gagged me. The pistol that was found on the floor belonged to my husband. It was put there by us as part of our plan to make it appear more like a robbery.

"I was in love with Mr. Gray and Mr. Gray loved me, and if my husband hadn't said that he would take my life, we would not have thought of taking his life. But after talking it over a number of times with Mr. Gray, we decided that the only way out of our difficulties was to take his life."

3

Judd Gray Confesses

When Judd Gray left the Snyder home that dawn, he was feeling strangely light-headed and dizzy, but not dizzy from qualms of conscience. He was feeling dizzy like someone who'd been caged up, then suddenly finds himself free. At that moment he felt almost happy.

That might explain why, when he saw an old man waiting at his bus stop at 6:05 A.M., he wasn't thinking about his alibi or that he had just murdered a man. Those phantoms had flown away. He did not care about the past or future. He was just grateful that the air was fresh and pure, and that there was someone at the bus stop to talk with. Gray asked the man about the bus—what time it arrived, if it was dependable, small talk—but enough to fix Gray's cleft chin and smartly tailored clothes firmly in the man's memory.

While they were chatting, a police officer who had been sweeping out a police booth near the bus stop began to take target practice at a row of beer bottles—admittedly, an odd thing to do so early on Sunday morning. Gray was fascinated by this display of marksmanship and told his companion, "I would hate like hell to stand in front of him and have him shoot me."

For some reason, Gray shared this observation with the policeman. Given that he had just killed his lover's husband and was trying to return to his hotel room in Syracuse without being detected, he had the most compelling of reasons to not share this, or any other observation, with the policeman. But Gray couldn't help calling out good-humoredly, "I wouldn't want you shooting at me." The policeman, of course, thought the comment odd and remembered him.

Gray got off his bus at the Jamaica station, where he found a taxi to take him to Manhattan. The driver remembered Gray's face, too. The cab fare was $3.50, and Gray left $3.55, the extra nickel being the tip. That five-cent tip made the driver curious. Till then, he hadn't really noticed this passenger, but after, Gray's visage was forever associated in his memory with stinginess.

Two more people identified Gray when he took the New York Central from New York City to Syracuse. The porter and the conductor found him alone in the train smoking car, where he handed his ticket over. It was a Pullman ticket to Albany, but Gray told the conductor he was not leaving the train at Albany. He was going to stay on to Syracuse. Why was his Pullman only to Albany? the conductor inquired. Because he wanted to ride the second half of the trip in coach. The conductor paused to digest this unusual request, then looked Gray over carefully, making sure he'd remember the passenger who planned on changing cars midway on his journey.

Why would Gray draw attention to himself at the bus stop? Why did he joke with the policeman, leave only five cents to the taxi driver, choose to sit in a train car that had no other passengers, and purchase

a Pullman ticket that only covered half his trip, requiring him to switch cars? These acts of self-exposure appear bizarre given all the effort he took to establish that he was in his hotel room when the murder was committed. Judd Gray arranged to make it appear that he was safely in bed and "not to be disturbed" at the time of the murder. Gray had given his room key to a friend of his from Syracuse, Haddon Gray (they had the same last name but were not related), with the understanding that Haddon was to go into Judd's room while he was gone and rumple the bed so that it looked slept in. He told Haddon he needed cover for a dinner engagement with Ruth Snyder in Albany, and that he probably would not be back that night. While Haddon was in Judd's room, he was supposed to telephone down to the desk, identify himself as Judd Gray, and tell the operator that he did not feel well and did not wish to be disturbed. Haddon was also supposed to mail some letters Judd had given him and place a DO NOT DISTURB sign on his doorknob.

Haddon did exactly as he was instructed, leaving a note for Judd that read, "Perfect—Call when you're ready. Had."

The following letter was one of those Haddon Gray mailed from the Onondaga Hotel on March 19, for the purpose of making it appear that Judd was in Syracuse:

Syracuse, N.Y.
Sat. 6 P.M.

Hello Momie:
How the dickens are you this bright, beautiful day anyway? Gee, it makes you feel like living again after that rain yesterday. If we only have a nice day tomorrow. Now we will be all set, as we have had so many

*miserable Sundays. They are lonesome enough as a
rule without adding rain.*

*Had. just came over for a few minutes for a little
smile, and wanted me to go home with him, but have
quite some work to do yet on the* [corset] *line, writing
besides. Then, too, I'm going up tomorrow for supper,
I don't want to rub it in.*

*If I get there in time after supper may run over to
a movie or vaudeville, but this warm weather doesn't
give me a heap of pep. I feel tired when the day is
done.*

*Tonight you go to the R's party didn't you say? Hope
you have a lovely time and have one for me—but see
you behave yourselves.*

*I want to call up Aunt Jule tomorrow and see her
before I leave, as I haven't seen her since Xmas time.*

*Well, old dear, I haven't much news so will get off
this and go grab a bite. Take good care of yourselves
and best to you all. As ever.*

> *Sincerely,*
> *Bud* [Gray's nickname]

Although it may be premature to draw any hard
and fast conclusions, one cannot help but notice that
Gray seemed deeply divided. His letter opened with
a hearty "how the dickens are you." He referred to
this "bright, beautiful day," but the next line, "Gee,
it makes you feel like living again," revealed a darker
perspective. There were "so many miserable Sundays" that "are lonesome enough as a rule without
adding rain." He was without "pep" and "tired when
the day is done."

Gray was divided also with respect to his crime.
After he left Ruth Snyder's house on Sunday morning, he made sure that at least five people—including
a policeman—could identity him, yet there is no de-

nying that he devoted a great deal of attention to making his alibi successful. Apparently, he wanted it both ways: to be exposed and to avoid exposure, to be punished and to go free, at the same time. Which may explain why, when Judd Gray returned to Syracuse on Sunday, the afternoon after the murder, instead of telling Haddon Gray what really happened and how he really felt, instead of risking saying something that might expose himself, he concocted a new series of lies.

"Haddon," he told his friend after dinner, "I didn't stay in Albany as originally planned, because when I got to Albany, there was a telegram there from Ruth asking me to meet her in New York at her house. That's what I did. But you aren't going to believe this, Had. While I was at Ruth's house a robbery was committed. She was assaulted and her husband was slugged and bound. I hid in the closet for, I don't know how long, for hours. At one point, this tall man and his companion went into the closet looking for something that was on the top shelf. I was down on the floor, behind the dresses that were hanging on the hooks, so they didn't see me.

"After matters had quieted down, I went into the bedroom and saw Mr. Snyder lying on the floor, and that either in picking him up from the floor or in bending over him to hear if his heart was beating, I had gotten a bloodstain on my vest and also on my shirt." Judd showed Haddon the bloodstained shirt and vest, adding that the shirt belonged to Snyder.

"How did it come about that you had his shirt on?" asked Haddon.

Judd mumbled something about his own shirt getting ruined, that he knew it looked bad. In fact, he wouldn't be surprised if someone accused *him* of the murder! That's why he needed help.

Haddon, his friend from childhood, swallowed. He agreed to help Judd get rid of the bloodstained garments, and promised to hold up his end of the alibi.

Later that night, when Judd Gray returned to his hotel room, he fell asleep quickly, but just as quickly awoke. It seemed to him that he had been lying on his bed a long while without knowing who or where he was. Ages seemed to pass, but in spite of himself, he could not remember anything.

Then there was a loud knocking at his door. With the suddenness of chains breaking, he could feel his memory fill like a jug under a fast tap. One after another, images flooded his consciousness.

In a strange house. In a dark room. *Dead!* It was a terrible revelation.

He looked at his clock—1:50 A.M. He knew that someone calling at this hour could only mean one thing. The police had found him.

"What is it?" he gasped, opening his door to six men, three of whom were uniformed patrolmen.

"We have to ask you some questions about Albert Snyder. He's been murdered. We need you to come back to New York City with us."

"Ridiculous," Gray bellowed. "Do you think I'm crazy? Why I never even met Albert Snyder. The woman must be crazy when she involves me in this thing."

Gray insisted that he had been in Syracuse all weekend. He said he registered at the Onondaga Hotel on Friday, the 18th, and never left town. On Saturday, he arose at about 7:30 A.M., had a bath, then took breakfast in the hotel. After that he visited various customers, went back to the hotel to have lunch with a friend, Haddon Gray, then went to the Elks club. He said he got back to his room at about 3:30.

The proof was that he had written three letters and

mailed them in the chute on the seventh floor of the
Onondaga Hotel. He also telephoned downstairs to
the office that he did not wish to be disturbed. He
was not feeling well and had hung a DO NOT DISTURB
sign outside his door. He went to sleep at about 7:30
P.M.

He said he rose again on Sunday morning at 7:25
A.M., that he went across the street to breakfast in a
lunchroom, took a walk, dropped by the Elks, returned to his room, wrote some more letters, and
worked on his samples.

When asked if he knew Ruth Snyder, he said he
did. He said he last saw her about the second week
in February, and last phoned her on Thursday evening, March 17, from Rochester.

The police then asked Gray to go to New York City
with them to pursue the homicide investigation.

"What's the word homicide mean?" asked Gray.

"Murder."

"Well, the only thing I ever murdered was a little
liquor." He winked.

According to Lieutenant Michael F. McDermott,
who questioned Gray on the train, "He took the
whole thing as a joke." Ruth Snyder had said in her
confession that Gray murdered her husband so that
he might marry her, but how could he marry her, he
laughed, if he was already married? She was obviously
naming him in order to shield someone else. After
all, his alibi checked out. Haddon Gray came forward
to support his story. A check with the hotel switchboard revealed also that the calls he claimed he made
had indeed been made from his room, and back in
New York, Judd Gray's employer was receiving a special delivery letter from Gray, postmarked from
Syracuse at the very time he was supposed to have
been in Queens committing murder. In fact, another

letter from him postmarked the day of the murder
should be arriving at Ruth Snyder's house about now.
How ironic!

He was holding up nicely. Fielding every question.
Bantering with the police. Even charming them. At
least, that's what the police led him to believe.

When more police boarded the train at Albany to
accompany Gray to New York, the prisoner rose to
his feet to give each new arrival a hearty handshake.

Maybe he really was innocent, he let himself think.
Maybe it was a mix-up, some kind of bizarre misunderstanding, a hoax more serious than anything he'd
ever experienced before. Why not? Every other alternative seemed just as unreal to him now.

"My word, gentlemen, you certainly find me in a
peculiar position," he said, smiling. "When you know
me better, you'll find how utterly ridiculous it is for
a man like me to be in the clutches of the law. Why,
in all my life, I've never been given a ticket for speed-
ing."

The conversation with Gray ranged from the vicis-
situdes of the corset business to the trials of detective
work, to the ups and downs of the life of the traveling
salesman. At one point they even reminisced with
him about college days.

"Where did you go to college?" asked James Con-
roy, Assistant District Attorney of Queens, who was
also on the train.

"Cornell," Gray lied. He had never gone to college.

"Why, that's my college," the D.A. exclaimed.

According to the New York *Herald-Tribune,* Judd
Gray and the D.A. then launched into a discussion
of old professors and college chums. Only occasionally, and in a good-natured way, did the conversation
return to the topic of the Albert Snyder murder.

While Gray was pouring some ginger ale for his captors, playing the part of the perfect host, Lieutenant McDermott mentioned as casually as he could that they found something interesting when they searched Gray's room at the Onondaga Hotel in Syracuse. In his wastepaper basket, amid scraps of paper, cigarette butts, sales tapes, and what have you, they had found a piece of a ticket.

"Did you know, Judd, that we have the Pullman ticket you went back on?" He showed him the stub dated March 20 from New York to Albany.

Complete silence followed. Gray's face became white, his smile disappeared, all of his hostlike vivacity vanished. Suddenly the atmosphere shifted and in words that were barely audible, he said, "Gentlemen, I was in Queens Village that night. Yes, gentlemen, I was there."

And so he confessed.

Once he started, there was no holding him back. Speaking in a dry, high voice, his words and emotions flowed in a gushing, ice-cold torrent that mixed shame, terror, and the clarity of vivid recollection. He talked almost nonstop from the moment he began in Poughkeepsie till the train came to a halt in Grand Central Station.

"My name is Henry Judd Gray and I live at . . . Wayne Avenue, East Orange, New Jersey. I make this statement voluntarily of my own free will, without fear or coercion, knowing that anything I say may be used against me.

"I was introduced to this Mrs. Snyder about two years ago in town by Harry Folsom. I believe that he had picked she and another girl up at the restaurant. I came in from a trip and he introduced me to her.

I didn't see her, I don't think, for two or three months after that. I would say probably it was two months when she wrote me and asked me to get her a corset. I am in the corset business. I am a salesman. I did that."

One of the main differences between Ruth Snyder's and Judd Gray's accounts of their relationship, it quickly became apparent, was in the characterization of his feelings for her. Whereas Ruth Snyder in her confession remembered every meeting with Judd Gray, he indifferently stated he could not say for sure when their affair began. He was also careful to state that a friend of his picked her up first—as if she were cheap goods. Nowhere did he mention love.

He acknowledged being attracted: "She is a woman of great charm—I probably don't have to tell you that—and I did like her very much and she was good company and apparently a good pal to spend the evening with," but, as Gray remembered, she pursued him. She was the motivated one. "She called me considerable and wrote to me very often," he testified. "To use the slang, she played me pretty hard for a while."

According to Gray, he told her that "there could never be anything between us as far as we were concerned, as I was happy at home and had a very fine wife." Which raised an interesting question—namely, why Ruth Snyder would have pursued a man like him in the first place. There was nothing romantic or exciting about him, nothing that seemed capable of inspiring even the most middling sexual response, and there was hardly a shred of evidence to suggest that Snyder needed someone to be dependent on her in the way Gray was. Why would she play the corset salesman "pretty hard"? Why make him her confidante and permanently tie him to her through the act of murder?

If no answer was forthcoming, Judd Gray more than compensated by sharing this startling revelation—that Ruth Snyder had repeatedly tried to kill her husband before March 20, the date of Albert Snyder's actual murder. "As this thing kept growing," Gray told the police, "she made several attempts upon his life. She told me and I told her I thought she was terrible. That was some time ago. I think this last December, and January and February there were more attempts made. I think in two instances she gave him sleeping powders, or so-called sleeping powders, and turned on the gas. I think she gave him bichloride of mercury at the time he was sick with hicoughs. Also after that more was given.

"She wrote me. I think—that is if I recall it—she gave him four at one time and six another and all her plans seemed to fail."

Gray claimed that Ruth Snyder continually hounded him to assist her, and he had every intention of turning her down. "I have always been a gentleman," he protested, weakly. "And I have always been absolutely on the level with everybody. I have a good many friends. If I ever have after this I don't know. And I absolutely refused at first to be a party of any such plan, and with some veiled threats and intents of lovemaking, she reached the point where she got me in a such a whirl that I didn't know where I was at." (The "veiled threats" consisted of Ruth Snyder's intimations that she would inform Gray's wife of the nature of their relations unless he helped her get rid of her husband.)

Despite all of Gray's intentions to resist her, he always gave in. He couldn't refuse Ruth Snyder anything. "During the past two weeks since this plan was concocted I have been in literal hell. That is the truth, because I have a very fine little wife and a wonderful mother. You may say that it is strange to say that now."

It was, indeed, strange to say. Why he acquiesced to Ruth Snyder's scheme remained the profoundest of mysteries. After all, this was a man who the arresting detectives said was "as nice appearing a gentleman as you'd want to meet." As the *Herald-Tribune* described him, "He was a Red Cross worker in the World War, was an assiduous worker for the Sunday school of the First Methodist Church, was quiet mannered in the home and a local country club man. He golfed and bridged and motored. He was a member of the Orange Lodge of Elks."

As Judd Gray described himself, "I was a morally sound, sober, God-fearing chap. . . . I met plenty of girls—at home and on the road, in trains and hotels. I could, I thought, place every type: the nice girl who flirts, the nice girl who doesn't, the brazen out-and-out streetwalker I was warned against. I was no sensualist, I studied no modern cults, thought nothing about inhibitions and repressions. Never read Rabelais in my life. Average, yes—just one of those Americans Mencken loves to laugh at. Even belonged to a club—the Club of Corset Salesmen of the Empire State—clean-cut competitors meeting and shaking hands—and liking it."

Here was a man who had a loving family. Here was one who was liked by everyone. Here was a triumph of American normalcy, and here was one who committed murder.

How was such an enigma explained? How was Judd Gray's senseless crime reconciled with his prior record beyond saying, along with H. L. Mencken, that "sin is a dangerous thing in the hands of the virtuous.

It should be left in the hands of the congenitally sinful, who know when to play with it and when to let it alone." Was it possible that this God-fearing Elk believed he was already damned for committing adultery, and so had nothing left to lose by committing another sin? After all, he wrote in his memoirs that "if you break one of God's Commandments, you are under the curse of a broken law as truly as if you had broken them all." Could it have been his stubborn refusal to differentiate between the wrongness of adultery and murder—believing that you can be blinded as easily by an eyelash as by a rusty nail—that did him in? Perhaps Judd Gray's crime "was a sort of public ratification of his damnation," hypothesized Mencken in an article titled, "A Good Man Gone Wrong." Perhaps it was his way of confessing.

In any event, this perfect model of the Y.M.C.A alumnus claimed he went over to the Snyder house two weeks before the murder with every intention of telling his lover to count him out. "I walked Queens Village for two hours and a half and absolutely gave up any idea of it." But like a man stupefied by some diabolical drug, he turned back, completely unable to mount a defense. "I started to hear from her again when I got out on the road and called her up and she said this night of last Saturday when they were going to a party, that she would leave doors open and I might get in."

That was all the instruction Gray needed, because he arrived at Grand Central Station that Saturday night at 10:20, carrying in his briefcase a bottle of chloroform, some cotton waste, and two pieces of picture wire. As he walked down Fifth Avenue, in a state of shock over the wickedness of the world, he was so dizzy that he could barely manage to stay upright. The buildings, cars, passersby—everything—danced and rotated before his eyes. For a moment, he contemplated sitting or lying down somewhere on the sidewalk, but thinking that someone might be following him, he hurried his pace. When he got to Penn Station and caught the Long Island Railroad to Queens, he noticed a scrap of Italian newspaper that had fallen from a passenger's bundle. On a sudden whim, he picked it up and placed it in his briefcase alongside his other murder paraphernalia.

Shortly after midnight, Judd Gray was in Queens Village. The side door of the Snyder house was open, so he let himself in. A package of cigarettes was on the kitchen table. Ruth Snyder had written him that if a package of cigarettes was on the table, they would not be at home. If there were no cigarettes, he was to wait in the kitchen, but Judd Gray could not remember what the cigarettes meant—home or not home. His head was numb. He felt he had to rest. At last, he went up to Ruth Snyder's mother's room, as she had instructed. He removed his overcoat and threw it in the closet and fell into a chair.

It was as though a cloud had descended on Gray and enclosed him in a dark and dismal loneliness. In recalling his thoughts afterward—several months afterward—he realized that he was delirious, perhaps even drugged. "Ruth had written to me to look under the pillow and find the weight, a bottle of whiskey, and cutting pliers (the telephone wires were supposed to be cut). I took a drink from the small bottle she left for me. I finished it in one drink. I started to perspire, took off my coat and was so dizzy I had to sit down on the floor. What was in the bottle I do not know, but my head went round and round—and the room seemed to expand—into space. My legs felt as if they were stilts—wood. I cannot tell how long I sat there—I had an impulse to go—to fly. I picked up my briefcase and coat, forgetting my overcoat and hat, and started downstairs. I heard a machine, an automobile, and fled up the stairs again. I say fled—stumbled, rather, on those long wooden pegs of mine. I flopped unnerved on the floor—lay there. I reached out and took a drink from the quart bottle. Again I had that wild impulse to run—and made the landing facing the front door. Their car drove up, and I just reached the room again as Ruth and Lora entered the house. I dropped to the rug, motionless."

Ruth Snyder and Lorraine passed down the hallway, past the room in which he was hiding. His door was slightly ajar. There was no light in the hall, so no one could see him. "The youngster and Mrs. Snyder came up first, I think, and she went into her bedroom and came back into her mother's room. Mr. Snyder, I imagine, had driven up his car with his wife and the little girl and he was in the garage when they came up. *I was trapped.*"

After Ruth Snyder put Lorraine to bed, she came into the room where Gray was. "She said, 'You are going to do it, aren't you?'

"I said, 'I think I can.' "

Her calm determination—no, her *excited* determination—filled him with an incongruous terror that not even the purchase of the window weight had aroused. He told her to go back to bed, figuring he could steal away. "But she didn't go," he recalled, a wave of futility breaking over him, smashing him. "She stood right there in the doorway, and I started after her."

Ruth Snyder claimed Gray kissed her and walked into her husband's room on his own while she remained in the hall, but Gray said "She went first. I followed her to the bedroom and it was I that hit him the first blow with the window weight. He started to fight me and she got very excited. I scarcely knew what did happen for a short time. He got me by the necktie and I think—I am positive that she started to belabor him with this sash weight after that."

Ruth Snyder had characterized Gray as the active one, the leader. In Gray's version of events, though, Ruth Snyder was in charge. Whatever potion this Momie-spider gave Judd Gray turned him into a paralytic who could only use his body on her orders, to enact whatever evil she designed for him: "She had the handkerchief and the bottle of chloroform which she poured on the bed. . . . She passed me a necktie and I tried to tie his hands and I couldn't. She tied his hands with a towel and . . . gave me a necktie to tie his feet and she covered up his head. He was still alive the last that I heard.

"She said 'Is he dead?'

"I said, 'No.'

"She said, 'This thing has absolutely got to go through or I am ruined.'

"I said, 'Well, I am through.' "

Another glaring discrepancy was over the question of who applied the picture-wire tourniquet to Albert Snyder's throat. Ruth Snyder said it was all Gray, from first to last. Gray saw it differently: "I am pretty sure, if you gentlemen said that there was picture wire around his neck, that it must have been tied by her. I don't know whether it was around his neck or not; this I don't recall. I went right back to the bathroom."

Ruth Snyder and Judd Gray even disagreed regarding the presence of the paper wrapping on the window weight. Snyder claimed that "in the darkness the white paper on the weight stood out." But Gray said that his lover refused him (and the murder victim) even this tiny gesture of humanity: "I had the weight wrapped in paper because I didn't think it would hurt so much. She evidently stripped that because it was bare."

After Albert Snyder had been murdered—and then murdered again and again—Ruth Snyder said that Gray took charge of destroying evidence and re-arranging the crime scene: "He went downstairs and burned the shirt and the paper with the bloodstains on it."

By contrast, Gray claimed he was disoriented and helpless after the murder and that Ruth Snyder had to take care of him and everything else: "I had blood on my shirt and hands and came back to the bedroom when I noticed the blood on my shirt and vest. I had my coat off because it was hot in there. Things were just a bit hazy during that period. I didn't know where I was. I couldn't seem to collect my brain for a minute.

"She brought me in a shirt of his and it was a new shirt. It was blue. I took off my own shirt and I didn't know that she also burned a robe of hers which was all covered with blood. I think she also burned a nightgown.

"I was not there at the time. I was putting on my shirt. She called me down to the cellar and told me what she had done and she had hidden the weight. . . .

"I put some coal on the furnace and came downstairs and started to throw things about, as you know, to make it appear as though it were a robbery. I know that I sat there and had three or four drinks.

"She gave me this bottle that went to Syracuse. She had given me, I guess a small bottle [actually a flask] together with a larger bottle, which I think was probably my undoing, as far as I was concerned, because even when I was sitting there, I firmly in my own mind absolutely said it would not go through.

"But it did, unfortunately. I went downstairs and this story was then thought of. She said that a man with glasses had been peeking into the house and this is how the story came into mind that two foreigners had come in to rob them.

"I happened to pick up this piece of Italian paper in a train coming over that night and I put it in my pocket, which accounts for that part of it. It was around the bottle of chloroform when she took it into their room.

"I sat there and said, 'I don't think you better make it one [Italian thug], you better make it two.' That is as far as plans went.

"I stayed there, sat more or less in a daze, until I suddenly discovered it was getting daylight and I left."

At this point in his confession, Judd Gray began to cough violently. "Boys, my throat is hurting me," he said hoarsely. "May I take some of my cough medicine?"

Nobody interfered while Gray fumbled at his suitcase with his handcuffed hands. He opened it, rummaged inside, and drew forth a flask. He was about to draw the cork with his teeth when one of the detectives reached over and took it from him. Gray coughed again and looked appealingly at the detective. A week later, a toxicologist found the flask to contain twenty grams of bichloride of mercury.

4

The Murderee

Albert Snyder, born Schneider, was one of six siblings. He was quite close to his mother, and enjoyed painting and papering for her. He was considered quite artistic, was encouraged to study art, and even enrolled in the Pratt Institute for a couple of years.

In 1913, he was hired by *Motor Boating* as a freelance artist at a salary of twenty-five dollars a week. The next year he married Ruth.

The match was doomed from the start. Following the wedding, when Ruth Snyder moved into her husband's small, wood-frame home in Brooklyn, her eyes fell on the photograph of a sad young woman, regally tall and gowned in white, hanging above the staircase landing. She asked Albert who the woman was. His former fiancée, he replied. He and Jessie Guishard had been engaged to be married, but she caught pneumonia. He was at her bedside when she died.

Three years later, when the Snyders moved to the Bronx, Albert unwrapped the portrait of his former fiancée and hung it in the living room. Six years later, when they moved to Queens Village, he again conveyed the portrait to their new home. This time, however, Ruth forbade him to hang it up. It wasn't appropriate for a married man to display portraits of former girlfriends, she said.

Albert Snyder quietly went along because, as the years passed, he had become used to his wife telling him what he could do and what he couldn't, what was permissible and what wasn't.

First, she asked him to give up his family name of Schneider. She felt it sounded too Germanic. Snyder was better, she said, more American.

Albert agreed.

She also asked this lifelong boating enthusiast to sell his beloved craft. Wouldn't the money be better used if invested in one of those new seven-passenger Buicks?

Albert agreed, again.

Once the new Buick was purchased, the question came up as to how to make best use of it. Ruth thought it would be wiser for Albert to leave the car home during the week and take the train to work. That way Ruth could have the car for running errands.

Albert agreed yet again.

Ruth next said she needed more money to cover daily living expenses—$85 each week from his $115 per week income should cover it.

Ruth also asked if her mother could move in. She could occupy the spare bedroom and help with Lorraine and the house. Taking care of such a large house on her own was quite a lot of work, Ruth protested.

Ruth mentioned to Albert that she sometimes had difficulty getting money when she needed it. She suggested that he convert the checking and savings accounts into joint accounts, so she could get cash and write checks on her own, without bothering him.

Albert Snyder always agreed to everything. If one hadn't known that a man lived in the Snyder home, one would have thought it the residence of two or three prudish older women with a taste for knitting and fluffy upholstery. There was hardly any evidence that he lived in his own home—no fishing trophies, no tobacco jars or old pipes lying around, no golf clubs, fishing tackle or adventure books. Instead, feminine artifacts were everywhere: knickknacks with ribbons tied to them, ornamental dishware, vases with flowers, frilly things neatly displayed in toilet cases, lace curtains on the windows, rose-colored bedspreads on the beds. Instead of finding pictures on the wall of boats and ships, as one might expect from the art editor of *Motor Boating* magazine, there were paintings of pale young women knee-deep in fields of daisies or lingering windblown, but not less pale, beside a blustering sea.

Where did the unobtrusive Snyder spend his time amidst this feminine bric-a-brac? Mostly in the cellar where there was a small workbench and some tools. Before he was murdered, he devoted three or four evenings to putting together a small birdhouse. People were surprised how pretty it was. It was sitting on his workbench.

The attic also contained some signs of his existence. In the corner were some neatly labeled boxes where he kept his things. One was inscribed SEEDS FOR GARDEN, another was MEDICINE FOR BABY, and yet another ODDS AND ENDS.

His pattern of existence, it seemed, was to go to the cellar or attic each evening, work on his projects, and then go quietly to bed, apparently unaware that his wife was at a nightclub or hotel with her lover, Judd Gray.

When members of his family visited at night and

found Albert alone, he would simply say, "Ruth had to go out," and that would be all. He did not dare to lodge a complaint because, after all, he had Ruth to thank for his home and the stillness of his life. Just think how peaceful it was with Ruth gone in the evenings, with nothing to keep him from retreating to his workbench, where he could dream the sweet dream of tranquility, of satisfied desire, of achieved ambition, for he was by himself.

How, people asked, could anyone be so perverse? How could he be so stupid? To fail to recognize that he was being forced out of his own home, to fail to read the meaning of his wife's frequent overnight absences, to fail to recognize that on many occasions, on the bed in the room adjoining his, separated by only a few inches of lathe and plaster, his wife lay in the arms of a strange man? How could he come home every evening, acting as if nothing was wrong, when his wife was treating his very existence as a reproach, plotting his extermination as if he were a bug?

Part of the answer, surely, was that most people go through life denying that anything terrible can happen or that anyone in their immediate circle would deliberately harm them. Call it foolish, but Albert Snyder felt safe within his family.

Another part of the answer, no doubt, had to do with Albert Snyder's attitude toward life. He never complained; he never questioned what life gave him. "A house to live in, enough food to eat, a good job—what more do you need?" Worry and dissatisfaction were not included in his philosophy, and he had no sympathy for either. As his boss at *Motor Boating* magazine described him: "First of all, let me say right here that he was a man, a real man, a man's man, like scores of your own good friends and mine; a quiet, honest, upright man, ready to play his part in the drama of life without seeking the spotlight or trying to fill the leading role. Our world is made up of countless good, solid men like this. . . . Perhaps he was slow to make friends, though in his bowling club he was the life of the party."

Many people thought that Albert Snyder's passivity came from the fact that Ruth had cast some sort of spell on him, much as a snake hypnotizes a bird. That was a notion that Judd Gray would have supported, based on his own experience with Ruth Snyder's powerful gaze—"The eyes that were so completely thrilling, so reassuringly and genuinely honest. . . . I sympathized—I pitied her—but something deeper stirred within me—a sort of blind hunger to just sit there and look across the table into her eyes. . . ." As the *Daily Mirror* put it on one occasion, "Love, overwhelming love for the woman who was so unworthy of his devotion, made Albert Snyder putty in her hands."

"I forgive you, Ruth," Albert was supposed to have said. "I can't help it—I love you."

For those who still wondered why this man hung around like a lapdog while his wife figured out how to murder him, there was another theory. The criminologist F. Tennyson Jesse suggested that Snyder remained silent despite his wife pressuring him to take out an accident policy, despite her arranging everything, even payment of the premiums, because he was a murderee. He was indifferent to the sudden rash of accidents, the string of curious overdoses and near misses, that coincided with his life becoming insured, because he wanted to die. According to F. Tennyson Jesse, Snyder was as responsible for his own death as his wife—no, he was more responsible—because he enticed her to do it. According to her theory, Albert Snyder was not a personality so much as

a caricature, a born victim, one for whom self-anni-
hilation appeared to be a natural destiny. He existed
in a completely segmented way—as a stimulant of
Ruth's homicidal desire.

Albert seemed to be possessed by an inner demon
pushing him toward his own murder. That he allowed
himself to be elbowed out of his house, out of his
income, his boat, his name, and finally, out of his life,
showed that nature is a composite system of related
parts, that murder is not simply a result of choice or
of some random events, but a matter of total cosmic
organization. Those who followed this interpretation
saw that the two levels of the crime—the criminals
and the victims—corresponded to each other in detail, that there was some underlying necessity, something in the nature of things, which made this
murder—Albert Snyder's murder—inevitable.

Judd Gray's confession raised the possibility that
Ruth Snyder had attempted to murder Albert repeatedly over the past year, and that this most obliging
victim stood by passively as she administered sleeping
powders, gas, and bichloride of mercury.

That possibility was confirmed the day after Gray's
confession when a large quantity of bichloride of
mercury was found in a bottle of whiskey taken from
the Snyder home. A toxicologist heated up a piece
of copper wire, dipped it in hydrochloric acid and
thrust it in the whiskey—the standard quick test for
bichloride of mercury. If the poison is present, mercury deposits should appear on the copper wire in
minute globules. Usually a microscope has to be used
to detect the deposit, but in this instance, no microscope was needed. After the copper wire was removed
from the whiskey, it seemed silver-plated, so thickly
was it coated with mercury. The toxicologist in-

formed the police that the whiskey contained so much poison that a teaspoonful would have killed.

One of Albert Snyder's brothers then came forward to relate an incident to which no significance was attached at the time, but after Gray's confession, loomed as another murder attempt. On the occasion in question, Ruth Snyder left the house while her husband was taking a nap on the living room sofa. She went to the corner drugstore, where she lingered for more than an hour in conversation with clerks and in half-hearted dabbling at a soda. When she returned, she found the house full of gas and her husband in the backyard gasping for breath. "Oh, I thought you were sleeping," she exclaimed, according to Albert Snyder's brother. It soon became apparent that a tube from the gas stove had been disconnected. "I must have kicked it off accidentally," Ruth Snyder said. Snyder's brother and two sisters became suspicious. Examining the gas tube, they concluded that it could not have been disconnected unless someone had deliberately pulled it off.

Was Albert Snyder determined to die as a martyr to love? Perhaps, but it is also important to consider that his saintly image existed beside a much darker portrait, one that made him appear mean and overbearing. To Ruth Snyder's mother, Mrs. Josephine Brown, Albert Snyder was not a pathetic soul; indeed, he was quite headstrong, demonstrating a distinct persistence and creativity in the pursuit of his own death. As she told the newspapers, "The other side— the prosecution—has said so much. They have made Ruth out a bad, vicious, common woman. But I speak for her. I lived in her home for many years, and I know the neglect and indifference that made her life with Albert a miserable disappointment."

Speaking with few gestures and little change in fa-

cial expression, an effect which was heightened by
the fact that she had no eyebrows, or almost none,
Mrs. Brown described Albert Snyder as a mean and
callous father: "He was always finding fault with Lorraine. He expected a little girl of nine to have the
mind of an adult of twenty-nine. If Lorraine put her
elbows on the table at meals, Albert bellowed at her.
If Lorraine wasn't up in the morning when he was
ready to leave, he punished her. The child avoided
him all she could. She wanted to keep out of his way.
Ruth was afraid to leave Lorraine alone in her own
father's care."

In confirmation of Mrs. Brown's view, on April 4,
the New York *Daily News* reported that Mrs. Brown
said that "Albert Snyder always wanted a boy," and
that "when Lorraine was born, he was disgusted and
disappointed." Beside the article was a photo of Lorraine Snyder as a five-month-old baby. The caption
read: "The innocent cause of the murder of Albert
Snyder . . . Little Lorraine." If Lorraine hadn't been
born, the *Daily News* would have its readers believe,
Albert Snyder would not have been so surly and ne-
glectful, so rude and inconsiderate, and therefore so
deserving of death.

His neglectfulness was the least of it, contended
Ruth Snyder's mother. He was physically threatening.
Only a week before he was murdered, he menaced
her daughter Ruth with a hammer. "Albert had been
trying to fix the radio unit in the piano, which was
out of order," she told reporters. "He fussed with it
for some time, but it refused to work for him. Then
Ruth came along, tinkered with it for a moment, and
pushed the piano back. It started to work at once.

"Albert was furious. He raised the heavy hammer
he had in his hand and shook it over his head. 'You

damn buttinsky,' he roared. 'You don't give me credit for anything.'

"I threw in a few quieting words," said Mrs. Brown, "trying to make peace, and finally he subsided.

"That was typical of their home life. Albert flew into a rage about the slightest thing.

"Another time he became angry over some fancied slight—I can't recollect what it was. One word led to another. Finally, he rushed upstairs where he kept his revolver.

" 'I'm going to blow my brains out,' he yelled. Ruth ran after him. She threw her arms around him, kissed him repeatedly, and assured him over and over of her love. He finally quieted down."

In Mrs. Brown's view, Albert Snyder was a tyrant who wanted his way about every detail of family life— regardless of how small. "Once we had a lovely little French bulldog," said Mrs. Brown. "Ruth called her Babe. Lorraine was crazy about her. Albert grumbled so much about the dog that for the sake of peace we had to give the creature to the Society for the Prevention of Cruelty to Animals."

The tales of Albert Snyder's permissiveness and generosity with his wife were all grossly exaggerated, said Mrs. Brown. "I don't suppose she went to the city more than three times a month. He always kicked when she wanted a little recreation or wanted to visit her folks."

As for him giving her eighty-five dollars a week, that too was a lie. "I know because I lived in the house and noticed Ruth's economies. It has been said he gave her eighty-five dollars a week for the house. He was supposed to give her eighty dollars, but week after week sometimes passed when he failed to give her anything. All expenses—clothes and everything— came out of the household allowance."

Ruth Snyder was an excellent mother and house-keeper, despite the fact that her husband gave her no support at all, said Mrs. Brown. To prove it, she led the reporters through the house, pointing to the signs that the woman who presided over it was a faithful housewife, utterly devoted to her home. "Look at these curtains," said Mrs. Brown, lifting the warm red drapery for the reporters to see. "Ruth hemmed all these. She made all the curtains in the house by hand."

In the kitchen she pointed to her daughter's immaculate white-enamel gas stove. "Four years old, but it looks like new, doesn't it? Ruth kept it as clean as a dish."

When they got to the basement, the tour guide indicated the rows of jellies, preserves, cherry and elderberry wines. Everything had on it a small label designating what it was. "All made by Ruth," exclaimed the proud mother. "How many housewives nowadays put up fruit?"

A canary's chirping was heard in the background. Mrs. Brown marched the reporters to the dining room, pointing to a gilded cage.

"Was that Ruth's bird? Did she care for it, too?" the reporters asked.

Ruth Snyder's mother nodded so vigorously that her glasses almost fell from her face. "Oh, yes, she loved Pete. She fed him every day. She was very, very good to Pete."

Ruth had a special feeling for animals, said her mother. "Why, Ruth cried for three days and made herself sick when her dog, Babe, died. She was too faint-hearted to send her old cat, Tab, away. I had to do that."

Ruth Snyder's nine-year-old daughter, Lorraine, added more data on her mother's caregiving. "Do you see my new shoes?" she asked a reporter from the *Daily Mirror.* "Mamma got me these about two weeks ago—for Easter, you know. They were terribly expensive—'most seven dollars they cost. You see, I wear lady's size now, and you can't get lady's size cheap. When Daddy saw 'em, he said, 'Aw, why did you pay so much? It's silly to pay so much for a child's shoes.'"

A reporter noted an Easter egg stuck in the corner of Lorraine's mirror depicting a rabbit going to church. "From Mr. Gray," Lorraine said, giggling. "He was nice to me. Once I met him and Mamma in New York. We went to lunch there."

Then Lorraine shared a letter she had written to her mother. The childish characters read:

Dear Mother,
I hope you will come home soon. I am very lonesome without you. I pray for you every night. I have nobody to read the Three Bears and Cinderella as you useter. I still have the candy for your birthday and it is getting stale. I send you a lot of love and kisses to you. Your loving baby,
XXXXXXXXXXXXXXXXX, Lorraine Snyder.

"No, I didn't love my daddy," Lorraine continued, "not like I love Mamma. He never read to me or helped me say my prayers. Mamma used to read to me. I like fairy stories best, Cinderella and The Three Bears. Every night after I say 'Now I lay me down to sleep,' I say, 'please God, bring Mamma home.' I hope He does it real soon."

Mrs. Brown conceded there were times when Albert took his wife to the theater or to a restaurant, but "he kicked for a week afterward about the price of the tickets, and grumbled about how much more cheaply they could have eaten at home.

"Naturally Ruth, being young and lighthearted, tired of her humdrum life. She is thirty-two, you know. Albert was forty-six, and set in his ways." Then Mrs. Brown pulled Lorraine to her feet. "Look at how nicely Lorraine is dressed. Ruth made this outfit by hand. She was a perfect housewife and probably would never have noticed Judd Gray if Albert had given her a little affection."

Albert Snyder did not possess a winning personality; nonetheless, most observers took Mrs. Brown's characterization of him with a grain of salt. She was Ruth Snyder's mother, first of all. Second, for every negative image of Snyder she offered, the tabloids came up with a series of counterimages which portrayed him in a very sympathetic light. Consider, for example, the way the press represented Albert Snyder's relationship to his dead fiancée, Jessie Guishard. To them, that story proved that Albert Snyder was a highly romantic figure, a veritable reincarnation of Heathcliff, with Jessie Guishard, his Cathy. She was "a ghostly presence who dominated the Snyder home," the papers said, "haunting Ruth and Albert with the memory of a sad and wistful woman who was as kind and generous as she was beautiful." Albert Snyder had loved her since childhood, and he could not stop loving her, not after she died, not after he married, not after more than a decade passed. Like the tragic hero from *Wuthering Heights,* Albert Snyder continually reproached his wife for not being his lost love, for not being as slim, for being less beautiful, less intelligent, less cultivated and gentle, until Ruth, overcome by hurt and jealousy, finally mur-

dered him. Perhaps the most ironic feature of this
tale was Ruth Snyder's claim that the metal pencil
used to twist the picture wire around Albert Snyder's
throat—the pencil originally thought to belong to
Judd Gray because it had the initials J.G.—was purchased by Jessie Guishard as a memento for her fiancée, Albert.

Another story—this one from the *Daily Mirror*—
had Albert Snyder as the muscular protector of his
wife and family. That Albert Snyder and Judd Gray
met only once—on the night Gray murdered him—
did not prevent the papers from claiming that the
cuckolded husband beat his rival "within an inch of
his life" when he caught Ruth in the corset salesman's arms.

"He flung open the door of his wife's room and
there he beheld them—they had heard him enter
and had jumped to their feet in alarm. A whiskey
bottle was on the table.

"Fear, yellow and cringing, came into Gray's eyes.
Mrs. Snyder, holding her dressing gown about her,
ran screaming to a corner.

"Snyder grabbed Gray by the throat and buried his
fingers in his flesh. Snyder's lips curled in hate as he
framed the fitting epithet:

" 'You . . . dirty . . .' "

Albert Snyder was a very tragic person, but he was
also, according to the newspapers, a very complicated
one, possessing many personalities, both good and
evil, nested inside each other. That he was described
as a (1) death-seeking murderee, (2) martyr to love,
(3) devoted husband and father, (4) spouse abuser
and child abuser, (5) the life of his bowling club, (6)
a man's man, (7) guardian of his wife and family, (8)
sensitive artist, (9) assiduous employee, (10) avid
sportsman, (11) petty complainer and whiner, and

(12) haunted lover, made it appear that there was no male experience or emotion which failed, sooner or later, to connect with some part of him. Whatever role people needed a husband to play, Albert Snyder was there, fitted to their needs until they could no longer grant him any attribute. In the public's imagination, this pure, virtually empty figure, represented every husband and every father.

5

Mother Love

Ruth Snyder remained in police custody, where she felt sadder and more helpless than ever before in her life. It wasn't simply that she was in jail, accused of first-degree murder, nor was it that she had little to do—no exercise, no radio, few magazines, and even fewer visitors. It was that she had to remain silent while her name was being dragged through the gutter. She was being compared to Lucretia Borgia, Medusa, Messalina, Jezebel, Lady Macbeth.

"Fiend wife," journalists called her, the "blond fiend," the "marble woman," the "faithless wife," "flaming Ruth," "ruthless Ruth," the "Viking ice matron of Queens Village." "If Ruth Snyder is a woman," thundered one columnist, "then, by God! you must find some other name for my mother, wife, or sister." The *New York Post* described her as hard-faced, heavy, and coarse, and the *Herald-Tribune*, after criticizing her for having rough skin, straight hair, and wearing a wrinkled dress, issued the most damning judgment of all, "She is not well-groomed." A phrenologist hired by the *Mirror* said Ruth Snyder's eyelids have "a compressed or flattened appearance," and her mouth is "as cold, hard, and unsympathetic as a crack in a dried lemon." He concluded that she has "the character of a shallow-brained pleasure-seeker, accustomed to unlimited self-indulgence, which at last ends in an orgy of murderous passion and lust, seemingly without parallel in the criminal history of modern times."

She was furious—and frustrated. If only she could challenge the lies that were being written about her, if only she could publicly explain her side of the story, then everyone would know that she was not the wicked person that was being portrayed in the press. After all, she had convinced her mother of her innocence and her attorneys, "who knew the truth," believed her. Surely she could not make things any worse for herself if she took her case directly to the people.

Unfortunately for Ruth Snyder, she and her attorneys decided that this impulse had some merit. It was a mistake that would haunt her forever. Before she began holding press conferences, people could only speculate on her personality and motivations. She was a fantasy figure, a storybook character, but afterward, as one self-serving quotation followed another, they fleshed out the picture of a relentlessly high-minded and moralistic woman whose principal mode of address was self-congratulation. She patted herself on the back all day long. She not only felt no sadness or remorse over the murder of her husband, but was indignant when others indicated she should. Moreover, this prickly, touchy, self-absorbed woman—so easily irritated by reporters' questions, yet so quick to describe herself as tenderhearted—appeared incapable of saying anything genuine. It was nearly impossible to tell when or whether she was telling the truth, not only about the murder and her role in it, but about anything at all. It would have taken a polygraph expert, some kind of criminal cryptographer, to authenticate what she said.

Ruth Snyder's first press conference was held on the afternoon of March 26, in the "Bridge of Sighs," the small visiting room which connected the Queens County Jail to the courthouse. Wearing the same green hat and muskrat coat she had worn at every public appearance since her arrest, she began by announcing, "I had nothing whatsoever to do with that murder. Judd Gray lies when he says I did have. My only anxiety now is for my child. My sweet little girl. When this is all over, my only plan is to devote the rest of my life to her. The trial will be an ordeal, but when I emerge, I shall give every hour to my child.

"Meanwhile, I ask the public to refrain from judging me. Wait until the story is told."

"Mrs. Snyder," she was asked, "did you acquiesce to Gray in any of his demands, including your love and the murder?"

"I opposed him as much as I could," she retorted. "He is an arch coward. He looked to me for the initiative in everything, and at first I thought it was just sweet consideration for my wishes. Now I know it was cowardice. I hate him. I hate Judd Gray.

"Any affection, any love that I may have had for Judd Gray has turned to hate," she declared, her eyes flashing, her well-shod foot tapping nervously. "I detest the sight of him for two reasons—for the cruel and barbarous murder of my poor husband, and secondly, because he is not a man and tried to entangle me in this sordid mess.

"Must I say I am innocent?" she asked, as if such a thing were unnecessary.

"Must I? Need I?" Ruth Snyder looked at her attorney, Edgar Hazelton, who sat beside her nodding encouragingly. Then she looked at the press corps, some of whom stared at the floor to avoid her challenging gaze.

"The police have told you a number of things about me that are untrue. These stories point me out in a very bad light. I wish the public, the women, every mother, every daughter, every wife to withhold their final judgment until they have heard all, and I am sure then that they will find some crumb of sympathy, some understanding, some consideration for me in this terrible sorrow that is mine.

"My little daughter, Lorraine"—her voice broke as she uttered that name—"thank God, she does not know anything about all this. She does not know that I am a prisoner. She does not know that her mother is charged with killing her daddy. She does not know that if I am proven guilty, I will be taken away from her, never to return. I am a weak and broken woman."

She hesitated a moment, then suddenly brightened.

"My mother came to see me today. She kissed me and threw her arms around me and it helped me to hear her say, 'I know you didn't do this—you couldn't. Why you wouldn't even hurt a fly when you were a child.'

"And that's true. I have always been tenderhearted and loved nature and life too much to hurt any living thing. I have been used to having pets, and even now we have two canaries at home.

"I will see my little girl tomorrow and, God help me, I am going to be cheerful, and when I kiss her good-bye, I will tell her this: 'Darling, Mother is awfully sick and am in a hospital and will have to stay here a long, long time.' "

Someone in the sea of faces smiled when she said,

"Long, long time." She fixed a stern glance upon him, then resumed. "When Lorraine goes, after I have had a hug and a kiss from her, I am going to tell her to be a big girl and I will be home soon."

She ended abruptly, as an expired tape recording would. She had had enough of this recitation of her feelings, her motives, her hopes—the unfairness of it all. She was weary. Her jailer escorted her back to her cell, where she napped.

The problem with Ruth Snyder's performance, as anyone (except Snyder herself and her attorneys) could plainly see, was that almost none of it was really convincing; almost nothing that she said made people feel that they had touched some literal truth or been in the presence of authenticity. Equally galling was that she showed little sign of sorrow or contrition over her husband's death. Instead, she focused almost solely on how she had suffered—how she was misunderstood and misrepresented.

There was also the way she characterized Judd Gray. Any chance she had of gaining public sympathy was destroyed by the promptitude with which she betrayed him. One minute she was claiming that she loved him—describing the murder of her husband as a crime of passion—and the next, she was squealing on Gray as if he were a gutter rat. Why Snyder blamed him was fairly easy to understand as legal strategy. At its core was a simple premise: since he was being portrayed as a love-mad boob completely dominated by her, why not reverse the order of blame, and portray him as the dominant, evil one, and herself as the trusting innocent? The problem there, of course, was that this was no way for a trusting innocent to treat her former lover. Would Isolde have called Tristan an "arch coward"?

Most troubling—although it did not at the time

seem to have the significance that it would later acquire—was that such statements forced Gray into a corner. Her efforts to shift the blame to him, left him with no alternative but to attempt to shift it back to her—if not immediately, then during the trial, when he had to defend himself. Without realizing the consequences, she had initiated a vicious cycle of accusation and retaliation.

Perhaps Ruth Snyder's most damaging press conference was the one held on April 16, 1927. Despite having had ample opportunity to consult with her lawyers and prepare in advance, she assumed the very tone most likely to do her harm. What inspired the negative reaction was not that she came across as capable of murdering her husband. Everyone already saw her that way. It was that she had the nerve to claim common cause with all wives and mothers. She represented herself as a feminist crusader and martyr, a stand-in for all good, warm, self-sacrificing women everywhere.

"This is a message to my friends and to the people who know me only as a woman whose name has been printed in the headlines of the newspapers since my husband met his death," she began, reading from a prepared statement.

"Mrs. Ruth Brown Snyder, my name is on everybody's lips and undoubtedly there are hundreds who accuse me with helping Henry Judd Gray to kill my husband.

"But I know there are thousands who refuse to believe the evil things that are being said about me, and who realize that because my name is being dragged in the mud and slime of notoriety is no proof that I am not innocent.

"All I ask is that the public withhold its judgment

of me until the jury that will be chosen next week can pass judgment upon me when it returns a verdict.

"I have no fear of the outcome because I know I am innocent. They can't send an innocent woman away for a crime which she did not commit—not in this country.

"How many mothers are there in this country who have read the things that have been said about me? How many of them sit down and think how they would feel if they were enmeshed in a lot of false dodges made upon my name and character by an unscrupulous and vicious man like Judd Gray?

"I knew Judd Gray as well as any woman knows a man. I know him better now than I ever did before. I know that he is a coward, a low, cringing, sneaking jackel, the murderer of my husband, who is now trying to hide behind my skirts to try to drag me down into the stinking pit that he himself willingly wallowed in; to brand me as a woman who killed her husband.

"I AM A MOTHER!" she shouted. "I love my child and I loved my child's father. God! Can you mothers and wives read this and appreciate the terrible, stifling ordeal I am going through at this time? Easter Sunday. Holy Week!

"I wish I was home with Albert and Lorraine. Oh, what a tragic difference a few months make.

"I feel sorry for Mrs. Gray. She is a wife and her lot must be hard to know that her husband could be sent to the depths that he has, that he is a coward so low and rotten that he seeks to drag himself to safety over the body of a woman he wronged.

"I defy Gray to disprove his relations with scores of women. His conscience must be of iron if he has any conscience at all. The women in his life! And he reads the Bible! What a fantastic lie.

"Please, mothers and wives, abide with me in your thoughts. Do not think of me harshly. Your sympathy will not help me before the bar of Justice, but it will comfort me to know that I am not an outcast in the eyes of the women of the world."

People could not believe the audacity. She appeared scarcely human. Wife, mother, murderer, and widow of a murderee—what sort of woman was she? If you met Ruth Snyder on the street, she looked like almost any blond, blue-eyed woman going to the corner grocery for the canned goods. Her muskrat coat, green felt hat, navy blue dress, and beige stockings— garments that could be worn by any woman—were bought with money which her husband, who lay cold and dead, had worked for. The light blue handbag she was carrying on her arm was a Christmas gift from her lover, the very man who had murdered her husband.

The key thing—at least for journalists and their readers—was that this bringing of the wrong images together in the wrong ways made great copy. This chronicle of the sex bombshell, who also happened to be a hardworking housewife, amounted to the most compelling cautionary tale, though it was sometimes difficult to make out what it was warning people against. The evils of adultery and the dangers of greed and the consequences of family breakdown were obvious choices—how they left virtually no one untouched, how they could reach into the lives of the most ordinary individuals, no matter who or where they were, but it was also possible that Americans were being shown how successful they were at resisting sin and temptation. Perhaps, through the tragedy of Ruth Snyder and Judd Gray, Americans were being given an opportunity to see what, in large part, they were not.

In any case, the newspapers knew a good thing when they found it. This mixing of the mundane and the exotic—motherhood and murder, Holy Week and jury selection week, Pete the canary and Judd the jackal—sold newspapers almost as fast as the story of Valentino's death. It even rivaled Lindbergh's crossing the Atlantic. That is why, day after day, alongside the language that described Ruth Snyder as a cold, calculating, remorseless killer, journalists maintained a continuous flow of images of Ruth Snyder doing motherly things, appearing housewifelike, looking demure and innocent.

Nobody knows how Snyder's family album got into journalists' hands—whether someone in the Snyder family sold it, whether it was stolen, or whether Ruth Snyder herself in her passion to improve her public image, came upon the idea of sharing it with the press as a means of generating goodwill. But by the time she was executed, her entire photographic history, including the most personal details of marriage, childbirth, work, play, and death, was as publicly well known as if she belonged, not simply to the Snyder household, but to everyone's. Hundreds of curious facts were known about her more fully than most people knew about their own relatives. In particular, the details of Ruth Snyder's motherhood were a source of endless fascination, resulting in newspaper stories on such mysteries as the contents of Lorraine's prayers, how Lorraine was adjusting to life without her parents, which parent had treated her better, how much she knew about her mother's affair with Judd Gray.

Every aspect of the Snyder-Gray press relations was a sideshow, though a revealing, fascinating, and frustrating one. At the same time Ruth Snyder was calling reporters, Judd Gray was running from them. He refused to speak to the press, a policy he adopted the day after his arrest, when about forty newsmen eavesdropped on his first meeting with his wife, Isabel, in the Bridge of Sighs. How reporters got into the jail and obtained permission to observe this reunion, was not entirely clear, but from the moment Judd Gray and Isabel caught sight of each other and rushed into each other's arms, they were not allowed a moment's peace. Reporters swarmed about them, threatening, waving pencils, trying ineffectually to close in on them. The following exchange, though barely whispered, appeared in print the next day, in every paper in the City.

"I can't understand it. . . . I can't understand it," were the first barely heard exclamations from Isabel. She was a heavy-set woman, almost fat, with a dignified, solemn expression, especially in profile. Her sharp Roman nose and prominent chin clarified a face that was not conventionally, nor even unconventionally, pretty.

She looked directly into her husband's eyes. "Did you do this thing?" she asked.

"Yes."

"Did you make a confession?"

"Yes."

"Did you make it under pressure?"

"I did not," said Judd. "They have treated me like a gentleman."

"Were you in Queens?"

"Yes."

Then Isabel grasped Judd by the arm and said, "Don't forget that all your friends will stand by you. We will assist you in every possible way."

Silent for a few seconds, she finally asked, "But

how is it possible—how could someone like you do a thing like that? Why did you do this thing?"

Judd looked at her, and lowered his head.

She continued staring at him in silence, then said his name, as if not believing the man next to her was really Judd.

Moments later, when Isabel tried to leave, reporters pursued her like sand crabs following the tide. Would she remain faithful to Judd? Would she stand by him? Did she still love him despite all that he had done?

Yes, yes, yes, she answered. "I will stand by my husband no matter what happens. He was insane when he did this. I have engaged a counsel for him and will see the case through. I will spare no expense to save him." She even told them that she saw his relationship to Mrs. Snyder as a sign of his essential goodness. "His insistence upon telling the whole truth has revealed his true character and convinced me he was ensnared in the clutches of a woman responsible for his downfall by his profound sympathy for everyone. This Snyder woman said that Judd was the only one who sympathized with her. It was like Judd. Everybody received his kindest thoughts and consideration. He simply couldn't help sharing the troubles of others."

Her magnanimity appeared unreal. Not only was she offering her husband a forgiveness he did not deserve, she was giving the press, the very people who had only moments ago invaded her privacy, a different sort of undeserved gift. By telling reporters that she had completely forgiven her husband, sharing with them her honesty and humility, she made it possible for them to turn her into an allegorical figure. If Ruth Snyder was this story's seductress, dark lady, and spider woman, then Isabel Gray would appear in the next day's papers as the redeemer, saint, and pro-

tector of traditional values. She would stand for perfect virtue—perfect sacrifice, perfect humility, and
forgiveness. As the *Daily News* described her, every
article of her clothing, every nuance of her expression represented light, truth, and moral rightness:
"She wore a beaver coat of inferior quality, and there
was a long rent on the right shoulder. Her blue hat
was not smart. Her black oxfords were a far cry from
the nifty cream-colored slippers that Mrs. Snyder
wore in court." Her nose, the description continued,
was without powder, her eyes "swollen" with "deep
circles" underneath, and her red face "bleak with
misery as though every emotion she had known in
her better days had been knocked out of her by the
blow just fallen." This shabby little wife, "this miracle
of love known as wifely loyalty," whom Judd Gray
"had shamed and cast out of his heart by his long
amour with the other woman, journeyed from her
home in East Orange, New Jersey, to his prison cell
to tell him she was standing by."

The only problem was that Isabel Gray didn't return to the jail for a second visit, nor did she attend
her husband's trial. It was too painful—and too public. She needed to withdraw to a quiet, gentle place
where she could sort things out. As she explained in
a letter to him:

> I don't know how I have the strength to live from
> day to day, but God gives me courage and my true
> faith in Him is my only salvation.
> All my friends have been so wonderful to me. I never
> dreamt I had so many friends. From all parts of the
> country I get letters and such expressions of sympathy
> and kind wishes for Jane and me!
> It is terribly hard for me to have this unbelievable
> trouble to bear—but poor Jane.

She is all I have and when I look at her my heart aches. She is so innocent and such a darling child.

What can I ever tell her? Now she knows her daddy was in a terrible accident and we won't see him for a long while.

I can't go out. I haven't the strength. I try to sleep, but that fails me, and I think and think, hoping that my thoughts are just a nightmare.

As I sit here the 91st psalm is before me. Read it and you will know my thoughts. I sit and think of anything wrong I have ever done but there is none. I have tried to be a devoted wife and mother to you and dear Jane. I only have the memories of the one loving and kind husband you have always been to me.

YOUR WIFE

With Isabel on the sidelines and Judd Gray refusing interviews, another person came forward as his spokesperson and defender. She was Gray's mother, Margaret Gray. It was a natural development, explained the *Daily Mirror,* for "no wife can sincerely uphold her husband who has sacrificed her, their children and home—in his preference for another woman," but "it is natural for a mother to stand by her child through good or evil—for nothing on earth can change the tie that binds them."

Like Judd Gray's wife, his mother gave love, understanding, asked little in return, and was stoic and long suffering. In addition, she projected those qualities visually. Her face always appeared heavy with sorrow, as if tiny bags of sand had been painfully sewn beneath her features, dragging her skin away from her bones.

During the first of her press conferences, at her daughter's home in West Orange, New Jersey, Mrs. Gray told reporters, "I don't see how Judd could have been sane at the time of the murder. I saw him for the last time before this awful crime on March sixth. He seemed quite all right then."

A few more reporters entered. Gray's mother rose to get chairs for them. She remained standing, an anguished look in her eyes. It was obvious that she was profoundly unhappy, that she wanted to explain things, to put her feelings into words and defend her son. A kind of desperate compassion was expressed in her face and voice.

"Judd never displayed any abnormal tendencies nor vicious temper. He had a normal temper, like most boys. I did everything possible a mother can do and his father, who died only six years ago, was very close to him and instructed him in all phases of life.

"As a boy he was fond of reading, but he divided his time between study and sports. He played tennis and football and was a good student, but left high school in Newark before graduation because of illness. There was a siege of pneumonia that left him with an affected lung. He didn't think he was strong enough to go to college, so he went into business with my husband. But he didn't like the jewelry business and changed over to my own father's establishment in the corset business."

"Did your son drink much?" someone asked.

"He was not what I would call a drinker. He took a glass of wine or liquor socially and we always had wine in the house before prohibition, although Grandfather Gray never touched a drop in his life. But he never came home drunk.

"Judd's home life was ideal. He married Isabel at twenty-two. She was the same age. They had been childhood sweethearts for six years, although theirs was a short engagement.

"I have no explanation whatever to make of his

intrigue with Mrs. Snyder, his participation in the murder, or his complete disregard of his wife and child. I can only say that we never suspected anything. When conditions in the home seem perfect, there is no suspicion. My daughter-in-law never had any cause to believe he was carrying on an intrigue with Mrs. Snyder.

"They never quarreled. There was no dominant personality in the house—they had a fifty-fifty arrangement in which they were both equal in their home. I know she never suspected anything, for if she had, she would have told me. We were and are very close.

"He didn't bring many business friends into his home, but he didn't exclude us from his business. And there were no unexplained absences. He would frequently return home before he was expected and whenever he was in town, he was always with his wife.

"I think he repents strongly of the crime now. I know that I shall do everything that my mother love dictates to help him and not from a sense of duty." Then she added emphatically, "But because I love him."

"Do you love the Judd Gray of today as you did the one you knew?" was the next question.

"I love the son I have known for thirty-five years. The Judd Gray today is a boy I don't understand. But he is one I must help. I am trying to understand, I am trying to help. He must be brought back. I am trying to reach through this strange personality and—" her voice wavered. Tears streamed down her cheeks and her eyes looked inconsolable. She could not continue.

Judd Gray's mother's press conference took place three days before the one in which Ruth loudly proclaimed, "I AM A MOTHER!" Whether Ruth Snyder was in some way responding to Mrs. Gray or was inspired by her, was impossible to say, but these two versions of motherhood contrasted sharply. To the degree that Ruth Snyder appeared self-absorbed and arrogant, Mrs. Gray appeared giving and self-deprecating. One mother was impervious to self-doubt, ready to step over the dead body and march on steadily, resolutely, wherever she had to go; the other, Margaret Gray, was a mother of sorrows—broken, anxious, profoundly troubled.

What made this opposition deeper and more complex than it at first appeared, was that Judd Gray's mother was, in some odd way, too good. Her ever-present warmth may have represented an incredible bounty for Gray, but it diminished him, too. Consider that Gray was over thirty, married, with a nine-year-old daughter, when he received this letter from his mother on April 10, 1927:

> *My Darling Boy:*
>
> *I must talk to you a little before I go to bed. You seem, O, so very far away. I never dreamed my precious boy could get so far away that I could not touch him when I was near him, or that he could ever be in trouble that his mother could not be near to hold his hand and comfort him. It seems so impossible—so carefully reared and loved. O, so much.*
>
> *I think of you as I know you, not the deed I know you in your right mind could never have done. Every one who ever knew you says you were always so kind and loyal a friend and always a gentleman.*
>
> *Dear, if you could have only come to me—you know we always had and still have the perfect understanding—I know this never would have happened. It could not have.*
>
> *Tuesday is our birthday, and I will know that, if*

*my boy could, I would get some lovely card (of which
I have many kept in my desk), so I will think of you
all day, darling, and think of all the years of happy
love we have had together, and leave the rest to the
heavenly Father. I know grandpa, grandma, and
daddy are watching over you, too.*

*My arms are always about you and God will keep
you and make you peaceful, as He has made me—and
all of us—with no bitterness.*

*Darling boy, keep calm, peaceful and manly, as you
have always been until this came into your life—and
praying, praying always for forgiveness. Your mother's
arms are close about you and her loving kisses are on
your lips.*

> *As ever,*
> *Devotedly,*
> *Mother*

To his mother, Judd Gray was "my darling
boy," "my precious boy," "my boy and my pride."
What Gray was not, in any sense, was his own man.
He belonged to his mother. So much so that when
she referred to her birthday, she labeled it our birthday, as if her life and her son's were inseparable. Judd
Gray's mother comforted her son when he was in pain
("Your mother's arms are close about you and her
loving kisses on your lips"), built him up ("You were
always so kind and loyal a friend"), and protected him
("so carefully reared and raised"). She was the nurturant center of his nightmare world.

Was it any surprise then, that Gray's most compelling fantasy while he was in prison was to return to
childhood, to babyhood even, to awaken with his
head on his mother's lap, her dear and tranquil fingers stroking his hair? "I was about four," he recalled,
writing in his cell, "a persistently whirring fly lights

on my nose and I move my head. . . . She strokes my hair with her gloved hand. . . . If I raised my head, Mother would fan me with a cardboard fan that had a beautiful girl pictured on it. She had very red cheeks, blue eyes, and yellow curls, and I fancied she was eating a heaped up plate of ice cream. My sailor suit stretched stiffly, it pricked through my under-clothes. . . ."

Oddly, that fantasy illustrates why this story, though it contained no mystery, no riches or social glam-our—none of the elements ordinarily associated with "successful" popular journalism—caused so much commotion. It makes it clear why Snyder-Gray dou-bled the circulation of every paper in the City, and why even that most respectable tome, the *New York Times,* printed every word of the trial transcript.

More than a bungled murder involving a fattish housewife and a baby-faced corset salesman, it was a story about the complexities of mother love, the ur-gency of a stiffly stretched sailor suit, the threat of a son becoming "the unholy husband of his mother," and a mother becoming a wife to her son. It was about the mingling, melding, and braiding of sin and inno-cence, guilt and salvation, fate and free will, and it was about the telling of a story to witnesses who could not withhold their anger, pity, merriment, and revul-sion. The tragedy of Judd Gray and his "Momie" was a dramatic performance. Its audience consisted of newspaper reporters and readers, a judge and jury, and a chorus of courtroom spectators who collapsed in laughter and dread at the show that was staged for them.

PART II
The Trial

6

Queens County Courthouse

The opening of Ruth Snyder's and Judd Gray's trial on April 18 was like the first day of a long-awaited festival. It was as if all of Queens had declared a holiday.

By eight o'clock, a crowd of several hundred was stationed outside the courthouse, scanning every person who walked up the steps and passed through the main entrance. It would be difficult to exaggerate the degree of frivolity, excitement, and malice manifest that morning. Never before had the vicinity of Long Island City been deluged by so many celebrity hounds. All morning they waited, riveted in place, standing on tiptoe, craning their necks, in the vain hope that they might catch a glimpse of Snyder and Gray as they were escorted from the jail to the court. Now and then the crowd surged as rumors started. "They're coming!" But the only reward they received was from the thirty-odd photographers who, unable to locate any celebrities, began snapping pictures of the crowd itself.

Crowd members, who consisted almost entirely of women, found themselves agreeing on all things, from Ruth Snyder's meanness to Judd Gray's innocence. They were dizzy with the extreme maudlin joy that the trial had awakened in their glowing souls. So fresh and vigorous was their pleasure in having Snyder and Gray—two people so like themselves—to stand in judgment over, that they felt an irrepressible urge to communicate. "I hope the Snyder woman gets the electric chair," was the most common sentiment, closely followed by, "She was much worse than Gray because she put him up to it."

Here at last was confirmation of the myth of the mysterious, insidious influence wielded by a woman over a man! Here was proof that an upstanding and solid man—one who was a faithful and hardworking husband—had no power of resistance once a female viper sank her fangs in him!

Yet the news that Gray's last-minute effort to escape trial by pleading insanity had fallen through was greeted with universal delight. A quartet of court-appointed psychiatrists said he may be a "mama's boy," but was sane enough to be held accountable for murder. Which meant that the public would not be denied the spectacle of seeing the modern Jezebel and her nearsighted lover confront each other in open court. Because they were charged with conspiracy to murder, with aiding and abetting each other, they had to be tried together.

The only problem was that ordinary folk didn't have a chance to get into the courtroom. Not with celebrities such as Fannie Hurst, playwright Willard Mack, philosopher Will Durant, Broadway producers David Belasco and Sam Harris, and the Marquis and Marchioness of Queensbury vying for seats. Only the most select were allowed admission to this theater, a room which contained no fresco or ornament, and had the shape and dimensions of a large, tall box. It seated about 500 people, at least 150 of whom were journalists. The journalists sat in folding chairs, their yellow pads resting on three rows of tables which stretched the entire breadth of the courtroom. Behind them was a railing, and behind the railing, were seats for the spectators, most of whom, during the first few solemn days, sat in pin-dropping silence.

Immediately in front of the journalists were the representatives of the families, the defendants, the lawyers, and then, finally, in the seat of authority, Supreme Court Justice Townsend Scudder. What was most striking about Judge Scudder was that in spite of the tawdriness of the spectacle he was overseeing, there was no doubt of his own dignity and reserve. Coming from one of Long Island's oldest and wealthiest families, his manner was marvelously refined, as if through some sort of astrological confusion, an Oxonian scholar had mistakenly landed in the midst of one of the most bourgeois murder trials in the annals of crime.

No such error seemed to have produced Ruth Snyder's lawyers, Edgar F. Hazelton and Dana Wallace, who were as gritty and perspiring as Judge Scudder was aristocratic. Well-known in Queens for their record of eleven straight acquittals in murder trials, their trademarks were pugnacity and enthusiasm. Instead of leading juries by force of reason and evidence, they led with their heart and lungs. Nobody could match them for roaring and spluttering and bawling—especially Hazelton, who entered so completely into the defender role that he was known to tremble and shed tears for his clients.

During jury selection, Ruth Snyder's attorneys moved about continuously, making quick little gestures with their hands, passing notes to one another, putting their glasses on, then immediately pulling them off, whispering in voices that had all the sonority of barbed wire. Mrs. Snyder sat between them, the center of everyone's rapt, goggle-eyed attention. The general opinion was that she looked more attractive than her photographs, and somewhat younger than her thirty-two years. Although she had a full figure, her lower jaw was a trifle too broad and set forward, and her face a bit puffy and wrinkled, it was very, very hard to stop looking at her. She was remarkable in this way. Despite the fact that she was not a beautiful woman, nor even always pretty, she had a peculiar power of attraction, not exactly sexual, but a certain grace, a way of resting her chin on her hand, for example, as if she was balancing on it something quite likely to fall. She somehow managed to look different every time she was seen—one moment posing, the next grimacing, and the next playing primly coy; sometimes she even appeared regal, dignified by long suffering. She was a carnival to watch.

Another reason she riveted attention was her style. Her trial motif was deep, heartbroken mourning. Instead of colorful silk stockings, she wore sheer black hose and plain black slippers. Her gloves were black, too—kid leather. A floor-length black silk coat with a narrow sealskin collar covered her body, and on her head was a snug black satin hat, the latest thing in Paris that season. The "skyscraper silhouette," they called it, because it rose upward and backward in a flattened sweep. A few tendrils of blond hair peeked out, forming a striking contrast against her hat's somber hue. The final touch was a string of jet black glass beads that fitted tightly about her throat, accentuating its whiteness and delicacy.

Where had Ruth Snyder obtained these clothes? She couldn't have made them in jail. That wasn't possible. But if they were purchased, how could she have selected them and been fitted? "We don't know when she got them," one of Mrs. Snyder's prison matrons told reporters. "But I imagine she has had them some time. They are all bought clothes." Which raised the fascinating possibility that Mrs. Snyder had rushed out on a shopping expedition immediately after murdering her husband or had purchased her mourning attire somewhat earlier, with complete foreknowledge of her husband's brutal death. In any event, her chic widow's weeds, far from winning any sympathy, were added to the already formidable list of evidence against her.

As for Judd Gray, dressed in a smartly tailored, double-breasted blue suit with a triangle of white linen peeping from his breast pocket, he looked calmer than he had since his arrest on March 21, the day after the murder. Freshly barbered and smelling of cologne, only his stubby fingers and posture betrayed his anxiety. His fingers moved continually from his lips to his cheeks and back to his lips again, and his body, slumped low on his spine in his chair, couldn't have looked more despairing. It was a mood which seemed to have spread to his attorneys, William J. Millard and Samuel L. Miller, who spoke, took notes, rose and sat down with the hesitancy and lethargy of performers who believe their work is futile.

In contrast to Gray, who sat all day like a man in a trance, silent, immobile, his back to the courtroom, Ruth Snyder's eyes continually darted around, repeatedly staring at the artists who were sketching her, examining spectators' faces, making comments to her lawyers, giving them her opinion about the potential jurors. Now and then she would rest two fingers on the sleeve of one of her lawyers, who would then turn and consult with her. Both of Snyder's lawyers seemed much interested in their client's opinions, and, indeed, she appeared to have a hand in vetoing the five talesmen who were peremptorily challenged by her lawyers.

But it would be unfair to blame her for the fact that not a single juror was selected from the first fifty who were examined. Ten were excused because they did not believe in capital punishment, and another thirty-one as a sort of tribute to the power of the press—because they had already formed opinions as to the guilt or innocence of the defendants.

By Tuesday, only one juror had been selected from a total of eighty-seven who were questioned. On Wednesday, seventy-four more potential jurors were used up, a new record. In obvious frustration, Judge Scudder left the bench and sat near the jury box in order to expedite the selection process. When a juror professed himself unable to make an unbiased judgment, Scudder asked, "Do you feel that your quality of mind is such that you cannot put aside an impression formed on rumor, gossip, and newspaper reading? Do you really feel that you have that kind of mind?"

The talesman squirmed a little and then announced in a grave voice, "I'm afraid so, Your Honor."

"You feel quite certain that you are so lacking in mental control and strength that you could not give up your present impression of the case and decide the issues strictly on the evidence?"

More squirming, a gulp, then the fatal admission that yes, his intellect was of the inferior sort described by the judge.

A few, unwilling to confirm Judge Scudder's analysis of their brain capacity, changed their opinions and declared that they would be able to suppress their already formed opinions. But most of these, under further questioning by Snyder's lawyers, reverted to the story that their minds were already made up about this case based on newspaper reading and discussion, and so did not qualify as jurors.

"You are excused," Judge Scudder would say, with an undertone of contempt, and the bailiff would swing open the jury box for their exit.

Contrary to what one might imagine, this quizzing was not entirely disappointing as theater. What spectators gained from it was a preview of how Mrs. Snyder's attorneys planned to argue her case. Over and over, Hazelton asked talesmen if they could accept the law of the state which forbade the conviction of a defendant on the uncorroborated testimony of an accomplice, which meant, obviously, that Mrs. Snyder's strategy was to make Gray's accusations appear as lies.

The case for the prosecution depended entirely on establishing that Ruth Snyder planned her husband's murder, but if Gray's testimony was dismissed, then the only compelling evidence against her was her own confession, the one she gave to the police in the early morning hours following her husband's murder. Which explained Hazelton's next question to potential jurors: Were they prepared to dismiss Mrs. Snyder's confession of guilt if it was shown to be given under duress? What Hazelton planned to prove, it was now clear, was that Ruth made her damaging admissions to the police only after they had used some sort of physical and mental coercion on her.

Jurors were also asked if they could accept Mrs. Snyder as innocent of murder, even if it was shown that she plotted and prepared for it, if it was also proven that she changed her mind at the last minute and notified her accomplice that she wanted to withdraw from the plot. Her attorneys were therefore pre-

pared to acknowledge that she collaborated with
Judd, that she encouraged him, but then they would
argue she didn't follow through, that she had some
sort of change of heart.

The relative apathy of Judd Gray's attorneys during
jury selection indicated that the case against him was
as clear as any case of murder could be. The only
thing his counsel could do, it seemed, was to attack
Mrs. Snyder and embarrass her defense—to show (1)
that she desired her husband's death, (2) that she
was for a period of several months engaged in bringing it about, (3) that she was in a conspiracy with
Gray up to the moment of the murder and immediately after, and (4) that she was not only present when
the crime was committed, but participated in the killing herself.

By Monday, April 25, a jury was assembled, and
Judge Scudder directed District Attorney Richard
Newcombe, a short, stout man with a large bald spot
in the center of his head, to open. What Newcombe
told the jury, in flat, businesslike tones, was essentially
a rehash of the story everyone had been reading
about for the past month—how Ruth Snyder liked
gayety and good times, and not getting them from
her husband, looked elsewhere. He described her affair with Gray, how they became intimate and stayed
in hotels, and how Albert Snyder became more and
more an encumbrance, more in the way, so that eventually these two decided to get rid of Albert Snyder,
the encumbrance. This was not a crime of passion,
Newcombe emphasized; the critical motive was the
$96,000 in insurance that Mrs. Snyder expected to
gain after her husband's death. He concluded by
promising to prove beyond any reasonable doubt that

the defendants were guilty of the "premeditated, deliberate murder of Albert Snyder."

Judge Scudder asked Snyder's and Gray's lawyers if they wanted to make their opening statements. Hazelton rose from his chair and declined, saying they preferred to wait till later in the trial. Millard, representing Gray, also waived an immediate opening. Judge Scudder told the prosecution to call its first witness.

This was Warren H. Schneider, brother of the murder victim, Albert Snyder. He stepped to the witness box merely to testify that he had identified his brother's body.

The second witness was Dr. Howard W. Neail, the assistant medical examiner of Queens County, who was called to the Snyder home after the murder was discovered. Dressed in a hound's tooth coat, and sporting a small, well-trimmed mustache, Neail said he was a veteran of "several thousand autopsies," then proceeded to describe at great length all the minor contusions and bruises on the body of "the white male adult" found in the Snyder home.

Dr. Neail testified that neither Albert Snyder's pajamas nor the sheets on which his body lay were at all disheveled, an observation that undermined Gray's contention that the murdered man flailed around before succumbing. Nonetheless, Gray's attorneys found some comfort in Neail's observation that the murdered man's hands had bruises on them, evidence which supported their argument that Snyder had grappled with his killers.

In the midst of describing Albert Snyder's wounds in the most exhaustive language, Neail inserted his second significant discovery: the cause of Snyder's death was not battering from the window weight or poisoning from chloroform, but asphyxiation from the tightly drawn picture-wire noose.

Dana Wallace, one of Ruth Snyder's attorneys, cross-examined him, asking if any of the blows from the window weight would have been sufficient, by themselves, to cause death.

"No," said Neail.

"Would the two, taken together, with the one on the back of the head, have been sufficient?"

"No."

"You maintain, do you, that all of these other wounds were what contributed with them in causing death?"

"They did."

"Would this strangulation have been sufficient to cause death if none of the other injuries existed?"

"It would have."

"That alone would have been sufficient, could it?"

"That alone."

Wallace swung away from the witness in triumph. He believed he had scored a major point for Ruth by establishing that the critical weapon was the picture wire, a murder device that Mrs. Snyder had all along attributed to Gray.

Next came Joseph M. Farrell, office manager at the Waldorf, who testified that he knew Ruth Snyder as Mrs. Henry Judd Gray. He said that she and Gray had been coming to the hotel for longer than a year. Two floor clerks and a bellboy also identified Mrs. Snyder and Gray, prompting Hazelton to jump to his feet.

"We object to this," he roared. "The defendant Snyder is not on trial for adultery!"

District Attorney Newcombe said that this testimony was to show the motive for the crime, why the two of them wanted to get rid of Albert Snyder in the first place. Judge Scudder overruled the defense and Hazelton sat down.

The tan suitcase Snyder and Gray kept at the Waldorf was introduced as evidence. At Newcombe's direction, a list of the contents was read to the jury. When the book title, *Gentlemen Prefer Blondes*, was read, the courtroom collapsed into laughter. Mrs. Snyder seemed to enjoy the joke, too. Here she was, Ruthless Ruth, the Marble Lady, as newspapers called her, laughing like a child. At that moment one would have thought her most simple and ordinary, a good-natured, kind woman, so completely like other women. The bailiffs had to hammer repeatedly before the room was quiet again.

With the conclusion of the Waldorf-Astoria testimony, the district attorney called to the stand Leroy Ashfield, a nearly bald man with patchy red skin and a scarred neck. He served as the Snyders' insurance agent.

"Did you have any talk with Mrs. Snyder, the defendant, in reference to life insurance upon the life of her husband, Albert Snyder?"

"I did."

"Where was that?"

"In her home."

"When?"

"I believe it was when I was making my monthly collection in the first week in November, 1925."

"At that time was Albert Snyder present?"

"No, he was not."

"What did she say to you in reference to insurance upon the life of her husband?"

"Mrs. Snyder told me that she would like to have her husband have a large insurance policy. She stated that he would be home on a certain night. I think it was later in the week, and she requested that I call and see him in reference to insurance. She stated I should try my best to sell him a policy. In the event that he was not interested, to at least get his signature and that she would possibly be able to persuade him later to take a policy."

As Ashfield testified, when he finally met with Albert Snyder, Snyder was interested in the thousand-dollar plan, and that was all. That plan was filled out and signed, but Ashfield had him sign a blank form, too.

"The next day I heard from Mrs. Snyder," Ashfield continued. "I called again at her request. Mrs. Snyder said she wanted me to make out a $25,000 or $50,000 policy with double indemnity for accidental death. She said she wanted a large policy on her husband's life and she would pay the premiums herself. She had an income, she said, from her father's estate, but wasn't saving any money. It would be a good way for her to save money."

On March 13, when the policies had almost lapsed, and the days of grace were about to expire, she sent a letter to Ashfield. "It contained a check made out to the Prudential Life Insurance Company," said the insurance man. "The space for the amount was left blank. I threw the letter away. But the letter was in her handwriting. She requested me to take the check and ascertain the amount of premiums due on March 13, for me to fill in the check for that amount. I filled it in for $261.20. This represents the premiums due on both policies for three months."

"You do not know whether or not the husband wanted her to have the additional insurance taken out, do you?" Hazelton asked on cross-examination. "No."

"And you do not know whether or not at any time they felt the policy had become burdensome and that she called at your office to have it canceled? You do not know that as a fact, do you?"

"Not as a fact."

"You just heard rumors to that extent, hadn't you?"

Newcombe was on his feet. Hazelton was putting his own words into the witness's mouth, he said. The objection was sustained, but Hazelton refused to give ground. He assumed a gallant smile and took a couple of steps toward the witness.

"Well, you heard such a conversation going on in your office, hadn't you?"

Judge Scudder shot a surprised look at Hazelton, for this was another grievously leading question. Again, Newcombe objected, and again he was sustained, and again Hazelton refused to give up. He rephrased the question.

"Haven't you heard such a conversation from your superiors to the effect that Mrs. Snyder had called there to have those policies canceled because the premiums had proved themselves too burdensome?"

Once more, Newcombe was on his feet, "I think it improper for counsel to have asked that question in that way after Your Honor has already ruled on it."

Judge Scudder, reserved as ever, said, "I will sustain the objection."

But it would take more than a simple ruling against him to quiet Hazelton. Trying a detour, he asked, "Naturally, as an agent, you had an interest in the premiums that were paid, did you not?"

"Yes, sir, I did."

"So, naturally, you were concerned as to whether or not those policies were canceled, weren't you?"

"I was."

"And, of course, then, naturally, you heard that she applied to have them canceled and was told to keep them for three years so she would not lose her premiums, didn't you?"

"Your Honor, Your Honor!" Newcombe was shouting, nearly beside himself. Hazelton's line of questioning was "highly improper," another attempt to lead the witness by the nose. Once again Judge Scudder sustained him, and Hazelton, scowling, wrote something in his notebook, at the same time moving his lips rapidly, whether in profanity or silent rebuttal no one could say.

The second day of witnesses for the prosecution was even more damaging for Ruth Snyder and Judd Gray than the first. By the day's end, their situation looked hopeless.

Three distinct setbacks occurred in rapid succession. First, there was the testimony of Police Commissioner George V. McLaughlin. When this large, affable man took the stand, there was no need for the microphones and loudspeakers placed around the court. His voice and message boomed like an earthquake. Ruth Snyder's confession, he testified, was given voluntarily, with no coercion whatsoever. He said that Mrs. Snyder had first attempted to lie her way out of it, giving the well-known story of the mustachioed robbers. Then she became tangled in the details of her story, especially concerning the extent of her prior acquaintance with Judd Gray. In the midst of one of these tangles, Ruth Snyder was asked to wait in another room while the police conferred among themselves. That was when a patrolman conveyed the message that Snyder wanted to talk to McLaughlin.

"Mrs. Snyder came in. She had a handkerchief to her eyes, and she stated to me that she had not told the truth, and that she now wanted to tell the truth. She expressed sorrow for keeping us there all those hours, and she stated that she could see that she was getting deeper and deeper in her answers to the questions that I had been submitting, and the district attorneys from time to time had submitted questions. I had in my hand a slip of paper on which there was written the name of H. Judd Gray, Thirty-seven Wayne Avenue, East Orange, New Jersey. That was based on the information which I had received from one of the detectives. And that was handed to her, and she said, 'That is the party. Has he confessed?' I then directed your two associates, Mr. Thorton and Mr. Gautier, I think it is, to come in, and I asked her to tell the story, and she related that she was having difficulties with her husband over a period of nine or ten years, that she was introduced to H. J. Gray by a friend in a restaurant in New York—I believe it was Henry's Restaurant—that after that they had the most intimate relations, had stopped at hotels registered as man and wife. . . ."

That was the first catastrophe for the defense. The second landed directly on Judd Gray who, according to the testimony of Police Lieutenant McDermott, treated his arrest at first as a most congenial misunderstanding. "We'll all laugh over this someday," Judd told the detectives who rode with him in the train from Syracuse to New York. McDermott said that Judd called him "Mac" and that he called his prisoner "Judd," and that it was "Mac" and "Judd" all the way from Syracuse to Poughkeepsie, and that everything might have continued in this merry way, if McDermott hadn't turned himself into a killjoy by telling Judd Gray that the police knew he went to New York on Saturday night, because they found the

stub of his Pullman ticket in his wastebasket in his
Syracuse hotel room. Upon hearing this, Gray's
cheeriness disappeared and he proceeded to tell the
story of the murder to the stenographer who had
accompanied the detectives onto the train. According to McDermott, far from being browbeaten and
coerced by the police, Gray was effusive in his praise
of them. "I want to thank you personally," said Gray
to Commissioner McLaughlin, "for the courtesies
which the New York Police Department has shown
me."

Through all this, Gray stared fixedly at a spot high
on the courtroom wall. He was completely silent and
his features immobile. A physiognomist studying his
face might have called him cataleptic. Once or twice
he shifted his position, but so slowly and wearily that
he appeared more like a bear going into hibernation
than the "peppy" fellow his neighbors and business
acquaintances said he was.

The third setback was against Ruth Snyder. Her
side had attempted to block the admission of her
written confession as evidence. Wallace and Hazelton
objected to everything about it. Not only did they
claim it had been given involuntarily, they said the
entire document was a sham. This came out during
the testimony of Peter M. Daly, the assistant district
attorney in charge of obtaining Ruth Snyder's written
confession. He said that he and Ruth worked together on the preparation of the confession, reading
it aloud together until Ruth agreed that the words
on the page were an accurate representation of her
story. She then signed the pages, writing the letter
"R" on the final drafts.

"Are all of the corrections initialed 'R,' her initial,
Mr. Daly?" asked Wallace, on cross-examination.

Daly said that they were. In addition, he said he

distinctly remembered asking Ruth Snyder why she killed her husband. According to Daly, she objected to the term *kill*. "It sounds so cruel, I don't like to use it," she said.

"Well, that is what you did, is it not?" he recalled saying.

"Yes," she replied, "but I don't like to use that term."

"Use whatever term you want to use," said Daly.

And Ruth Snyder replied, "Get rid of him."

At this, Wallace almost leaped into the witness box, thrusting some papers he was holding into the witness's face. "Why are not pages five and seven in this confession initialed?" he shrieked.

Daly hesitated, and the next five minutes were taken up in a wild scramble of objections and recriminations. Wallace contended that pages five and seven, which dealt with the actual murder, were planted, and that Mrs. Snyder had not approved them.

"Your Honor, I can't believe Mr. Wallace is serious in this," Newcombe appealed to the bench.

Taking the questioning into his own hands, Judge Scudder finally straightened out the matter by showing that Ruth Snyder had indeed initialed every copy of the original document. Confusion arose because the uninitialed pages five and seven were actually carbon copies. The stenographer, it seems, had inadvertently mixed them into the originals.

What resulted from all this testimony was simply that Snyder's and Gray's confessions could be read in court and admitted as evidence. The judge was not going to treat them as spurious.

Ruth Snyder's was read first. Surprisingly calm during the recital, she gave a slight nod of confirmation during the part of her confession that said her husband, Albert Snyder, had threatened to kill her.

There were no tears, no demonstrations. The lurid details of the murder, including her description of how she helped Judd Gray tie her husband's hands behind his back and attempted to suffocate him with chloroform, left her utterly unaffected.

This was not the case when it came her turn to listen to Judd Gray's confession. In that instance, she was beside herself with rage and disdain. She was literally writhing in her seat when Gray described her as "a good pal to spend an evening with," who "to use the slang, played me pretty hard for a while." When it came to his descriptions of the preparations leading to the murder, a smile of contempt and anger passed over her face, and she shook her head, silently mouthing the word, "No." When his confession said, "She got very much excited. . . . I am positive that she started to belabor him with this sash weight after that," Ruth turned to face the spectators, and shaking her head, whispered "No!" in a low, but vehement voice. Then she glared at Judd, who sat motionless at the opposite end of the defendants' table, his back facing her, his head propped up by his hands. The only evidence that he was listening came from the twitching of his fingers against his face. Staring at his back, she narrowed her eyelids and screwed her face into an expression of fury and disgust. Then she once again glanced around the courtroom as if to share the feeling of loathing and outrage inspired by Gray's document.

A journalist for the *Daily News* claimed that "the sheer horror of that document read in court caused veteran reporters to shudder. And while spectators sat aghast at the cruelty and cold-bloodedness revealed there, Gray himself well nigh lost consciousness." As he was being escorted back to his cell, he collapsed in the corridor and had to be carried up-stairs by attendants.

There was another figure in court who appeared to suffer as much as he—who cringed when he cringed, feeling the very same pangs of misery. That figure was his mother, Mrs. Margaret Gray. Sitting three feet behind Ruth Snyder, it was a wonder, the journalist from the *News* opined, "that the frantic mother did not rise from her seat and with her own small hands tear to pieces the doll-like blond who sat within her arm's reach."

She did nothing of the kind, of course. She merely sat where she was, looking stunned. Her only conso-lation was that she was allowed to visit her son in an anteroom of the trial chamber—"the strong mother sustaining the weak son. For five minutes after court adjourned, she was permitted to kiss and fondle him and whisper words of courage . . . while the guard gulped and tried not to listen to the pathetic conver-sation."

If Ruth Snyder was to be called as a witness, it was to be on Friday, April 29, after Hazelton opened the case for the defense, but a few other witnesses had to testify first. One was a youthful taxicab driver "with a voice and face like an altar boy" who claimed he could never forget Judd Gray. He drove Gray from Queens to Grand Central Station, Manhattan, on the morning of the murder.

"What was there," asked Gray's attorney, W. J. Mil-lard, "to attract your attention to his appearance more than when he got in the car?"

"Well," said the driver, "as he stood there and paid me off, it was $3.50 on the meter, and he paid me $3 in bills and the rest in change, and as I counted it, it was $3.55, and I sort of looked up from my hand to his face to see if he was dissatisfied with the ride, as it was only a 5-cent tip, and in a case like that it seems as if I didn't do the right thing or didn't give him an easy ride."

Another person who remembered Gray as left Queens on the morning of the murder was Nat Willis, an aged man who boarded the bus with Gray not far from Snyder's house. A third person was Charles E. Smith, the policeman who was taking target practice near the spot where Judd and Willis were waiting for the bus. They both testified that Gray was unusually excited and jocular for that time of morning. For some reason, he seemed full of pure, animal joy. They also noticed how odd it was that his overcoat was buttoned up to his chin on what they felt was an unusually warm morning.

The next witness was G. Van Voorhees, a conductor on the New York Central which Gray boarded at Grand Central four or five hours after the murder. He said he remembered Gray because he had a Pullman ticket for Albany, but was staying on to Syracuse. Quite unusual to take half the trip in the Pullman and the other half coach. Also, Gray was the only passenger in the smoking room of car 16, which was named "Crocus." This is what Voorhees said:

"The Pullman conductor said 'Albany.' I said, 'This passenger is going to Syracuse.' So then I turned to the passenger and said, 'Are you going through to Syracuse with us, or do you intend to stop at Albany? You have that privilege. That is why I asked if you would like to stop at Albany, or are you going to continue through to Syracuse.' He said, 'I am going through to Syracuse.' I then told him, I said, 'I will keep your railroad ticket, and wherever you are in this train after, I will remember you.' Then I looked him over, so that I would know him after we left Albany, and he had changed his seat to another car, or another seat in that car."

Yet another person claimed to remember Gray as he attempted to return to Syracuse. This was Patrick George Fullerton, the porter on the "Crocus," who said he observed Judd sitting by himself. Then there was the ticket salesman, Reginald Rose, who said he remembered Judd because he rarely sold a railroad ticket to Syracuse and a Pullman to Albany. People almost never did that.

Then, Haddon Gray, the Syracuse man who helped Gray arrange his alibi, spent an unpleasant hour on the stand. Toying with the Elk's tooth that dangled from his watch chain, he told the familiar story of how he put the DO NOT DISTURB sign on his friend's hotel room door, mussed his bed, mailed some bogus letters, and pretended to be Judd Gray—all for the sake of covering for what he was led to believe was his friend's rendezvous in Albany with Ruth Snyder.

When Judd Gray returned to Syracuse the next day, he said he had not met Mrs. Snyder in Albany, as planned. Judd Gray said he met Mrs. Snyder at her home, where he witnessed a robbery in which both Mrs. Snyder and her husband were bound and assaulted. He said he barely managed to escape by hiding in a closet. When he came out, he saw Albert Snyder lying on the floor and "either in picking him up from the floor or in bending over him to hear if his heart was beating he had gotten the bloodstain on his vest, and also on his shirt, that the shirt he had shown me, the blue shirt, belonged to Mr. Snyder."

Gray asked Haddon if he would help get rid of these bloodstained things, and Haddon, after suggesting that they take them over to a friend's office, took the suitcase containing the garments to the Onondaga County Savings Bank Building, where he went to the sixth floor, room 641, and placed the bag in one corner of the top row of some shelves. Then Haddon Gray drove Judd to his home, where Judd entertained Haddon's young children, playing marbles with them, and reading the Sunday funnies. Before going in for dinner, Judd read the children the Bible lessons they had received at Sunday school that day. He seemed just the same as ever, like nothing was bothering him.

Haddon Gray made it clear he knew a crime had been committed, though he did not report it to the authorities. Even after the news of Judd's confession appeared in the press on March 22, he did not go to the police. Choosing to shield his friend, he acted as an accessory after the fact. These developments prompted Judge Scudder to tell the witness that he could withdraw his testimony if he wished and refuse to answer further questions on grounds of possible self-incrimination.

"Thank you, Judge. I will leave it. I will let it stand," insisted Haddon Gray. "Yes, I kept it from the police. I believed he was innocent. I did not think he could have done it until I heard the story from his own lips."

That is why, he said, the Wednesday morning after Judd Gray's confession appeared in the newspapers, he visited his friend in his prison cell.

"I asked him, 'Have you done this thing?'

" 'Had, I did,' Judd said.

"Then I asked him why he did it, and he said, 'Haddon, I don't know myself.' "

By the time Haddon Gray's testimony was finished, it seemed that everything that could possibly be said against Judd and Ruth had already been said. Two or three more witnesses were called by the prosecution, but we will not go over their testimony because it only repeated and confirmed what had been said before. At this stage in the trial, the case against the defendants appeared beyond dispute. There was no doubt about it—these two were obviously and conclusively guilty. The only suspense was over the question of what a talent like Hazelton's could make of such a hopeless situation.

7

Ruth Snyder's Defense

Ruth Snyder's situation may have been hopeless, but you couldn't tell by looking at her counsel. Hazelton's confidence and exuberance were unmistakable. When he introduced the case for the defense on Friday morning, he made no attempt at humility, at self-effacement, or apology. He was like an old-time evangelist addressing a full tent. He spoke in long, eloquent sentences, and his voice, although not particularly soothing or sonorous, possessed an immediately perceptible vitality, an almost hysterical conviction, which he accentuated by removing his glasses and waving them about. His method "was not to work slowly, artfully, up to a climax," said the *New York Post*. "He got to the top immediately and stayed there on an oratorical plateau."

Hazelton first touched on the story of Mrs. Snyder's marriage, how she met Albert Snyder, was faithful and good to him, and in return, was cruelly neglected and abused.

Then, with barely a warning cough, he screamed, "We will prove to you that the defendant Snyder is not the demimonde that the people's testimony might have led you or had for its purpose to lead you to believe, but that she met the deceased when she was seventeen years of age or thereabouts, and he was somewhat eleven years her senior, that she was working in the same office with him at the time they met, and after a courtship of a few months, they married. But that the deceased before he met the defendant had had another fiancée with whom he had courted several years. She died. And then the defendant Snyder came into his life, but he did not forget the other woman. The little album and other parts of her home were replete with the picture of a woman, Jessie Guishard, who had passed away. The deceased even went so far as to name his boat after his former sweetheart. They were only married three months when she [Ruth] attempted to bestow on him the love and affection that a wife of her years only could and wanted to and he repulsed her, the evidence will show, and told her that he wished she had never come into his life and that if his old sweetheart would have lived, he would have been happy and things would have been as he wanted them to be.

"That was the commencement of what little love existed in that union at its inception; that was the commencement of the act, aggravated by similar acts, that drove the love from that house.

"Bickering started; quarrels; dissatisfaction; just as bad there in the beginning—I might say worse—than it was at the time of this regrettable crime; but the wife did not err."

Hazelton, who had his arms crossed over his chest, suddenly flung out his hands, palms down and rigid. "We will show you she continued faithful to that—her husband and had a child—not a chance child by accident. No, but a child which, in order to bear, she had to undergo the torments and pain of surgical operation.

"And the sole purpose of having that child was to see if she could bring back into that home the essential fundamental of love which had been cast aside. And the child was born. For a time the little angel brought happiness, but the father was a man who in the requirements of the domestic state was not in many ways—and I will go into detail at this time—the compatible companion of the defendant. He was a man who, when he returned home in the evening, wanted it quiet. The child cried. The child annoyed him, with the result that not only did they start quarreling about old conditions, but about the child. Bickering, bickering, continually bickering over the child and other matters. The father was a good provider. I shall not stand here in our defense and heap coals upon the head of the departed. I shall only tell you, even though it be against the wishes of the defendant, what facts I believe are absolutely necessary for you to understand in this case. Quarreling continually, as I have stated to you. It became worse. All love was lost."

Hazelton began to pace the room with his hands in his pockets. "For social reasons appearances [were] kept up, but still the wife was morally faithful to that husband, morally faithful. I do not know whether it can be proven that she occasionally went out or was seen in the company of another man, but insofar as being faithful is concerned, she continued that way until she met the defendant, Henry Judd Gray. We will prove to you that Judd Gray found in that disorganized home, found in that home of no love, a willing victim for his nefarious purpose and design."

Hazelton flatly denied that Judd Gray was the passive nonentity everyone had all along said he was, and consequently, that Ruth was the sexually dominant one in their relationship. What Judd Gray really was, said Hazelton, was a gigolo. "He, we will prove to you, was a perfect lover; so much so, the defendant says, that he could talk to her over the phone and make her feel that she was in his presence.

"But no!" Hazelton shouted at the jurors, who were now looking as incredulous as Judd Gray himself. No, he was not describing the pathetic Judd Gray who now sat in court. "That Judd Gray is a sham, a pretense," said Hazelton. "He was not the man you see now at any time, we will prove. He showered affections upon her in abundance, such as she had not had at any time for the eleven years of her married life. And what happened? They gave way, as must have happened under those conditions, which perhaps no human evidence can portray and sufficiently investigate and solve."

What could Judd Gray have been up to? asked Hazelton. Why was he working Ruth Snyder so hard? Very simple. When Mrs. Snyder told him that her husband, Albert Snyder, had a couple of near fatal accidents at home, this smooth-talking corset salesman, whose wits had been honed to a razor's sharpness by selling corsets in a corsetless age, had a brilliant idea. Why not get Ruth Snyder to take an insurance policy on her husband?

"I believe it was in the latter part of 1925, yes, the latter part of 1925, the defendant, Henry Judd Gray, said to Mrs. Snyder, talking about the intimate matters of their home life—they confided everything in each other—he brought up the proposition of insurance and said, 'Why, I carry $30,000 worth of insurance. What does your husband carry?' And she said,

'None or very little.' I believe it was a thousand dollars. 'Well,'' he said, 'I think that is rather careless.'

"Well, Mrs. Snyder returned home, and she spoke to her husband about insurance—perhaps several weeks or several days later. And the husband said, 'Send for the insurance man.' The insurance man came, and all the matters of that insurance, just as the agent told you from that stand, we will prove to you were discussed in front of Mr. and Mrs. Snyder, and the husband, as the agent told you, signed two applications, one for the smaller policy and the other for the larger policy. You will recall the agent said that.

"No subterfuge, no concealment about it. The reason why the large policy was not signed up then, they both thought the premiums were rather too high, and they wanted to think it over. She talked it over with her husband after the agent left, and the husband told her to call up the agent and have the larger policies taken out. And the premiums, we will show you, were paid from a common bank account, a joint bank account, from which the husband and the wife both had the right to draw. No individual wife's bank account. The wife paid all the individual bills in the house. The husband knew all about it. We will show you the checks were drawn from the same checkbooks by both husband and wife, and the stubs filled in, so there was no mystery whatsoever about the insurance, insofar as Albert Snyder and his wife were concerned, as these checkbooks will show you. But after the premiums had been paid several times, or, in any event, after they had been paid, Mr. and Mrs. Snyder again arrived at the conclusion that that was a little too much money."

Here Hazelton, waving the checkbook in the air to emphasize his point, was interrupted by a juror. "You dropped a stub. There, on the table," the juror said, pointing his finger. Hazelton responded with the enthusiasm of a man discovering a long-lost friend.

"Yes," he beamed. "That is one of the stubs. Well, they talked about these premiums being burdensome. So what did she do? She went down to the offices of the Prudential Insurance Company on two occasions and made inquiry as to whether or not the policies could be canceled. We will have the managing agent and another agent testify that she went down there and spoke to them about an insurance matter, but that they do not know whether that matter related to the cancellation of the policies or not, because that is an ordinary matter, but she went down and spoke to them on two occasions, and she will tell you about canceling those policies, and she was advised, if I recall correctly, that she had to let the premiums remain there for three years, otherwise she would lose them all. The insurance man will be better able than I to tell you that is one of the provisions of the policy or requirements of the policy.

"So she came away and went back and told her husband, and they decided to leave that insurance there for three years, and then at that time, if they were in the same frame of mind that they were at present, to which I have referred, they would reduce the insurance, or perhaps might let it continue.

"That we will prove to you. That, we contend, is the proof insofar as the insurance is concerned. We will prove to you that Mrs. Snyder never had, as a motive, the need of obtaining insurance upon the life of her husband, and then killing him to get that insurance. We will prove he knew all about it, and it was a mutual matter between them, for the protection of herself as a wife."

Hazelton then described how Judd Gray introduced the idea of murdering Albert Snyder for the insurance money, and how murdering Albert Snyder became a constant preoccupation—how hardly an hour went by without Judd raising the subject to her, how he was always dreaming up new ways to kill him, and was continually pressuring her to help him. True, he said, Ruth Snyder has been accused by Judd Gray of turning the gas on her husband on one occasion. But "we will prove it to you how that little accident did happen with the windows open in the summertime. There is a little jet coming out of the floor. The husband was lying on the couch, snoozing. Someone hit that jet, the windows were wide open, and a little gas escaped. No one paid any attention to it, but Mrs. Snyder wrote Judd Gray about it, and he wrote back to her. This man who says he was drawn into this thing by her, he wrote to her, 'Well, why didn't you get a long tube and put it on the jet and put it under the Governor'—he called Snyder the Governor— 'under the Governor's nose while he is sleeping?'

"That is what he said. Mrs. Snyder viewed it more as a joke than anything else, but we will prove to you he had a motive in his mind. This idea that he had, and which was expressed in that letter about putting the gas jet or the hose under the Governor's nose, smoldered, became an obsession and fermented in his mind until he seized, we will prove to you, seized upon it, at least, that he was going to get rid of the Governor for a motive which we will explain to you. So a few months before this matter he wrote, or rather he said to her casually, 'Well, we can't go on any longer this way. You are living a very unhappy life, you ought to get rid of the Governor.' If Mrs. Snyder, we will say to you, wanted to get rid of him, she might have divorced him. She had not even arrived at that point. Judd Gray was the first man who caused her to be unfaithful and violate her marriage vows.

"This matter grew in his mind—it did—and he mentioned, as I have stated to you, 'You ought to get rid of the Governor.' She treated it casually, but on meeting her so often he pressed the point—sort of casually, too—then pressed it again, and then, on one occasion, if I recall correctly—she will be able to tell you better than I—he said, 'It must be done. And if it isn't going to happen, I will do away with myself and with you,' meaning Mrs. Snyder.

"She then, for the first time, realized that he was serious in that matter, in that objective."

The part of Hazelton's speech which came next was a bit hard to follow. In attempting to describe the luncheon meeting between Ruth Snyder and Judd Gray, during which Gray gave Mrs. Snyder the package containing the sash weight murder weapon, he seemed to get bogged down in needless detail—something about a "pinch whiskey" bottle and "hip rollers." Hazelton explained that Ruth had asked Judd to get hip rollers for her to help her lose weight, and the "pinch whiskey" bottle to convert into a lamp. Holding up the whiskey bottle, he added, "You fill it with colored water—I had the lady explain it to me—you fill it with colored water and then put an electric bulb and so forth on it, and it makes a lamp. I believe they are somewhat fashionable now in suburban homes."

Working his way back to Ruth Snyder's rendezvous with Gray, Hazelton described how she opened the bundle and found the whiskey bottle inside, with the hip rollers, a corselet, a sash weight, and a package of powders. There was also a letter, Hazelton said, which contained the message: "I'm coming Monday night. Put the sash weight under the pillow in

Mother's room." Regarding the powders, the note said, "Give these to the Governor before he retires."

"She took that sash weight," Hazelton continued, "and she left it in the paper in which it was wrapped—I believe she did. I don't know whether she told me she unwrapped it or not. But anyway, she put it down in the cellar, and she threw those powders away."

Here, Hazelton approached Gray, stared at him with bulging eyes, and his lips pressed firmly together. Then, shaking an accusing finger in Gray's face, bayed: "True to his promise, Judd Gray came back to that home on Monday evening, March seven, at about eleven o'clock, and came to the back door and asked her was she going to let him go through with the job. She said, 'Judd, you are crazy. This can never go through.'

"Well, Judd says, 'It will, for, as I told you, it will be you and me. We cannot go along this way any longer.' She said, 'No,' and would not let him get any further than the pantry, and his own confession at least partly corroborates that—any further than the pantry, and the husband was asleep upstairs. We will prove it to you that if she wanted to kill him, she could have done it that time, but would not permit him to do it, and before he left he said this: 'I will come back Thursday night then. If you do not want it done in the house, when the Governor has his bowling night'—Mr. Snyder bowled every Thursday night—'and when the Governor puts his car in the garage I will give it to him then.' She said, 'Judd, you can never do it, and do not come back here Thursday night.' She closed the door on him and he went away. I believe he wrote a couple of letters thereafter. He called her up and spoke to her, but still this matter was for some reason or other, so it seems to you and which we will explain further, kept smoldering in his mind. He kept thinking it over and planning it, we will show you."

Hazelton returned to his position in front of Judd Gray, his finger growing more and more menacing. Gray lifted his eyes to look at his accuser, but quickly lowered them. Then, turning to the jury, Hazelton described the letter Ruth Snyder received from Gray on Wednesday which declared his intention to "go through with this matter" on Saturday—the night she and her husband were going to a party. But Ruth Snyder wanted no part of Gray or his plan, said Hazelton. She was terrified of him, fearful for herself and her husband. A neighbor, knowing Mrs. Snyder had no one to look after her daughter on Saturday, "offered to have her 'park the baby,' as the saying goes, at that neighbor's house that night until she came home from the party. But, not having any desire to do away with her husband, she did not do it. She made up her mind she was going to have that out with Judd Gray that night if he went as far as that, and she went to the party, and she didn't drink, because she rarely ever drinks, and never to excess. She is temperate, not a teetotaler, but temperate, and she does not smoke either, and she dances very little."

Hazelton, seeming to have momentarily lost the thread of his argument, mentioned that Henry's Restaurant does not allow dancing, "contrary to what you may have heard here," and that Ruth Snyder "is not a butterfly," not "a woman of many loves." He mentioned that Albert Snyder was not what one would call an excessive drinker, even though "he would have a good time, perhaps, at a party, and take eight or ten highballs, even as you or I."

Just when Hazelton seemed to have forgotten that the topic at hand was the murder night, and not

Henry's Restaurant or Mrs. Snyder's faithfulness or
Albert Snyder's drinking habits, he was back on track.
Without any noticeable transition, he started re-
counting how Ruth Snyder "came home about two
o'clock, expecting to see Judd Gray there. No doubt
about that. Her husband went to put the car in the
garage, and as she passed her mother's door, taking
the child to bed (Judd Gray had been in the house
before, I believe on three occasions), she saw him
standing in the dark of the mother's room, and she
said, 'Shh, I will see you in a minute,' and he slumped
back. She then went in and put her child to sleep.
The husband came up after putting the car in the
garage and retired, and she retired, too. And in about
twenty-five minutes, she arose and went into the
room where Judd Gray was, and she says, 'You have
been drinking, Judd.' He says yes. She had purchased
for that party they were going to give the following
week five bottles, I believe, of Tom Dawson, or some
Tom whiskey, I believe, and she put one of those bottles—Judd liked to drink when he came; he always
did—under the pillow; no sash weight or no pliers,
as he said in his confession, a sash weight and a pair
of pliers. We contend that is ridiculous. Nothing like
that was done. Judd was drinking. He was not paralyzed drunk, but he had been drinking more than,
perhaps, he should have. We contend it was to nerve
him up for the objective he had in mind and which
he was going to consummate and put through that
night. She sat down on the bed and he came over
and kissed her, he did, and as he kissed her, she felt
those rubber gloves that he had upon his fingers on
her face, and she said, 'My God, Judd, you are not
going to do that, are you?' and he said, 'Well, you
don't want me to go through with this, Momsie, do
you?' She said, 'No, Judd, I don't.' He said, 'I know

you didn't, there is no weight under the pillow, but I am going to go through with it,' he says, 'myself.' She did not know whether he meant to shoot, whether he had a weight, or what he had at that time, and her story, we will maintain, is just as reasonable and possible of being believed as his, indeed. He says, 'I am going to go through with it myself.' She begged with him, she pleaded with him, she cried. He had his hat and his overcoat off. She got him as far as downstairs. While up there he had told her, 'If we don't, I'm going to do away, as I told you, with you and myself.' And that revolver that was found broken in on the bed—Judd Gray at that time had in his hand and threatened Mrs. Snyder with, and she pleaded with him and cried with him—she did—and got him to go downstairs, and again talked to him, and caused his mind to abandon the thing, and she took the revolver, if I recall correctly, and placed it on the piano.

"She thought things were safe. She ran upstairs to the bathroom to adjust herself, due to a condition which you heard the doctor describe, and which the nervous excitement, brought on by the threat of Gray and his fixed determination to do this matter, brought on and aggravated it more than ever. She went up to the bathroom—she did. You see from the diagram it is at the end of the hall. The room in which Albert Snyder was is at that end, with twin beds in it. She went into the bathroom—she did. He was downstairs. She heard him come up quickly and believed he was coming up to the mother's room for the hat and coat which was there. While she is in the bathroom, she hears a heavy thud, the door is a little ajar, not tight. She rushes out. She is in the hall looking down from the bathroom, towards the room, the death room, in which Snyder is, and there she sees

Judd Gray, not aside, not beside Albert Snyder, hitting him—no, not at all, but jumping up with one leg over him and striking him with this weight. Albert Snyder, we will prove to you, never moved after Judd Gray gave him that first thud on the head, and the doctor's evidence bears it out. Albert Snyder, we will prove to you, never arose, as is said in the confession of Judd Gray, and grabbed him by the collar and fought with him. He lay there unconscious. But the hand that grabbed him by that collar and pulled the collar, she told me, from the neck, was what? It was the hand of Ruth Snyder taking Judd Gray from off her husband, whom he is belaboring with that. Judd Gray jumping in, and he pushed her and she fell."

Hazelton spoke as though he was in a fever. He pantomimed continually as he talked, so that the jury not only heard his arguments, they saw them. Swaggering across the courtroom when imitating Judd Gray, he created the visual impression of the spruce lady killer pursuing his prey. When he described Gray on the murder night, Hazelton bent his body like a hunchback's, jutting out his chin, twisting his mouth into an enormous grimace. Then, scurrying back and forth in front of the jury box, he stuck out his arms, extending and contracting his long fingers as though he were about to dart at his listeners and strangle them. When Hazelton came to the part of his speech where he described how Ruth Snyder fought with Gray, risking her own life to protect her beleaguered husband, fighting him to the very limit of her physical capacity, he grabbed his own collar and, falling to the floor, proceeded to pull, pound, and tug, stopping only after tearing it from his shirt. His face blanched, Hazelton stood in front of the court with his collar in his hand.

What was taking place in the court was incredible.

As long as anyone could remember, no attorney had ever argued before Judge Scudder without the profoundest respect. Almost everyone who had him as a judge felt a great favor was being shown him, so that such buffoonery amazed and bewildered the spectators, or at least most of them. The district attorney and his assistants seemed at the point of standing up and objecting, but waited in silence to hear what Judge Scudder would say. As for Judd Gray, he looked on the verge of tears. Ruth Snyder remained quite unmoved, apparently waiting with interest to see how it would end. But Judge Scudder said nothing, and Hazelton went on.

"She is a woman who faints easily," he continued, hunching up his shoulders and blowing out his cheeks. "And she fell. She fell, she did, and she swooned, in spite of what anyone may think, and her story is just as reasonable and probable as his. She swooned, she did, and when she came to, Judd Gray was not in that room. She got up. She went in to look at her husband and there he was covered, covered. She went to pull down the blankets, and that man rushed in and said, 'Come out.' He said, 'I have done it, and it is over with.' And, looking down upon her nightgown, her bathrobe, what did she see? You have not heard this. What did she see? The brand, the brand of Cain, of blood, his four or five fingers upon her white nightgown where he had pushed her. He had touched his face, and in his drunkenness he fell upon him, and when she came, we will prove, he pushed her, and that is how the blood mark got upon her. It was over.

"The man was dead. Gray says—now, for the first time he mentioned the plan of burglary—'We have got to go through with this.' She says, 'No, I won't.' He says, 'You know what I told you. We have got to go through with this. You're in it now. Look at the blood on you. If I am caught, you're caught, and you will be in it as bad as I, and you will be ruined.' And he briefly portrayed to her all the sordid, terrible possibilities of her having been found in those incriminating surroundings and conditions.

"He said, 'This is going to be a robbery. We will now upset this house, make this rather look like a burglary, that a tall dark man came in and got you.

" 'No, no, no,' she says. She wouldn't do it. He stopped and went in and washed his hands. We claim that she reacted to those conditions the same as you would react to those conditions, or I would react, or any of our wives would react to any of those conditions. He went in again and washed his hands. His shirt was bloody. He got a shirt himself and changed it, and he burned his clothes, and she in fear—guilty people usually run away—she could not. He did. She burned the nightgown. He told her that he had chloroformed her husband to make doubly sure. Ha! She never knew that an eight-ounce bottle of chloroform or anything like that was with him that night. We will just contend and prove, too, that it was impossible for her to know it. Then, while seated downstairs, he says, 'Well, I will make this sure.' So after the fellow was dead, he goes up to murder him for the second time and takes the picture wire that he brought with him from Syracuse and ties it around his neck and, I believe, fastens it with that little pencil. I believe that is why the pencil was found, his pencil was found in the bed. I maintain that is the logical conclusion. Fastened it with that little pencil and strangled him to death for the second time, if it could be done. Then he said to her, 'Now, if you have got some jewelry—this will not look like a robbery if I do not take your jewelry.' Yes, he was always after money, and he took the $100 or $115, Snyder's money, that was in his coat hanging on the chair, and he took that off with him, too, to Syracuse, together with the money he had borrowed in different sums before."

Judd Gray's motive in killing Albert Snyder couldn't have been to have Ruth Snyder for himself, contended Hazelton. He already had Mrs. Snyder "to the fullest extent that he could have her." He didn't want to marry her—he couldn't have—because he was already married. No, Gray only wanted Albert Snyder's insurance money, and he would get that money out of Ruth Snyder by blackmail. If she didn't go along with him, he would use their affair and his threat to incriminate her as a club over her head. "Is it not according to the facts?" asked Hazelton. "Her story and contention is just as reasonable as his and just as reasonable as the state's."

Hazelton slipped one more piece into the growing mosaic of Ruth Snyder's defense. Her confession was not freely given, but torn from her in the most brutal, medieval style: "They questioned her for several hours, brought her to the station—no sleep all day Saturday, up all Saturday night, we will prove to you, up all day Sunday, continually being questioned. One officer would leave her, another—as those who have prosecuted crime know, and I have prosecuted a few—one after another the officers stepped in and took the place of the one who had left, questioning her." Then they brought her back to the district attorney's office, Hazelton said. Still no sleep, no food. When Ruth Snyder dozed off for a little while, they would wake her up, questioning her.

Why was Mrs. Snyder questioned and requestioned for forty-eight hours, with no food or rest? Because, Hazelton said, she did not tell the police what they wanted. Only if she gave them the confession that fit their theory, one that dovetailed with Gray's, would they ease up on her. What she told the police, he said, was wrung from her by torture.

"We will prove to you"—Hazelton's voice rose—"that this crime happened exactly as I have portrayed to you, and twelve—my twelve peers—I will show you that she was not a gay butterfly, but that she loved her home, that she taught her little daughter her evening prayers, that she taught her child her little Sunday school hymns, and sent that child to Sunday school, that she made that child's little clothes; dolls, and she dressed them for her, that she made most of her own clothes, that she kept a seven-room house out there.

"Oh, if you could see it, with the curtains made by her own hand. The pretty lamps made by her own hand, draperies made by her own hand, and she was known as an excellent cook and did all the cooking for the family. She was immaculate and careful and successful as a wife. Her cellar she filled each year with row after row of preserves that are still there.

"We will prove to you that she is not the demimonde that Gray would like to paint her, that she is a real, loving wife, a good wife; that it was not her fault entirely that brought about the conditions that existed at that home; and Judd Gray took advantage of a condition that offered him the opportunity that he was used to and was himself looking for upon this occasion."

Then Hazelton uttered what was to become the most quoted line from the trial. "Woman is just as God intended her, were it not for some man. And we will prove to you," he said, stepping up to the jury box and unbuttoning his jacket, "that Mrs. Ruth Snyder is just as God intended her to be were it not for her incompatible husband and the deceiver Gray, who, taking advantage of the conditions that were there, stole himself into the house. And we will prove him to be a coward, who first was untrue to his own wife; second, he stole the affections of another wife; third, used her husband; fourth, brought his friends from Syracuse and all over, even by a letter to his own wife, into this crime, to serve him as an alibi and get him out of it; and again, that he is a coward because in the last moment, when his mistress is caught, he squeals and throws the blame, the same as Adam, upon the woman that he deceived and made his."

So spoke Hazelton for Ruth Snyder, offering a defense that was as significant for its omissions as it was for what it contained. For he made no mention of Albert's Snyder's threat to kill Ruth—behavior described by Ruth in her confession and supported by Ruth's mother, Mrs. Brown. Despite the fact that witnesses could have testified to Albert Snyder's violent temper—he slept with a loaded revolver under his pillow—self-defense was never introduced as an explanation for Ruth's actions. No effort was going to be made to prove that Albert Snyder planned on taking Ruth's life, nor even that Ruth believed he planned on killing her. In fact, Hazelton made it appear that Mrs. Snyder had lied when she made this assertion in her confession. Now, instead of proving that Albert Snyder threatened to kill her, he had to prove that Ruth was forced to say that.

What did Hazelton's defense of Ruth Snyder rest on? The argument that she was a good, dutiful wife and mother, and was helpless against the connivances of Judd Gray. Unfortunately for Hazelton and Ruth Snyder, every time jury members glanced at her, they saw how absurd that characterization was. The idea that a "real, loving wife," could also be an adulterer, conspiring with her lover to murder her husband was a joke, a source of endless amusement to courtroom spectators and newspaper readers. It was also impossible to imagine Ruth Snyder as helpless, as dominated by anyone, least of all the diminutive figure with the cleft chin who sat all day at the defendant's table with his head in his hands. Although journalists were awed by Hazelton's theatrics, they were at a loss to understand what purpose they served, for everyone felt the case against Ruth Snyder was airtight, and was growing more and more so by the hour.

8

Judd Gray's Defense

To understand clearly the ins and outs of this trial, it is important to keep in mind that it was three cornered. There was one prosecution and two defenses, and each defense was opposed to the other. Any doubt that this was so—that any gain for Ruth Snyder or Judd Gray could only come at the other's expense—was quickly dispelled when Samuel L. Miller, a short, youthful man, who might have been nice looking if he had not been rather fat, opened the defense for Gray.

Glancing at his notes, and speaking with deliberate slowness, in a voice that always seemed to tremble from forced restraint, Miller made a few introductory comments about the "great importance" of the task at hand and how "we must not falter in our duty." Then he declared that Gray's defense team would prove that Gray's confession was "involuntary, obtained by duress, by compulsion, by threat, and by force." He then proceeded to describe Gray in the most pitiable terms. Making little petulant movements and intense ejaculations, Miller proclaimed Gray's "the most tragic story that has ever gripped the human heart, a story of the human triangle, of illicit love and of unnatural relation and of dishonor, that ever fell to man to submit in a court of justice."

Judge Scudder interrupted to warn Miller that this wasn't a summation, but was supposed to inform jurors what the defense intended to prove.

Miller bowed slightly before the bench, then half turned toward the jury: "There will be presented to you evidence that the defendant was not, and could not have been, of rational mind at the time that this crime is alleged to have been committed. That he was hopelessly intoxicated, that the mind of the defendant never conceived, never realized, and never comprehended what his hands were doing."

Significantly enough, Miller made no mention of mental illness or insanity, nor did he suggest that expert witnesses would be summoned to certify that Gray's mind was not sound when he committed the murder. Instead, the defense was going to prove "that the defendant was driven into this tragedy by a force not his own, dominated by a will not his own, commanded by a brain not his own, and powerless to struggle against that controlling superpower which was gripping him and driving him and directing his energies and faculties, and he struggled to loosen himself from this domination and from the catastrophe it was leading him into, but without avail. There could never have been any motive on the part of the defendant Gray to do it. There never could have been any intent on the part of defendant Gray."

After touching on the idea that Judd Gray could not have committed this crime "were he of rational mind at the time it is alleged to have been committed," Miller turned his attention to Ruth Snyder's effect on his client: "He was dominated by a cold, heartless, calculating mastermind and master will. He

was a helpless mendicant of a designing, deadly, conscienceless, abnormal woman, a human serpent, a
human fiend in the guise of a woman. He was in the
web; he was hemmed in the abyss; he was dominated;
he was commanded; he was driven by this malicious
character. He became inveigled and was drawn into
this hopeless chasm, when reason was gone, when
mind was gone, when manhood was gone, and when
his mind was absolutely weakened by lust and by passion and by abnormal relations."

Everyone was looking at Judd Gray, but he was immobile, clenching his teeth, with hands clasped, head
bowed.

"The defendant will present the most heartrend-
ing, the most woeful and the most tearstained drama
of human helplessness, human dominion, and human fallacy. We think that the story told by Gray himself on the witness stand," said Miller, "will be the
most interesting, human, tragic story ever told and
narrated in a court of justice. We shall paint a picture
of human life that you will never, never forget. Judd
Gray will take the witness stand and he [will] tell you
every detail of his life from the time that he can remember down to this catastrophe which engulfed
him in this chasm of tragedy. He will bare every simple detail of his life and this tragedy of illicit relations,
truthfully told by Judd Gray with his own lips, right
on the witness stand, gentlemen, the defendant Gray
will tell the simple truth; he will not color the truth;
he will tell you a straightforward story as he can remember it and he knows it. And we will come to you
later before God, who renders justice to that poor
victim of [a] designing, malicious human serpent of
a woman. I thank you."

So concluded Miller for Judd Gray. The most striking feature of the speech was probably its repetitive-

ness—Gray was "driven into this tragedy by a force not his own, dominated by a will not his own, commanded by a brain not his own. . . . He was in the web; he was hemmed in the abyss; he was dominated; he was commanded; he was driven," on and on. This may look somewhat bizarre in print, but in court, spoken out loud by Judd Gray's excited attorney, it was quite dramatic. Although he spoke for only ten minutes, Miller's speech produced a mystical, otherworldly sensation. The deliberate obscurity of his language—"He was a helpless mendicant of a designing, deadly, conscienceless, abnormal woman, a human fiend in the disguise of a woman"—pushed the trial from the brink of Alice in Wonderland into a world of shimmering fantasy, into meanings beyond the grasp of the human mind to verbalize or define.

Legally, Gray's situation presented a classic case of premeditated murder. As things stood, all the law was against him. The notion that Ruth Snyder was a dominant person and Judd Gray a passive one, was not, and could never be, construed as a lawful justification or excuse for killing. That Gray was drinking heavily when he killed Snyder may have suggested, on the surface, a defense against the charge of premeditation, but the fact that Gray had arrived at the murder scene with so much murder paraphernalia on his person—the picture wire, the chloroform, the gloves—coupled with the amount of time and effort devoted to setting up his alibi, made it clear that whatever effects alcohol had on him, they did not include destroying his capacity for deliberation. Miller was banking on the jury declaring Gray innocent, not because of a legal defense, but despite the lack of one. The twelve jurors would let Gray go, Miller hoped, because they felt so sorry for him—because this man was broken in mind and body by the woman he loved, obeying her every whim. No doubt Miller also hoped that jurors would declare Gray innocent because they were so angry at Ruth Snyder—because they would be dying to blame her for everything.

9

She Takes the Stand: "Judd Did It."

Whether to call Ruth Snyder as a witness in her own behalf was the most critical and difficult decision Edgar Hazelton and Dana Wallace had to make. Even though she had an absolute constitutional right not to testify at her trial, there was the risk that if she failed to do so, the jurors would think she had something to hide. Worse still, if she did not take the stand, the jury would decide her guilt after having heard extremely damaging evidence from her own mouth—her confession. On the other hand, if Ruth Snyder did testify, she would become available for cross-examination, in which case every discrepancy between her current story and her original one could be held up to microscopic scrutiny. Not only would she have to make her new story plausible, she would have to explain why she withheld the truth from the police in the first place, choosing instead to falsely incriminate herself.

Viewed from this perspective, the decision to put Ruth Snyder on the stand assumed the dimensions of a Hobson's choice. There was no risk-free resolution. Of course, knowing everything we know now (including the fact that she was electrocuted), Hazelton and Wallace would probably not have put her on the stand. But knowing what they knew at the time—that the defense had very little to work with, was already losing in a spectacular fashion, and needed to do something dramatic to recover—Mrs. Snyder looked like their only hope.

When Hazelton called her to the stand, Judge Scudder leaned forward and cautioned her in slow, sonorous tones—in "a voice which a radio announcer would give ten years of his life to achieve," said the *New York Times:*

"Now madam, you are not required to take the chair as witness. The law privileges you, and you only can take the stand of your own free will and accord, by your own consent. If you do take the stand, you are subject to the state's cross-examination as is any other witness. The court now affords you an opportunity to decide whether you will take the stand or whether you would prefer to avail yourself of your privilege and remain off the stand."

"I will take it," she said softly, at which point several spectators—some clutching opera glasses—stood to get a better view. Ruth Snyder's face, ivory gold against the morning sunlight that shone through the courthouse windows, had a quality spectators had not seen before: her soft features, her almond eyes, her faintly luminous skin, had the serenity of a Vermeer portrait. Her outfit, as before, was all black. She wore a long satin coat with a black fur collar over her high-necked black dress. About her throat was a set of black glass beads. A small—minutely small—lock of blond hair appeared under her black felt hat, which had an inch of brim. She held in her hand a tiny linen handkerchief.

Ruth Snyder was followed to the witness stand by

a prison matron assigned by the deputy sheriff to safe-guard her. The matron, Irene Wolf, was a rectangular-shaped, doughy-looking woman of about fifty who wore an expression of unwavering compassion. She continually hovered about Mrs. Snyder, patting her back, putting her arm around her, comforting her, as though she was not a murderer but a grieving widow.

Hazelton was respectful and gentle, too, as though out of consideration for Mrs. Snyder's deep unhappiness. In his softest voice, he eased into the topic of her marital troubles. How long after you were married, he asked, did you have your first domestic disturbance?

"About two or three months," Ruth Snyder replied in a low, dignified voice.

Hazelton then asked if the name of her husband's first fiancée, Jessie Guishard, ever entered into these disturbances. "What did he say about her?"

Mrs. Snyder sighed and breathed deeply before she spoke: "That she was the finest woman he had ever met." She added that her husband named his motorboat after her, calling it the *Jessie G.,* and only changed it to Ruth's name a month or two after they were married.

"Did your husband ever mention the name of that Jessie Guishard to you upon any other occasions?"

Again the sighing, deep breathing: "Yes, every time we had an argument."

"Were there pictures of her in your house?"
"Yes."

"Would you say that there were many pictures?"
"Well, there was an album filled with them."

"Did your husband wear a pin at all times with the initials J. G. on it?"
"Yes."

"That pin was the pin of Jessie Guishard, wasn't it?"

"Yes."

"Your husband's former sweetheart, is that right?"

"Yes."

"And that pin your husband wore at all times until his death?"

Mrs. Snyder frowned and breathed deeply, clutching the arms of her chair until her knuckles turned white. "Yes."

"When was baby Lorraine born?"

"November fifteen, 1917."

"Did you have to undergo an operation before you were able to conceive that child?"

Trembling: "Yes."

"And after your child was born, would you say that you and your husband had any disputes after that?"

"Yes," she answered with the voice of a small, sad child, "because it was not a boy." Then she burst into tears, shuddering into her tiny handkerchief, stopping only after Judge Scudder handed her a glass of water and asked her to compose herself.

Ruth Snyder had been on the stand for barely ten minutes, yet two persuasive points had been made. First, that she was not the Marble Lady or "demimonde" people said she was. Second, that even if she had been unfaithful with Gray, her husband had been unfaithful, too, with a ghost named Jessie Guishard. He had obviously worshipped her as the one real love of his life. The third point, which Hazelton was about to make, was that despite Ruth Snyder's marital misfortunes, she wanted to be a good wife and mother—facts which he illustrated by questioning Mrs. Snyder on her housework and her role in "baby" Lorraine's religious training. Naturally,

Hazelton suggested, Mrs. Snyder had Lorraine attend Sunday school.

"Yes," she confirmed.

"Did you teach her morning and night prayers?"

"I did."

"Did you teach her hymns?"

"Yes."

"Tell me different things that you would do about the house."

"Well, I did everything pertaining to the household, making up draperies and curtains. I made all the baby's clothes, most of my own. I did almost everything that went with the house."

Hazelton nodded gravely as he listened, looking at the wooden floor, like a priest at a confessional. "Did you make any lamps?" he asked.

"Yes, months ago, for the house."

"Did you stock your cellar with preserves in the fall?"

"Yes." The mention of preserves in the cellar stimulated a distinct titter in the courtroom, but Hazelton, unaware of the joke, appeared profoundly impressed.

"You did the same this fall?" he asked.

Solemnly: "Yes."

More tittering, which disappeared only because Hazelton switched the topic to his client's affair with Gray. "You were unfaithful to your marriage vows with Henry Judd Gray, were you not?"

Eyes downcast: "Yes."

"Was this the only man who ever knew you carnally or knew you in that manner?"

"Yes."

"Excepting your husband."

"My husband."

Hazelton asked her if she was in the habit of drinking much with Mr. Gray.

"Very little," was her reply.

"How many highballs would you say you had in a night, assuming that you drank highballs."

"Well, I would try to make what I did get last most of the night. Possibly one or two drinks."

"But not more than two?"

"I very rarely finished what I got."

"Did you in your entire life drink to excess?"

"Never."

"Did you ever smoke?"

"No!" She said this in the tone one would use to say "How could you imagine such a thing of me!" which provoked still more laughter. Everyone was thoroughly enjoying themselves—everyone except Judge Scudder, who glared into the audience. The bailiff pounded his gavel to restore order, but the laughter didn't fully recede until Hazelton had abandoned Ruth Snyder's personal habits in favor of her insurance policies.

Was the insurance on her husband taken with his full knowledge? asked Hazelton.

"I had been after my husband for years to take out insurance, particularly after he had the two accidents in the garage. I encouraged insurance, and he said, 'Well, we will see, we will see.' And I finally got him to consent to having Mr. Ashfield [the insurance agent] come up and talk insurance to him."

She explained that her husband had consented to the insurance, even though he felt the premiums were too high. At his urging, she had called the insurance company to try to get the policy reduced or canceled, but was told that it could not be reduced, and if she chose to cancel, she would lose all that had already been put into the policy. Only if they kept the policy another three years could they get their money back. She said she and her husband discussed the matter and decided it would be better to continue the policy another three years.

Hazelton asked about the accidents which prompted Mrs. Snyder and her husband to take out the insurance in the first place. "When was it he had those two accidents in the garage, would you say?"

"In the summer of 1925."

"And what were they, please?"

"Well, at one time he was fixing a spring, a broken spring, and the jack of the car had slipped, and the car had rolled, and if I hadn't come in and started the car going again he would have been crushed." Ruth Snyder explained that a second accident also happened in the garage, when her husband tried to start the car with a hand crank. As he was turning the crank handle, "it flew and hit him in the head, and I came in, wondering why he had stayed in the garage so long. We were getting ready to go out, and I found him in a heap in the corner, with a big mark on his upper lip, where the crank handle had hit him."

"Was he unconscious?"

"He was unconscious and the motor was going."

"When was that?"

"That was in the spring of 1925."

"Then you administered to him and resuscitated him?"

"Yes."

"Well, you heard stated here something about gas being turned on your husband. Do you remember any such episode or accident or whatever you might call it?"

To this, Ruth Snyder replied that when her husband was sleeping on the couch one afternoon in January or February, with the radio going full blast, she leaned over to turn it off, and in doing so accidentally stepped on the gas pipe, opening it up. Unaware of what she had done, she then left the house to run an errand. "When I came home, he was on the street, and I asked him what the trouble was, and he said that he was almost asphyxiated, that the tube had left the cock on the floor, and I wrote Mr. Gray about this."

"And what did Mr. Gray write back to you?"

" 'It's too damn bad the hose wasn't long enough to put in his nose.' "

Mrs. Snyder explained that this was typical of Gray, that he had repeatedly talked about getting rid of her husband. She said that she had intended to break with him, but he threatened "that if I ever stopped going with him he was going to expose me to the whole world and tell them what kind of woman I was."

Hazelton asked how she came to possess the window weight used to murder her husband.

Gray gave it to her without her knowledge, she answered, when they had lunch together at Henry's Restaurant on March 5. He ate quickly that afternoon, saying, "I am in an awful hurry, Momie. I have got to get the 1:25 train." Then, as he was about to leave, he added, "There's a package on the chair. Take it home." Ruth Snyder said she did as she was told, thinking the package probably contained the "flesh reducer" (a rolling pinlike gizmo that Judd Gray's corset company marketed) that she had expressed an interest in. She said it did indeed contain the "flesh reducer," but at the bottom of the package there was also a window weight and a letter from Gray. It said, "I am coming over Monday night." Ruth Snyder could not recall whether it said to "do the job" or "finish the Governor."

"Were there any powders in that letter?" asked Hazelton.

"Yes, there were."

"Did he say anything about the powders?"

"He said I should give my husband one of those powders when he went to sleep or at supper time."

"What did you do with those powders?"

"I threw them down the sink."

"What did you do with the sash weight?"

"I didn't know it was a sash weight until I unwrapped it, and I put it down the cellar."

Then, according to Ruth Snyder, Gray came to her home the following Monday, saying he had come to "finish the Governor."

She said she immediately protested: "Judd, you can't do such a thing."

"Well, if I can't do it tonight," she said he responded, "I am coming back Thursday and get him in the garage."

But Gray, perhaps aware that Thursday was Snyder's bowling night, did not come back on that date. Instead, a day or two later, Ruth Snyder received a letter from him containing the message, "I am enclosing two powders. Give one and a half or possibly two to the Governor before you go to the party Saturday night." The note also said that he was coming down Saturday "to finish the job," instructing her to leave the two back doors unlocked.

"Had you left the doors open?" asked Hazelton.

"I had."

"When you got home that night did you and your child enter the house before your husband or after?"

"Before my husband."

"What did your husband do?"

"He put the car away."

"When you entered the house, whom did you see?"

"I went upstairs to put the baby to bed. While she was getting undressed, I passed up the hall passing Mother's room and I saw Mr. Gray, and he—"

"And did any conversation take place between you and he?"

"Just a word, that I said, 'Be very quiet, I will see you later.' "

"What did your husband do?"

"My husband came in a few minutes afterward, and came up and got undressed and went to bed."

Ruth Snyder said she stayed in bed about twenty minutes, until she thought her husband was asleep, then went into her mother's room, where Gray was waiting. She immediately noticed the rubber gloves on his hands.

"I said, 'Judd, what are you going to do?' and he became semi-mad to think that things had not gone as he supposed they were to have gone, as he had planned."

"What did he say to you?"

"He said, 'If you don't let me go through with it tonight, I am going to get the pair of us.' And he then had my husband's revolver, that he had gotten from under my husband's pillow, and he had it in my mother's room, and he said, 'It's either he or it's us.' I grabbed him by the hand and I took him downstairs to the living room."

"Did you give him any weight that night?" asked Hazelton.

"No, he took the weight away with him Monday night that he was out to the house."

"Did you put any weight under the pillow that night?"

"I put a bottle of liquor under the pillow, no weight."

"After he got downstairs, did you and he have any talk?"

"We did. We talked for quite a while, I trying to plead with him to try and get him to change his mind and get the idea out of his mind." Ruth Snyder said she stayed down there quite a while, and in her excitement "said things to him that probably enraged him." She then went upstairs to go to the bathroom, "and while I was in the bathroom—I had been there about five or ten minutes—I heard this terrific thud. I immediately opened up the door and ran down the hall to see Mr. Gray leaning over my husband."

"Well, now, wait, was the light lit in your room or not?"

"No, it was not."

"When you saw your husband, was he lying down or was he up around Gray?"

"My husband was lying down. Gray was kneeling on his back."

"What did you do?"

"I ran in and grabbed Mr. Gray by the neck, pulled him off, and in the wrestling with me he pushed me to the floor, and I fainted. And I remembered nothing until I came to again and saw my husband all piled up with blankets. I pulled the blankets off—"

This is where Ruth Snyder had her second cry. She began with rapid little breaths which soon became faster and deeper, building and surging, like an enormous wave, until it seemed she was in danger of being carried away by it, but she wasn't, of course. As a reporter from the *World* put it, "Almost as suddenly as the tears had come, they disappeared. She lifted her face, eyes stained by weeping, but her chin was firm, her composure recovered." It was the seamlessness of this transition which, more than anything, was impressive. According to the *Daily News,* "Mrs. Snyder is either the greatest actress since Bernhardt, or she is the most wronged, the most maligned woman in history. . . . No Belasco star ever wept more effectively—more touchingly—more gracefully. And when she finished—the tears consumed three minutes— she did not look red and ugly."

"You may proceed," Judge Scudder urged.

"Are you sure that you grabbed your husband by the— or grabbed Gray by the collar?" asked Hazelton.

"I did. I tried to pull him off my husband."

"When you came to, was Gray in the room?"

"No."

"What did you do?"

"[When] I tried to pull the covers off his head and pull the bandaging that he had on his hands off, [Mr. Gray] came running into the room and said, 'What are you trying to do after me doing something? You are trying to undo it.' "

"What happened then?"

"He took me in my mother's room."

"Did you, that night, strike your husband with any weight?"

"I did not." Ruth Snyder uttered these words loudly and distinctly, looking squarely into the face of Judd Gray. Indeed, according to the *Daily News,* she "gave the impression of looking the whole world squarely in the face. She has that gift." In any case, Judd Gray responded by lowering his eyes and turning crimson.

"Did any talk take place between you and Mr. Gray?"

"It did."

"What talk took place there?"

"He said, 'I have gone through with it, and you

have to stand just as much of the blame as I have.' And he said, 'We can frame up a burglary.' And he said, 'We will both get out of it. They will never know that I did it anyway.' And we sat there, and I was in the mix-up, and I just had to sit and listen to what he told me when he made up the story of the burglary, the lie that I gave to the detectives all day Sunday."

"Now, did you notice anything, any mark on any of your robes when you came to?"

"I did not just then, but I did in my mother's room."

"What did you notice?"

"I noticed when Mr. Gray had said to me, 'My shirt is covered with blood. Let me look and see if you have any on you,' and I had a mark up here of blood"—she indicated the upper portion of her dress—"where Mr. Gray had pushed me when I went for him."

"What did Mr. Gray then do after he had spoken to you about this burglary matter?"

"He told me that I was in it just as much as he was and I would have to go through with it."

"Were you afraid at that time?"

"I was partly afraid. I saw what a terrible mess he had made of things, and I couldn't see any way out of anything, out any other way than to do as he asked me to do."

"Then tell me what Gray did. Was the house ransacked?"

"Yes, it was. He said, 'Momie, you stay up here. You are in no fit condition to do anything. I am going downstairs and mess up all the things, to carry out the idea that it was a robbery.' And he said, 'You stay here until I come back,' and I did."

Studio portrait of Ruth Snyder from the early days of her marriage. (*Photo courtesy New York* Daily Mirror)

Albert Snyder shortly before he was murdered.
(*Photo courtesy New York* Daily News)

Judd Gray on the stand.
(*Photo courtesy New York* Daily News)

Albert Snyder with his first love, Jessie Guishard in 1908.
(*Photo courtesy New York* Daily News)

The Snyder home in Queens village, New York.
(*Photo courtesy New York* Daily News)

An Artist Pictures the Snyder Murder

WHERE SNYDER WAS MURDERED IN BED

ROOM IN WHICH GRAY AWAITED THE SNYDERS' RETURN AND WHERE HE AND MRS SNYDER RETIRED TO AFTER THE MURDER

WHERE MRS SNYDER WAS FOUND BOUND IN HALLWAY

WHERE LORRAINE SLEPT AND WAS AWAKENED BY HER MOTHER'S CALLS FOR HELP

CONTENTS OF DRESSER DRAWERS STREWN ABOUT TO APPEAR AS ROBBERY

KITCHEN WHERE GRAY AND MRS SNYDER DRANK LIQUOR

MAIN ENTRANCE USED BY SNYDER FAMILY UPON THEIR RETURN FROM PARTY

(©*New York* Daily News, *L.P.* reprinted with permission)

I GAVE HER A SASH WEIGHT IN HENRY'S RESTAURANT.
LORRAINE WAS THERE.

The newspapers dramatized
Judd Gray's testimony with
illustrations.
(*Photos courtesy New York*
Daily Mirror)

SHE SAID SHE PUT
BICHLORIDE PILLS IN HIS
WHISKEY BUT THEY ONLY
MADE HIM VOMIT.

SHE TRIED OUT TWO VIALS OF SLEEPING POWDER ON ME
AND THEY LEFT ME DAZED.

That night he wrote a letter to Ruth Snyder.

Judd Gray writing a letter to Ruth Snyder which will be used to support his alibi. (*Photo courtesy New York* Daily Mirror)

His old friend, Haddon Gray, had not failed him.

When Judd Gray returned to Syracuse the afternoon after the murder, he saw that his friend, Haddon Gray, had rumpled his hotel room bed making it appear slept in. (*Photo courtesy New York* Daily Mirror)

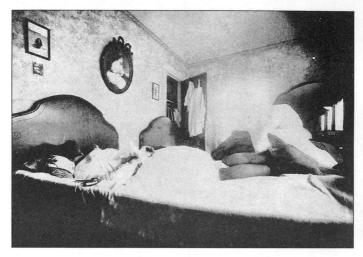

Police photograph of the crime scene. Snyder's head is on the pillow, his arms tied behind him, and the revolver is on the edge of the bed. (*Photo courtesy New York City Police Department and* Daily News)

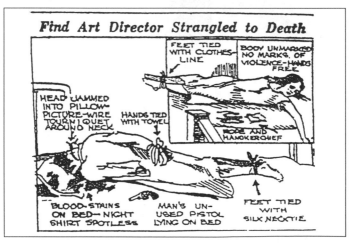

Diagram of crime scene was published in the *Daily Mirror* on March 21, 1927. The day's headline was the single word: Strangled. (*Photo courtesy New York* Daily Mirror)

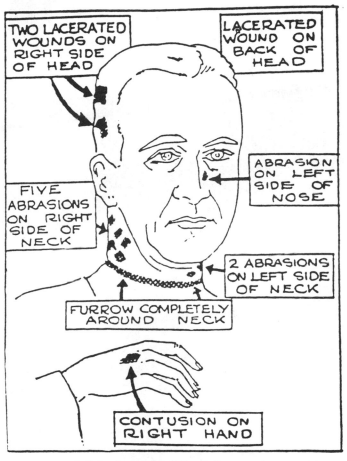

Artist's depiction of Snyder's wounds.
(*Photo courtesy New York* Daily Mirror)

Ruth Snyder testifying. Judge Scudder is to her right.
(*Photo courtesy New York* Daily News)

The photo of Ruth Snyder with her daughter, Lorraine, and her mother, Mrs. Josephine Brown, appeared on the front page of the *News* after the jury found her guilty of murder. (*Photo courtesy New York* Daily News)

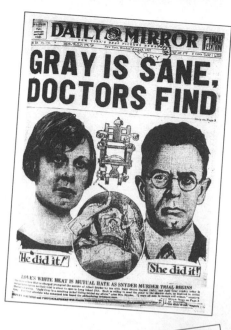

To the press, and to their public, the killers were known simply as Ruth and Judd, and they made front page news throughout their trial. (*Photo courtesy New York Daily Mirror*)

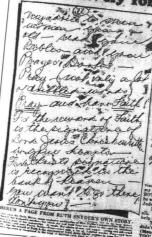

Ruth Snyder in Queens County Jail with her supportive
prison matrons, Nan Hart *(left)* and Irene Wolf (*right*).
(*Photo courtesy New York* Daily News)

In 1944, Fred MacMurray and Barbara Stanwick starred in "Double Indemnity", the first Hollywood film inspired by the Snyder-Gray case. (*Photo courtesy Paramount/Museum of Modern Art, Film Stills Archive*)

"The Postman Always Rings Twice", starring John Garfield and Lana Turner, another film based on the case, was released two years later. (*Photo courtesy MGM/Museum of Modern Art, Film Stills Archive*)

Ruth Snyder was executed on January 12, 1928.
(*Photo courtesy New York* Daily News)

"Did you tie any wire on your husband's neck that night?"

"I did not."

"Did you administer any chloroform to him?"

"I had no hand in that murder at all."

"What happened to your jewelry that night?"

"He said to me, as everything was all messed up and we sat there talking about it, he said, 'If the robbery story don't go through,' he said, 'you will have to think about something else.' He said, 'Whereby you can get yourself out.' He said, 'You will have to accept some part of the blame.' And then he said to me, 'Give me your jewelry.' He said, 'We have got to get rid of everything we can to make it look like a possible robbery.' And when he said that to me, it came to my mind that he was probably out to get more than my jewelry. So I ran into my room and took the jewelry from out of the box I had previously kept it in and threw it under the mattress."

"Did he say when you would again hear from him or see him?"

"He said at that time, too, 'You won't see me for a couple of months, and when you do,' he said, 'by that time the insurance will have been in your hands, or they will have saved it, or given it to me.' I don't know just the exact words he used, but he said it would take at least a couple of months for insurance to be settled."

"Did he tie you up that night?"

"He did."

Judge Scudder: "That is a leading question."

"What did he do to you? What also did he do to you, please?"

"Just before he left, he said to me, 'Well, I will have to bind your feet and your hands and put a gag in your mouth to carry out the story that you were probably hit and knocked unconscious.' "

"Why did you let him do that?"

"I did, I had to."

"Why did you let him do that?"

"Because I was afraid if I did not go in with what he asked me to do that he would finish me up that night."

Hazelton asked about Ruth's earlier statement to the police. Would she describe it as accurate?

How could it be? she retorted. "I was very, very weak, because I hadn't any sleep and I hadn't but very, very little food, and I was in a physical condition that would make me feel miserable without all this trouble that I had had."

The questions that followed were designed to show that at the time Ruth was interrogated she was physically and mentally incapacitated. Hazelton wanted the jury to see that she had been unfairly trapped into making her incriminating confession.

"Did you feel sleepy or did you feel like remaining awake?"

"Well, I was sleepy."

"Did you feel hungry or did you have no appetite?"

"I had no appetite."

"Did you have a headache at any time?"

"I did."

"Did you cry at any time?"

"I was weary all the time I was down there."

Ruth Snyder could not be held responsible for what she said to the police, Hazelton argued—she was too tired and upset.

Then, attempting to cover all bases, he contended that Ruth Snyder could not have made the incriminating statements the police now attributed to her.

To make his point, Hazelton led her skillfully, back and forth, over her entire confession like a trainer with a circus dog. Ruth Snyder's trick consisted of barking on cue. Whenever Hazelton read an incriminating statement, she screwed her face into an expression of righteous indignation, and then uttered a peremptory "No!" or "I did not!"

"Did you say this," he demanded, " 'I want to make a full and truthful statement about the death of my husband, Albert Snyder, and I understand that anything I may say may be used against me'?"

"I did not!"

"Did you say in your confession that 'Judd Gray told me to take home a window weight in case we were going to do anything, that was the way we were going to do it?' "

"No, I did not. As I explained to you before—"

"Did you say, 'When I went into my mother's room, Mr. Gray had the window weight'?"

"I did not."

"Did you say, 'I had brought the window weight up from the cellar that afternoon'?"

"When I said that I meant—"

"Just yes or no. Did you say that?"

"No."

"Did you say, 'And when he went into my mother's room, he had the bottle of chloroform. He had a regular eight-ounce medicine bottle with one and one half ounces of chloroform in it.' Did you say that?"

"I—"

"Just yes or no!"

"No."

"Did you know how much chloroform he had?"

"After it was all over, he told me how much chloroform he had."

"Did you see any of this cheesecloth before the crime was committed?"

"No, sir."

"Did you see any waste or cotton handkerchief before the crime was committed?"

"No, I did not."

"Did you tell him it was either your going or your husband going?"

"I didn't say that."

"Did you say that you saw Mr. Gray tie your husband's hands behind his back?"

"I did not."

"Did you say, 'We tied his hands behind his back and put the blue handkerchief and the waste with the chloroform on it on the pillow'?"

"I did not."

"Did you say, 'He then covered his head with blankets to make sure of suffocation'?"

"I didn't say that."

"Did you say, 'We then went downstairs and took the weight and the shirt and the bloodstained paper down to the cellar and burned the shirt and the paper with the bloodstains on it in the furnace'?"

"I did not say 'we.' "

"Was any of your clothing burned?"

"Yes, my nightgown and my bathrobe."

"And who burned it?"

"Mr. Gray put them in the furnace."

"Did you say, 'We then put the window weight, sprinkled with ashes into the toolbox, and then we came upstairs to the living room and sat there'?"

"I did not. I said Mr. Gray put the window weight in my husband's toolbox and sprinkled it with ashes."

"Did you have any wire that was found on your husband's neck and has been offered in evidence in your home that night?"

"No, sir."

"Did you put any pair of pliers underneath the pillow?"

"I did not."

"Did you say, 'While Mr. Gray and I were in my mother's room before he went into my husband's room, we had planned that in order to avoid detection, to upset the house and throw the stuff in the house around so that it would look like a burglary or a robbery, and we had planned that I was to show the police that it was a robbery'? Did you say that?"

"I did not."

"Did you bring any Italian newspaper to your home that night?"

"I did not."

"Did you break the pistol in your husband's bed that night?"

"No, sir."

"Where did you put the pistol after you took it from Gray?"

"I laid it on the piano downstairs."

"Who brought it upstairs and broke it?"

"Mr. Gray did just before he left."

Hazelton paused. This was the crucial part of his case. He wanted to get it right and make sure the jury heard it. "Did you say, 'I make this statement of my own free will, without any fear or threat or promise, and knowing that anything I may say may be used against me'? Did you say that?"

"No, I did not."

Hazelton's examination of Ruth Snyder ended as it had begun—with the characterization of his client as a poor, abused child-wife. It was a creative and imaginative performance of the highest order, an interpretation of events firmly grounded in the old double standard that portrayed women as fundamentally pathetic, vulnerable, and in need of protection.

According to Hazelton, there had once been a sweet and inexperienced girl named Ruth Brown who was just like all women—*Just as God intended her!*—were it not for two male blackguards. One was her husband, Albert Snyder. He nagged her constantly and taunted her with the memory of his dead sweetheart. He even named his motorboat after this woman and wore a pin with her initials on it. The other was Judd Gray. But not the Judd Gray who sat in court looking so pathetic—Oh, no!—the real one, the perfect lover, the hypnotic, irresistible one. What chance would any woman have against such a forceful, sweet-talking, corset-selling schemer? None.

If the jury believed this, Ruth Snyder would go free.

10

She Holds Her Own—then Crumbles

In approaching the question of how to cross-examine Ruth Snyder, Gray's attorneys and the D.A. agreed on one essential point: they did not want the trial—and eventual jury deliberation—to turn into a referendum on hard and cold facts.

Because this murder was practically carried out in public, there was almost universal agreement on all points of physical evidence. Which meant, except for the fact that Ruth Snyder denied killing her husband and entering into a compact with Gray for that purpose, the questions of What? Who? When? Where? What with? and In what way? had long been settled or, at least, mainly settled. What remained to be resolved was: Why? The "inner facts" were still up for grabs.

There was, of course, the motivation that came from obtaining her husband's life insurance, but the most obvious answer is sometimes also the least convincing. Consider the thousands of dissatisfied wives who do not kill their husbands, and have no intention of killing them, although they stand to gain enormous insurance benefits. How was Ruth Snyder different? That was the real mystery of this case. Consequently, the most pressing question was not, How did she do it? but rather, How could she do it? What nameless god was hidden in her heart? What tangle of dark impulses set her apart from other housewives?

She was examined first by William J. Millard, the soft-spoken, elegantly dressed, senior attorney on Gray's defense team. Addressing Ruth Snyder in the manner of someone who had a sad but inevitable duty to perform, he directed almost all of his questions to her frame of mind. What could she have been thinking? Why did she do what she did? Why was his favorite word.

He began by asking her if she received a sash weight from Judd Gray in a package he passed to her at Henry's Restaurant.

"Yes," she said matter-of-factly, "but I did not know what was in the package until I brought it home."

"What did you do with that sash weight?" he asked.

"I took it and put it down in the cellar, after I unwrapped it."

"Why did you put it in the cellar?"

"Because I had every intention of giving it back to him after I read his note that he was coming out Monday."

"Did you know what the sash weight was for?"

"After reading the note, yes."

"Then why did you place it in the cellar?"

"Because I didn't want to have it anywhere around."

"Why did you not throw it away?"

"Because I felt it should go back to him, inasmuch as he gave it to me."

"Well, did you believe that that sash weight was to be used in killing your husband?"

"I didn't believe anything"—she paused, then

stumbled—"because I knew that if I gave it back to him that he would have to take it away again."

"You knew you were giving it into his possession when you gave it back to him?"

"Yes, but I also told him that I didn't want him to go through with it"—another pause, another stumble—"of getting away, of doing away with my husband."

"Let me ask you again, Mrs. Snyder, why did you not destroy or throw away the sash weight instead of giving it back to Judd Gray?"

Hesitantly: "I gave it back to Judd Gray because I didn't want anything to come to me from it."

"Did you believe that he wanted to use it to kill your husband?"

"Yes, I did."

"And yet you were placing it back in his hands?"

She had grown tense and pale. "I told him when I gave it back to him that I didn't want him to consider such a thought."

Millard's opening series had been designed to make only one point and it succeeded: Ruth Snyder was not comfortable with her own story. She stumbled, hesitated, strained. It wasn't so much that Millard had made the jury wonder why, if Ruth Snyder really wanted to protect her husband, she had handed the weapon over to her husband's murderer. It was that he demonstrated her lack of authenticity.

"Did you warn your husband?" Millard continued in the same sad, almost apologetic manner.

"No."

"Did you believe that Judd Gray wanted to kill your husband?"

"I thought I could talk Judd Gray out of it."

"But you never mentioned the subject to Albert Snyder?"

"I could not mention it to my husband."

"Why?"

"Because I was ashamed of the disgrace that might come out of it."

This was plausible. Surely, she would be ashamed to tell her husband that she was involved in an extra-marital relationship with a man who planned on killing him. Who wouldn't be? But why did she leave the rear doors open for Judd Gray that night? What could her thinking have been in making it so easy for Judd to get into the house? Those were Millard's next questions.

"Because I thought when I came home I could still talk Judd Gray out of the idea, and I was going to have it out with him that I did not want him around me anymore."

"Yet from the previous conversation with him you had learned, had you, that he wanted to kill your husband?"

"He had spoken of it several times."

"You were afraid he would?"

"I knew he would."

Slowly, easily: "And yet you left the rear doors open for Judd Gray to enter your home while you and your husband were at Fidgeon's party?"

"Yes."

Scratching his head, a look of utter perplexity on his face: "Why didn't you send word to him to stay away, Mrs. Snyder?"

"Because he had been sending me letters telling me of this thing that he had planned, or was planning, and I made up my mind that I was going to see him and break it off right then and there."

More head scratching: "Why was Judd Gray coming down from Syracuse to see you on the night you and Albert Snyder were going to the party?"

Ruth Snyder grew silent and looked up at the sky-light. The courtroom was hushed. Even the whispering celebrities seemed to sense that Ruth was having a hard time "remembering" her story.

"I don't know other than he was going home over the weekend and he was going away the following week, and he asked himself could he see me before he went away, and I made up my mind, too, that as long as this thing had been going on for weeks I was going to stop it."

Was Ruth Snyder planning to say to Gray what a mother says to her child? No, Judd, you don't want to reach for that candy, because if you do, you will be punished—and punished severely. It seemed so. Yet it was completely unclear how murdering Albert Snyder was candy to Gray—what was the allure there? Why in the world would Judd Gray want to get rid of Albert Snyder? Did Ruth Snyder have any suspicion?

"Yes," she replied, "for the insurance that he was after."

"Was there any insurance policy made with Judd Gray as beneficiary?"

"No."

"Who was the beneficiary?"

"I was." Laughter was audible in court, prompting Judge Scudder to lean forward and scowl.

"The money wouldn't go to Judd Gray in case your husband was killed?"

"No, but he would have eventually gotten it out of me."

"How?"

In a tone of weary patience: "Through the same means that he got money out of me before."

Ruth Snyder was convinced of Gray's determination to murder her husband. But if that was so, why did she do nothing to protect him? Could she please explain that?

"I did not protect my husband because I knew that I could talk Judd Gray out of it, which I had done on two previous occasions."

"Yet you had him come to the house, didn't you?"

"Yes, to break it off finally."

"Brought him near your husband so that you could break it off?"

"So that I could break it off, yes."

"Knowing your husband would be home?"

"Yes."

"And that Judd would be there?"

"Yes."

Shifting direction, Millard asked Mrs. Snyder if she would mind walking the jurors through the actual murder once again. Would she tell the jurors what she did on the night of the murder from the time she and her family got home, to the time her neighbor found her gagged and tied up?

Obediently, she described how she got home at two o'clock, put the "baby to bed," passed through the hall and stepped into her mother's room, where she found Judd wearing rubber gloves and carrying a pistol. After taking the pistol away from him and leading him downstairs, she said she "tried to plead with him, reason with him" for about an hour, then finally left him because she needed to go to the bathroom.

Almost word for word, she repeated the testimony she had given to Hazelton during direct examination: how she heard "this terrific thud," opened the bathroom door, looked down the hall and saw Judd Gray on top of her husband in bed, and then ran in and grabbed Judd Gray, who responded by pushing her, causing her to fall to the floor in a faint.

And almost at the same point in the story as before,

the point at which she described how she awakened from her faint to find her husband's body covered with blankets, Ruth Snyder dropped her face into her hands and cried. For nearly three minutes she sobbed, the same duration as before, sucking in air like a sprinter progressing through the hundred-yard dash, softly at first, then louder and faster, while her attorneys, Edgar Hazelton and Dana Wallace, looked on, profoundly sympathetic.

Then, just as abruptly as she broke into tears, she raised her head and resumed her look of assured control, explaining once again how Judd Gray ransacked the place and told her that she would have to help him make it look like a robbery.

"And you listened to all that?" asked Millard, who was now looking incredulous.

"Yes, I did."

"And when you knew your husband was dead, did you cry out?"

"I couldn't cry out. I was too frightened to cry."

"Did you notify the police department?"

"I notified none—no one."

"But you sat and listened to Judd Gray plan a method of throwing the police off the scent."

"I didn't know what it was all about. I was too confused myself. I didn't know what it was—what he was doing."

"But you were planning, were you not, to make it look like a robbery?"

"I was not planning it. He planned it."

"Did you disapprove of it?"

"Yes."

"What did you say?"

"I said, 'I don't want to go through with it,' and he said, 'I am going to leave and they won't know where I am.'"

"But you did go through with it?"

"I had to."

Why she felt she had to follow Judd Gray's plan, why she felt compelled to lie to the police for almost sixteen hours, despite the fact that Judd had long ago departed for Syracuse, why she did not dash out and tell the neighbors and call the police, was left unexplored. It seemed that Millard's way was to bring out an inconsistency and move on. Many people felt that he was letting Mrs. Snyder off the hook, that he wasn't pressing hard enough, which may explain why Judge Scudder interjected a question of his own. Why, he asked the witness, had she undressed and gone to bed knowing that Judd Gray was in her home?

"I had to get undressed, Judge," she replied. "I did not want my husband to get up in an effort to get Gray out of the house."

That ended Ruth Snyder's cross-examination by Gray's attorney. It was now time for one of the prosecution attorneys, Assistant District Attorney Charles W. Froessel, to begin on her. The drawback to this way of proceeding, at least for Ruth Snyder and Judd Gray, was that they were cross-examined twice—they had to defend themselves against each other, and against the legal team assembled by the D.A.'s office. But the positive side, from the public's point of view, was that Ruth Snyder would have a harder time getting away with anything. The general consensus was that Millard had been too easy on her—that he had been too much of a gentleman. What she needed, people felt, was a bulldog who would bore in on her and pelt her with questions.

That was exactly what Assistant D.A. Froessel was, a bulldog. Although he appeared mild enough in repose, with fleshy cheeks and an apple-shaped torso, when he started moving about and asking questions, he produced an entirely different—much more canine—impression. From the way he kept his legs widely separated as he strode around the courtroom, to the way words rolled furiously over his protruding lower lip, one had the feeling that he intended to maul someone.

"Now, madam," he opened, "the judge just addressed a question to you and asked you why you did get undressed when Judd Gray was in the house, and you replied because you wanted to use your efforts to get him out of the house."

"Yes, sir."

"Is that correct?"

"Yes."

"In other words, you wanted to get him out of the house that night, did you not?"

"I did, yes."

"You could have kept him out by locking those doors, yes or no?"

"I could have."

"Yes or no, madam?"

"Yes."

His back toward her, his eyes scanning the jury: "But you did not keep them locked?"

"No."

"As a matter of fact, you did not have one door open, you had two doors left open?"

"Yes."

"So that he would surely get in."

"Yes."

Abruptly changing direction, Froessel turned his attention to Ruth Snyder's married life. He had her acknowledge that she had no grounds for divorcing Albert and that he provided her and her daughter with a good home, an automobile, a motorboat, a

summer bungalow, and plenty of clothing. She testified that her husband gave her $85 a week out of his
$115 a week salary, and that he spent little money on
his own clothes.

"And yet you were unhappy?" Froessel asked in a
shocked tone of voice, as if he could not imagine how
any woman could be unhappy on eighty-five dollars
a week.

"Yes."

"Of course, you did nothing in your married life
to make your husband unhappy, did you?"

"No."

"You never did a thing to make him unhappy?"

"No."

"Madam, your answer is that you did nothing whatever to make your husband unhappy."

"Not that he knew about." There was more laughter.

Hazelton half rose. "Your Honor, the gallery is twit-
tering again!"

Judge Scudder repeated the warning that he had
given earlier—the court would be cleared if there
were any further demonstrations.

Froessel resumed, making the same point over and
over. "You knew that he didn't know about the life
that you were leading?"

"He didn't know."

"He never talked to you about his suspicions concerning your staying away at night?"

"He never did, no."

"He never talked to you about staying away for a
period of ten days with your paramour?"

"He did not know that."

"I did not ask you what he thought."

"He did not know."

Froessel was close to her, leaning forward. His

speaking voice, a gruff baritone, added to the impression of contempt he conveyed. "You have answered it. So that you thought that while you were carrying on with the defendant Gray you were putting it all over your husband, didn't you?"

"No," the witness replied, a defiant edge to her voice, "I did not think I was putting it all over him."

"You knew you were doing wrong, did you not?"

"Yes."

"And you did not think your husband had any suspicions concerning your remaining away nights or weeks or ten days at a time?"

"He did not."

"You made sure of it, did you not?"

"I did not have to make sure of it," she said with a half-smile, fending off Froessel's questions with calm insistence, appearing much more relaxed and sympathetic than when she was cross-examined by Millard. That afternoon's edition of the *Daily Mirror* was inspired to call her "the most remarkable witness that has ever warmed a witness chair." True, her story was still far from plausible, but her answers, under the hectoring, badgering, and nagging sarcasm of Charles Froessel, made her look spirited, steady, and resolute. Not once, not even when the questions were contemptuous and belligerent, did she seem shaken.

Desperate to humiliate her, to wound her, and place her on the defensive, Froessel tried to get Ruth Snyder to acknowledge that she was sexually indiscriminate and promiscuous.

"Do you know a man by the name of Bernard?" he asked.

"Yes."

"How long have you known Mr. Bernard?"

"I met him on one or two occasions when he came to my house to sell me an oil heater."

"I asked you how long you had known him."

"I met him about two years ago."

"Do you know his first name?"

"Yes."

"Do you know his address?"

"No, I do not."

"Then you never saw him at his home, did you?"

"No, sir."

"Did you ever go out with him?"

"I did not."

"Did you register with him in the Sydney Hotel—?"

"I certainly—"

"In New York City, at least six times?"

"I did not."

"Wasn't your acquaintance with him merely a pickup coming around to your house as a salesman for heaters?"

"No, it was not."

"That is how you met him, wasn't it?"

"I met him at my house. He was canvassing."

"In other words, he was another salesman, was he not?"

"Yes."

"He sold heaters?"

"Yes."

"Harry Folsom sold stockings?"

"Yes."

"Judd Gray sold corsets."

"Yes."

"Did you know any more salesmen in that way?"

"Yes. I did."

"How many of them did you know?"

"A number of them."

"Did you ever go shopping in department stores for your needs?"

"Very seldom."

"You usually went around to the salesmen, did you not?"

"I did not go to see salesmen. I went to wholesale houses."

"You know that wholesale houses do not sell at retail prices unless you know somebody there?"

"That is true."

"And you always knew somebody there?"

"Yes."

"And that somebody was a salesman?"

"Yes."

Back and forth they went, Ruth giving Froessel an answer for every question. When Froessel was indignant, she'd be indignant back; when he tried to make her back down, she held fast; and when he appeared at the point of trapping her into an admission, she'd either say she couldn't remember and end it there, or agree that what he said might be true, and then, with a toss of her head, brush it aside, as if to say, "Well, have it your way. What difference does it make?" She was beating the prosecutor at his own game.

Froessel next tried to break her on the topic of insurance. She wanted her husband heavily insured, did she not?

She did not.

She never did?

Never.

But she wanted her husband to take out more life insurance, didn't she?

She did.

What amount of insurance did she think was the right level for her husband?

Whatever amount he wanted.

Froessel took a breath and continued. "And you were the one to pay the premiums?"

"I was not to pay the premiums out of my money, except—"

"You can answer that yes or no."

"Yes."

"And you were the one to pay it out of your own private bank accounts?"

"No."

"Or were you to pay it out of the allowance of your husband?"

"I took twenty dollars a week—"

"I am asking you—"

"Out of my husband's money that he gave me."

"In other words, nearly one-fourth of your weekly allowance you paid to the insurance company."

"Yes."

After getting Ruth Snyder to admit that the insurance agent delivered the policies to her during the day, when her husband was not home, and that she placed the policies in a safety-deposit box under the name of Ruth Brown, her maiden name, Froessel asked if her husband had access to those policies in that safety-deposit box.

"Yes, he did."

"You mean to tell us that he had access to the safety-deposit box in the Queens Bellaire Bank kept in the name of Ruth Brown? Yes or no?"

"Yes, he did."

"You are certain of that?"

"Yes."

"Did he go down to the bank at the time that you ordered that safe-deposit box?"

"No."

"And gave his signature?"

"No."

"Did he give his signature to the bank on that particular box at any time?"

"No, he did not."

"And yet you want to tell us that he had access to that safe-deposit box?"

"Yes, he did."

"You mean that he had access to that box through Ruth Brown?"

"Yes, through me."

"Then, he did not have access to that safe-deposit box without your personal consent?"

"No."

"And it was in that safe-deposit box, to which he did not have access, that these policies were deposited by you?"

"Yes."

"And it so happens, does it not, that in that same safe-deposit box in your own maiden name there were placed the receipts for each one of these payments?"

"Yes."

After bringing out that all her other family papers—the papers in connection with the house, the deed, the fire insurance policies, the receipts on the mortgage—were in a different box under her married name, Froessel had his witness admit that she had issued instructions to the postman to deliver personally into her hand all mail from the Prudential Life Insurance Company. He also had her admit that she had the postman deliver into her hand all mail addressed to Jane Gray or Judd Gray, and her bill from the telephone company containing a record of her toll calls to Judd Gray.

Then, slowly and deliberately, he asked if the reason she had for telling the postman that he shouldn't deliver, except to her personally, the telephone company bills was because she didn't want her husband to see the toll calls to Judd Gray.

"Yes," she answered.

"And the reason that you told the postman not to deliver the mail to Jane Gray or Judd Gray or to anybody but you is because you didn't want your husband to see those letters?"

"Yes."

"And the reason that you told the letter carrier not to deliver the Prudential Life Insurance bill to anybody but yourself was because you didn't want your husband to see those letters?"

But to this, Ruth replied, "No."

"That is the only distinction you make?"

"Yes."

"You had another reason, did you not?"

"I did not."

"But you told the letter carrier without any reasons at all?"

"Without any reason," she answered because she had to, because there was no other answer. But before Froessel could follow with his next question, Ruth added with a toss of her head, "It was when we were on our trip that I asked him to be most careful—"

Cutting her off: "I didn't ask you anything else but a yes or no answer. You had a reason for the telephone bills?"

Chastened: "Yes, sir."

"You had a reason for the Jane Gray letters?"

"Yes."

"And that had no connection with your trip at all?"

"He kept them for me just the same."

"You had a reason for the telephone, and you had a reason for the Gray letters, but you did not have a reason for the Prudential letters?"

"I had no reason at all."

Bitterly and sarcastically: "Wasn't the same reason that you told the letter carrier to deliver to you only personally the Prudential Life Insurance Company mail, the reason that you kept the matters connected with the $50,000 policies in a safe-deposit box in your own maiden name?"

Tonelessly: "No."

Froessel stopped cold and closed his eyes. He was stalled. He had made his point; he had demonstrated Ruth Snyder's inconsistency; but instead of appearing crushed and exhausted, she looked as if she had just taken a walk through a field of daisies. Mrs. Snyder was a force, all right—not necessarily a positive or predictable one—but a force.

After a silence, Froessel asked her if she was at all interested in the policy to be obtained on the life of her husband.

"In what policy?" she asked with a child's searching wonder.

"The policy, or, we will put it in this way, the insurance as to which you invited Ashfield [the insurance agent] to come to your house?"

"I do not quite understand the question?"

Froessel tried to clarify. What he wanted to understand, he asked, was whether she was at all interested in what would happen—what payments she would receive—in the event that a fatal accident were to happen to her husband.

Partly, yes, she replied.

Did she try to become familiar with the provisions that were incident to the policy? Was she, perhaps, familiar with the term double indemnity?

She was.

Now, did she ever sit down and figure out how it would be paid or anything in connection to it?

No, she did not.

Well, then, said Froessel, with a quick little gleam of triumph in his eyes, "What do you make of this?"

Then he produced a scrap of paper and read a series of figures:

> First five years, $10,000, $199.70. After five years, $374.60. $50,000, 5—$998.50. $100,000 x .04, $4,000, equals $78.00 per week.

Ruth Snyder looked at the scrap of paper, then looked at Froessel, and then looked up at the skylight. Everyone's attention was riveted on her eyes, as she tried to read meaning into these barely discernible, cryptic figures.

"You were figuring out what you would get in the event of the maturity of this policy in case of an accident?"

"I figured that up—"

"Yes or no?"

"No."

Froessel snorted, then asked her who was the beneficiary of these policies.

"I believe myself," she answered.

"Well, will you look at the policies and tell us for a certainty, referring to the $5,000 and $45,000 policies?"

"Yes."

"And you were not sure until now whether you were the beneficiary or not?"

"I didn't—"

"Yes or no?"

"Yes, I did."

"Yes, you did know?"

"Yes, I did know."

"Well, then, you did not merely believe, did you?"

"No."

"You knew it."

Wearily: "Yes."

"Now, was there any reason for hedging?"

"No."

Froessel wheeled, arms extended to the jury, looking as exultant as a man whose horse had just won the Preakness. His persistence was paying off.

For some reason, though, Froessel did not go for the kill. Instead, he embarked on some new, subtle strategy, and began questioning Ruth Snyder on how she and Gray got along with each other. His tone of voice changed, too. Instead of sounding harsh and contemptuous, it was now soft, almost understanding.

"Did you [she and Gray] quarrel about other girls?"

"I would not say that, no."

"Did you quarrel about other men?"

"No."

"Did the quarrels amount to anything?"

"No."

"They were about petty things?"

"Yes."

"You really would not call them quarrels, would you?"

"No."

"Leaving aside the little understandings—the little misunderstandings or petty quarrels about minor things that did not amount to anything, you got along very nicely, did you not?"

"Yes."

"And thought a lot of one another?"

"Yes."

"Did you do him any harm of any kind?"

"No."

"I do not mean moral harm now. I mean something he resented."

"No."

"Did he do any harm to you of any kind that you resented?"

"No."

"So that you got along mighty well right up to the time of the murder?"

"Yes."

"You continued writing one another these affectionate letters?"

"Yes."

"You had never done him any injustice and he had never done you an injustice?"

"Not to amount to anything."

Froessel maddeningly repeated all his previous questions. Did she and Gray argue about men? About women? Did she threaten him? Did he threaten her? No, no, no, no, Ruth answered. It seemed that Froessel was trying to trap her into admitting that she and Gray had quarrels. No, she insisted vigorously, they had never had a serious quarrel.

Froessel now had his wedge firmly in place. Looking up from his notes, he inquired: What about the quarrel she described in court during direct examination? Had she forgotten that she testified that she was intending to break off with Gray last summer, but had backed down when Judd threatened to "expose her to the world"? Was it true that Judd threatened her or was that a lie?

For a moment, Ruth Snyder reeled as if from a physical blow. She saw with sudden, awful clarity the enormity of her blunder. It would injure her case irreparably if the jury believed that she had been lying when she earlier testified that she intended to break off with Judd upon learning of his plan to murder her husband. Her whole explanation for cooperating with him rested on the premise that she was coerced—that he was blackmailing her. Of course, they had quarreled, Mrs. Snyder should have said. Instead, she had denied the very thing she needed to insist upon.

"Madam, when I asked you whether there were any petty quarrels or misunderstandings of any kind between you and Mr. Gray, you said no," said Froessel, who was by now positively salivating. "Had you forgotten the incident of last summer?"

A hesitation. Then emphatically, "No . . . no, I had not forgotten it. That was a verbal argument."

"I did not ask you to distinguish between verbal and written argument," hissed Froessel, who saw that the witness was trying to wriggle free.

"Then I do not understand what you meant."

"Now you say he threatened to expose you last summer?"

"Yes."

"And you stood for that from him, did you?"

"Yes, I did."

He was livid. "Is it not a fact that your story in that regard is made of whole cloth?"

Hazelton shot up. "One moment, if the court please."

"I wouldn't say that," muttered Mrs. Snyder, beneath her counsel's objection.

"Indefinite, incompetent, irrelevant, and immaterial—" shouted Hazelton, goaded beyond all endurance.

Judge Scudder interrupted him. "This is a cross-examination. The question may be asked."

"Exception," said Hazelton.

Froessel attempted to clarify his question, but Ruth Snyder, now fully aware of his tactic, simply reverted to the position she had articulated on Friday. Yes, she had insisted on breaking off with Judd over this whole unfortunate matter. It was a horrible verbal disagreement.

Ruth Snyder was calmer now, even faintly confident, but Froessel was not about to quietly retreat into the dark night. This witness was still on the stand and Froessel still had plenty of ammunition.

"You testified here that you knew he was going to kill your husband the moment you saw the sash weight in the package?"

"Yes, but—"

"No buts, madam," he growled.

"So, knowing that he was going to kill your husband," Froessel went on, picking up the pace of his questions, "and basing your knowledge not only upon the correspondence and telephone calls and talks, but upon the giving to you of the sash weight, you returned it to him on that Monday night, did you not?"

"Yes."

For thirty minutes, Froessel threw questions at her, one after another, like a missile barrage before the final ground assault.

Hadn't she written Judd Gray at a rate of a letter a day the week before the murder?

Hadn't she also written him, the very week of the murder, that her husband kept a revolver under his pillow?

Didn't she write to him that on the night in question, the night of the murder, she was going to a bridge party?

And at the bridge party, didn't she give her husband extra whiskey, even though she knew he was at risk that night?

And didn't she leave both back doors open for Judd so that nothing would bar his access to her home and husband?

Froessel was hitting his stride.

After her family got home from the party, and she

made sure her husband was asleep, what happened then? Did she go to Judd Gray, who was hiding in her mother's room, and demand that he leave? Did they quarrel? Or was it the case that they kissed? Didn't he kiss her, and she kiss him, all the while knowing that Judd Gray was there to kill her husband?

Granted, she took her husband's loaded revolver away from Judd Gray, but where did she put it? Did she hide it, as she did her jewels, or did she put it on the piano, within easy reach, still knowing, or being afraid, that Judd Gray would kill her husband?

She testified, did she not, that she left Judd Gray downstairs alone while she went up to the bathroom, and that while she was in the bathroom, she heard "this terrific thud"? But didn't she also testify that the bathroom door was closed? And hadn't she heard the physician testify that her husband's skull was not fractured?

After Judd Gray had finished with her husband and went to the cellar to dispose of the murder weapon, she was alone with her husband's body, but what did she do? Did she examine her husband's body to see whether he was alive or dead, warm or cold—to see if there was something she could do to help him? Did she scream at any time or call for help? Or did she instead fetch the wallet out of her husband's coat pocket so she could give it to Judd Gray? Did she instead become worried about her jewelry and hide it under her mattress?

Froessel's deep voice began to rise, like a strong wind preceding a storm. She protected her jewelry from Judd Gray, said Froessel, but she did not see fit to determine if her husband might need her help.

"Madam," he shouted, his face deep crimson, his expression a prolonged sneer, his words evenly spaced like markers defining Ruth Snyder's guilt. "Madam—you—were—more—concerned—about —your—jewelry—than—your—husband's—life!"

An isolated tear escaped, though Mrs. Snyder's eyes lost none of their defiant immobility. Ruth Snyder could take a beating as a peasant took bread and salt, on every inch of flesh and spirit.

"Madam," said Froessel, "you realized that this story of yours—about trying to keep Gray from killing your husband was important enough to tell to the jury, didn't you?"

"Yes," she murmured in a voice so low and soft the amplifiers could barely catch it.

"Didn't you realize that you had to justify yourself to the police when they were questioning you?"

"Yes."

"And then, do you mean to tell me that when you realized they were getting to the truth and you decided to confess, you didn't tell Commissioner McLaughlin this very important fact, that Gray, not you, had killed your husband?"

She faltered and was lost. "I—I don't—I can't recall just what I told him."

Froessel concluded his cross-examination by going over the statements she made to the police the day after the murder. He led her over her confession, sentence by sentence, asking her to inform the jury which parts she repudiated, and which parts she accepted as true.

"Is this the truth?" asked Froessel, who then read from her confession, " 'Mr. Gray was the only one who would listen to my troubles'?"

Feebly: "Yes." Her voice had lost all its spirit.

" 'During the time that I had known Mr. Gray. I told him more and more of the troubles with my husband'?"

"Yes."

" 'Things became unbearable and I was looking for a way out'?"

"No, that is not the truth."

" 'That in talking with Mr. Gray, a method was proposed whereby we were talking about getting rid of him, and finally things came to a climax'?"

"No."

" 'Things became unbearable and he was looking for a way out, and in talking with Mr. Gray, a method was proposed whereby we were talking about his getting rid of him'?"

"Well, I cannot answer that."

"You cannot answer that?"

"No."

"What I would like to know is what is the untruth in this? The 'we' or the 'he'?"

"The 'we.' "

"In other words, he did those things, but you didn't?"

"Yes."

Unlike Hazelton, who only asked Ruth Snyder whether her incriminating statements were true, Froessel went over everything. Not a word was excluded. As a result, jurors could see a definite principle of selectivity operating. If a statement incriminated her, she said it was false; but if it didn't, it was true. Whenever the text of the confession stated that "we" had plotted or carried out any detail of the murder, Ruth Snyder said that the "we" should be changed to "he." All other "we's" were okay. No matter what parts were read which implicated her in the murder, she denied them.

At the beginning of this examination, Snyder's "no's" and "did nots" rang out—they were much more emphatic than her affirmations, but as Froessel bore on, her responses became progressively flatter, so that by the end any tonal difference between a denial and an affirmation had disappeared. Even Ruth Snyder—that most optimistic of liars—could tell her story sounded false.

She was limp when she left the stand, her face buried in her handkerchief.

11

He Takes the Stand: "Ruth Did It."

When people asked what kind of a man Judd Gray was, and what kind of person could have committed his crime, they were confronted with an utterly dismaying vision. Gray seemed on the one hand plain, honest, and direct. On the other hand, he invited the fanciest metaphysical musings. He was caught up in an endlessly complex plot involving a woman, he was over his head, bewildered and lost. Yet, his role in the trial was that of shameless truth-teller and unabashed confessor. The person least likely to understand this crime—the one least likely to know what really happened—was set up as the trial's most reliable expositor. Which may explain why his testimony often seemed so hard to follow, so incoherent, and at times seemed to erode right before people's eyes. What Judd Gray did on the witness stand was to lure observers into his shallow-appearing, artless world, only to violate all expectations. Having drawn people into his consciousness—a consciousness seemingly defined by its availability and simplicity—he pulled the rug out from under everyone, revealing how illusory his simplicity really was.

Immediately after he ascended to the stand, he wept, his thin shoulders shaking with awful sobs inside his tailored coat, his eyes redder than a drunk's. His face seemed strained, much grimmer than before, but he quickly regained his composure under the direction of his attorney, William Millard, whose initial questions were so innocuous and narrow, they could have put a hummingbird to sleep: "How long have you lived in the state of New Jersey?" "Till what age were you a constant communicant of the Presbyterian Church?" "What was your wife's maiden name?" "And how long did you continue with the Gray Homes Company?"

Things did not open up much when Millard turned to the topic of Judd Gray's involvement with Ruth Snyder. For some reason, Millard seemed chiefly concerned with capturing the statistical dimensions of that relationship. What hour of the day did Ruth Snyder and Judd Gray meet? Was anyone else present? What time did they part? If the answer could be formulated in demographic terms, Millard wanted it. Anything else was useless to him.

When Gray was directed to describe his second meeting with Ruth Snyder, for example, the time he had sexual relations with her in his office, what Millard wanted to know, above all else, was the office's address.

"Thirty-fourth Street and Fifth Avenue," Gray answered.

"What number Thirty-fourth Street?"

"Three-five-eight Fifth Avenue."

"What was the name of the concern?"

"Benjamin and Johns."

Then, expanding slightly, Millard asked, "Was the office open at the time?"

"It was not, sir."

"Did you have a key to the office?"

"I did."

"Did you open the door yourself?"

"I did."

Millard and Gray plodded along in this manner for about an hour, turning what promised to be the most interesting part of the trial into the dullest. Then, gradually, almost imperceptibly, Millard receded into the background. By the time they had worked their way to Gray's vacation with Ruth Snyder—their swing through New York State in October 1926—Gray's testimony was beginning to sound more like a monologue than courtroom Q and A.

Speaking quietly and slowly, Gray talked on and on, about Ruth Snyder and himself, what she said, what he said, without interruption. The problem everyone had, though, was it was almost impossible to say what details really counted and which ones did not, and how they did count if they did, and if they did, by how much? Small facts, odd associations, affirmations of intent, picturesque circumstances, what he and Ruth Snyder said to each other, how many drinks they had, their sexual habits, where they stayed, what time they got out of bed, what time they had luncheon—nothing was irrelevant to Gray, nothing peripheral. Trivia flew from him like snow from a blower, scattering without principle.

"We drove through Jersey, up through the Hudson River Valley section, stopping off at a little town above Newburgh for luncheon," he began his description of their "vacation"—what was in fact a business and pleasure trip, since Gray arranged to call on customers in each of the cities they visited. "She said she was never so happy in her life. She thought that the trip had already done her good. We drove from here on through to Kingston, arriving there about four-thirty. I left her at the hotel, telling her that I was going out to make a couple of appointments for the following morning. I put the car away and went out and called upon two customers and arrived back at the hotel about six o'clock. She greeted me, saying how glad she was to see me back again. Stated that this was the first honeymoon that she had ever known."

As he spoke, his fingers fluttered between his lips and cheek, going back and forth, up and down, like tiny tap dancers. That was one of his two gestures. Otherwise, you forgot he had a body at all. Listening to Gray was like listening to a tape recording of someone who had died a long time ago.

"At dinner she told me that she would have to write to her husband that night and mail the letter from there. I told her that I thought it was advisable to wait until the following day, inasmuch as she had gotten such a late start that it was only natural that a party that was driving through to Canada would be farther than Kingston, New York. [She had told her husband she was touring Canada with a married couple.] She thought this good advice and followed it.

"We sat around the room after dinner and had four or five drinks; went out for a walk. She then decided that she would—she told me that she had decided that she would call up her mother and see how things were at home. We stopped in a hotel uptown, chatting while we were waiting for this long-distance call to come through. She told the telephone operator not to tell where the call came from when she was connected with her home. She conversed with her mother and with her daughter for about four minutes; then came out and said that everything was fine at home, that the baby had said that she missed her and asked her if she was having an enjoyable time, and she said that she had been. We then went back to the hotel and retired."

Gray drew a long breath, like a baby's sigh after crying. That was his second gesture.

"That night again the question came up of her husband in a sexual way. She said she had never really known what sexual pleasures were with her husband. I sympathized with her, as I recall, that it was too bad, as I felt that was probably one of the greatest reasons for her unhappiness. She told me that when he came over into bed with her, that to her it was so disgusting and degrading that she felt like killing him. I told her that I could understand such a thing as that, because I was unhappy at home with my relations in that extent with my wife. We had considerable talk on sex that night. I recall I drank considerable. I do not remember falling asleep at all, which was my usual condition after being with Mrs. Snyder.

"The following morning I woke her up and told her that it was time for me to get up, that I had to attend to my business. I was in very much of a daze and told her that I did not feel like going out to work. She asked me if I could not stay in bed. I said no, that I could not, that this was a business trip as well as pleasure, that I did not feel that it was fair to my firm when I was out on business to lay down on the job. She said, 'Well, you go ahead and do your work and I will get up when I get ready.' So I left her in bed and went downstairs, having breakfast, returned to the room, took my two sample cases, went over and got the car and went out to call upon the trade. The first customer I called upon—"

The first customer he called upon? What did this have to do with the murder? What did it have to do with anything? No denying it, in the least likely places (that is: everywhere) his language sounded like tittle

tattle. Not only were his ideas unfocused, his delivery
was. None of his words were stressed above any others, there was no throb of emotion, nothing signaling
crisis, nothing that could be equated with life. It was
all flat, an unbroken legato incantation.

To be sure, some parts were mildly intriguing—for
example, Ruth Snyder's reaction to learning, when
they got to Albany, that they were assigned a room
with twin beds instead of a double: "We went upstairs
to the room," he said, expelling his breath. "I know
she started to laugh and chide me about this being
an old married man's honeymoon, inasmuch as we
had twin beds, as we had the night before. I said, 'It
does seem strange.' She asked me if I had asked particularly for that. I said no, that I had not. She said,
'It does not make any difference. I will push the beds
together,' and she proceeded to do so. We arranged
the room. I asked her if she would have a drink. She
said that she would. I had about four drinks. We conversed over the day's work, over the beauties of the
country that we had traveled. I asked her if she would
like to go down to dinner, and she said that she
would. We went downstairs for dinner, afterward going out for a walk. We returned to the hotel, and she
gave me two or three other drinks. We then went to
bed."

And they committed adultery. And later they committed murder. But the world Judd's language represented contained no passion; it contained no drama,
no music, no sensuality, no pretty words even, no
boughs, no veils, no impetuous hearts. No, Judd
Gray's threadbare phrases had about as much life
and beauty in them as Dick and Jane. I said, she said,
I remarked, she remarked, we conversed, we went
downstairs, we returned, we went to bed—he described things, all things, plainly.

One night, he said, they made love till two. "She asked me that night if I was going to come over to her bed. I said no. So she came over to mine. It was about two o'clock in the morning when I told her that I thought we had better go to sleep. She said she thought so, too, if I was going to get up and do any work in the morning."

And that's that. Ruth Snyder was the sexual predator, and poor Judd the prey. He said they made love, but he never showed them loving. What he displayed, instead, was his own reluctance and sterility—a sterility inherent not only in his behavior, but in his very method of explication. Dull, flat, repetitious and narrow, he cut off meanings, he did not add them on. He named, never rendered. One could not imagine a language more thoroughly and obstinately barren.

This frightened mama's boy, this death seeker, this prudish and terribly fragile fellow talked for another half hour, when he finally let slip something related to the murder, something about the "old crab" dying. "She called up her mother from this particular place that night," he said, "and found that her husband was ill. She said that he was feeling very bad and had been sick since she left. I asked her if she did not think that she better go home. She said, 'No, let the old crab die.' We went back, after purchasing a bottle, to the hotel. She went to bed while I did some work. She asked me when I was coming to bed. I said when I was finished. I do not recall the time when we went to sleep, but it was very early in the morning. I told her that I could not continue at this pace and still do my work. She said that she did not want me to feel that she was a burden on the trip, that if I must work, that we would try to be more careful of our hours and our intercourse."

Then, the next day, in Syracuse: "We went out for

a walk that evening. I showed her around the city, the department stores, and asked her if she would like to go to the theater. She said no, that she would rather go back to the hotel and go to bed. We went back to the hotel. She got undressed and I got undressed. We had quite a few drinks and then retired. I asked her if she did not think that she had better call up her home next day and find out how everything was. She said no, that she would write instead."

If one follows Judd Gray's tale, which was now beginning to sound moderately coherent, he continually pressed his lover to behave sensibly—for example, to go to bed at a decent hour and call her ailing husband—but all she wanted to do, it seemed, was have intercourse, party, and sleep late. He was the Puritan, she the relentless voluptuary. His impulses were all good, hers all wicked.

"The following morning," he continued, "we did not arise until pretty nearly noontime. She said that she had not slept as late as that in years. She only wished her home conditions were such that she could enjoy herself as she had enjoyed herself on this trip so far, that it was perfectly heavenly. We went down for luncheon, came back to the room. I asked her if she would like to go for a walk. It stopped raining. She said that she would. I took her down to show her the other hotel. We returned in the afternoon, remained in the room until that evening. That evening we went over to a chop suey place. She asked me if I would like to dance. I said that I did not care whether we did or not. She said, 'Come on, we have not danced since we have been away. The orchestra sounds so good I can hardly keep my feet still.' We got up and started to dance when the proprietor of the restaurant came over and told us that there was no dancing on Sunday. She told him that we came from New York where they could dance at any time. She forgot that she was in a small town.

"After our meal we took a walk and returned to the hotel. I asked her if she minded if I left her for a while. She said that she did not. She asked me where I was going. I said, 'Over to the garage to see about the car.' I returned in about half an hour. She was disrobed and in bed. Asked me if I was coming to bed. I told her that I had some work to do and would come to bed as soon as I could. I finished my work and I retired, so that we could get an early start in the morning. It was about two o'clock, I believe, when I told her that we would absolutely have to go to sleep if we were to get an early start in the morning. She said, 'Well, what's the difference? We are having a good time.' I insisted that I would have to be fresh for the morrow. We had a hard drive ahead of us."

True to the moral profiles that were emerging, when they arrived at Scranton, at the very end of their journey, Ruth Snyder said they had some liquor left, and that they might as well finish it up: "She said, 'Let us get good and plastered tonight, this may be the last evening that we are together.' " To which Judd Gray, prissy little fellow that he was, replied: "I told her that I had a hard day's work to do the following day. I did not think that I better get intoxicated. She said, 'Oh, go ahead, this will probably be our last evening together.' "

And what happened? Did he continue to challenge her, putting his whole being into the struggle, fighting to the last, or did he yield, melting in the face of her persistent pressure? The answer, predictably, is both. Their pattern of interaction was for Ruth Snyder to introduce some nifty bit of hedonism, to which Gray responded with peevishness and whining, reproaches and scoldings, but in the end, whatever she wanted him to do, he did. If he gave in to flesh and the devil, he did so protestingly, tremblingly, and helplessly, but he always gave in.

Thus: "We did get intoxicated that night. Stayed in the room all evening. I told her the following morning that this thing could not keep up. My physical condition was such when I woke I would apparently be in a daze—when I would call upon my trade I could not sufficiently collect to know what I was talking about. She said that she realized that we had been excessive in our intercourse, and the following night, if we stayed over, we would not have any."

A week later, after Judd Gray and Ruth Snyder returned from their trip, he said they met for lunch at Henry's. "Well, she said, during lunch hour, how unhappy she was after having such a wonderful time on this trip, that she was very unhappy at home, that her husband and she had had continuous quarrels since she had been back, and that she did not see how she could stand it longer.

"She said she absolutely would have to do something to get rid of him. She had reached the stage that life with him was unbearable. I told her that I thought that she was foolish to entertain such thoughts as this. I had taken her away on this trip with me to rid her mind of all such ideas, that it had not been spoken of at any time on the trip, and I thought that she had forgotten it. She said she couldn't forget it. It was uppermost in her mind. She asked me if I knew, on this particular meeting, anything about knockout drops. I said that I didn't. She said, 'You know a lot about medicine.' I said, 'Some.' She said, 'Well, you ought to know what they administer in liquor to put people out.' I said I knew nothing about such things. She said, 'Well, there is such

medicines,' that she had been out on a party one
night with some friends, and this man had given her
one drink and she had passed out for hours. She
asked me if I could give her anything of this type. I
said absolutely not."

Such was the art of conversation as Ruth Snyder
and Judd Gray practiced it, said Gray. She'd say the
Governor had to go, and Judd, in his best Y.M.C.A.
manner, would be horrified by the mixture of sin and
impracticality. Not only would she go straight to hell,
he'd argue, she'd definitely be caught. Then Ruth
Snyder, showing total disregard for his objections,
would ask for his assistance. From this point forward,
Gray's testimony was little more than a piling up of
examples of Ruth Snyder's homicidal designs and his
own almost unshakable resistance. What Gray was establishing, no doubt, was that he did not go out
eagerly and gladly to commit murder. Which left the
question, Why did he go out to commit the murder
at all? And why, if all his instincts revolted at the
thought of murder, did he listen to Ruth Snyder so
patiently day after day as she spun out her murder
plans?

Judd Gray did not say.

What he did recount instead, was how he followed
Ruth Snyder's orders, going to her house the following day, carrying some small bottles of liquor that she
had asked him to bring over. "I arrived, I presume,
about eleven-thirty. I called her up from the station.
She told me that it was all right to come up, that she
was home alone, and to come in the back way. So I
came up to her home, entered by the back way. She
kissed me and said it seems so good to see me again.
That her mother was not home. I told her I had
brought small bottles and lain them out on the
kitchen shelf for her. She asked me if I would open

them up, which I did. She brought me a large bottle and asked me if I would have a drink. I told her that I would. She asked me if I would have another drink, and I told her that I would. I left the small bottles open on this shelf. We went inside and talked in the living room. She then told me and showed me how she had kicked off the hose of the gas pipe—of the gas heater. Explained to me how he had laid down. Told me that when she came back, he had been walking up and down the street to get air. I said to her, 'I think you are absolutely insane to try such a thing as this in your own home.' She said she absolutely could not stand him longer, she had to get rid of him. I said, 'Did you try it before?' She said 'Yes, I did.' I said, 'When?' She said, 'Out in the garage.' I said to her, 'How did you do that?' She told me by taking liquor out to him while he was working on the car one Sunday the previous winter. Had given him two drinks while he was working in the garage, telling him he must be cold, that he had the motor running, but he had come out before anything had happened.

"I said, 'I cannot understand how anybody can do a thing like this.' She said, 'Well, that is because you don't know him and do not feel towards him the way I do.'

"I asked her what she was going to do with the little bottles. She said she was going to put some powders in them. I asked her where she had gotten the powders from. She said through a friend of hers who was a druggist. She told me at that particular time that she had other poisons around the house. I asked her if she had destroyed all the poisons that she had showed me on my first visitation there. She said she had not, that she had kept some of them.

"I told her that I thought she was very foolish to keep anything around the house that might be accidentally taken in the way of liquids. She said that she put them where nobody would find them until she wanted to use them herself. After luncheon she went upstairs and came down and gave me four or five powders, to put two in one bottle and three in the other. I believe I brought four bottles in all, if I remember correctly.

"I left them laying there on the kitchen table. We went back into the living room and talked for a while. We then went upstairs to her daughter's room where we had intercourse. I told her that I would have to leave early that day as I must get back to the office, that I was planning a short trip and must see to the packing of my trunk. I left her, as I recall, about four o'clock, going back to my office."

Gray recalled that the next time Ruth Snyder brought up the murder plan was during the third or fourth week in November. "She said she was going to make one more attempt, and if that failed, that I would have to help her with some plan. I said, 'This cannot do.' She said that she was at her wit's end to know how to get out of her difficulties. I said, 'I cannot help you because I don't know anything about these things.' She asked me if I would not find out from some friend of mine who was a doctor what was in the way of knockout drops. We had come back from Henry's Restaurant after dinner, and we sat and talked for quite a while. She brought the subject up again while we were in bed, after I had a number of drinks, and asked me if I would promise that I would find out what she could get to use."

Here, Gray pulled his hand away from his face. He seemed suddenly aware that his fingers were moving spasmodically, trembling and jerking, as if they were having bad dreams. He attempted to bring them under control by clasping them, prayer-style. Then he pulled them apart and sat on them.

"I told her that I would try," he said in a husky voice. "That she told me the next day. I did not remember making the promise. The next morning, when I awoke, I was in the usual haze. She recalled the conversation of the night before and asked me if I remembered that I had promised to help her. I told her I did not. She said, 'You would do anything for me, would you not?' I said I did not know. She said, 'You know, last night, that you promised me that you would find out what it was I could use in the way of knockout drops to put a person to sleep.' I said that I did not remember that I had promised, but I would keep it if she said that I had."

He didn't remember making a promise of this sort, but had to keep it. That was his excuse—not love for her, not fear for his life, not liquor or sex. To shrink from keeping his word, even though he knew what she asked was a mortal sin, would have been, in Gray's mind, the act of a puling and tacky fellow. He was a gentleman.

What was his reason then for allowing Ruth Snyder to experiment on his body? It was early evening, and they were in their hotel room in the Waldorf. "She asked me if I would try out these vials of sleeping powders to see what effect they would have on me. I asked her if they were poison. She said no, they would just put me to sleep, and she wanted to see what effect they would have upon me. I had three or four more drinks, and tried first one bottle." He said it tasted very bitter. "She gave me three or four more drinks of whiskey and then I tried the other bottle." That one tasted "sickishly" sweet. "I didn't know very much what happened thereafter until about eight o'clock next morning," said Judd. "My brain was very dazed and numb."

On and on they went, said Gray, following the same pattern month after month, Ruth Snyder preoccupied with poisonous powders and gases, and he begging her to abandon her crazy plans. Then toward the end of December 1926, she explained her murderous fixation in a way that made a certain amount of sense to him. She told him that her husband had just purchased a gun and that he had threatened her with it. "I asked her if she really felt in her own mind that he would kill her. She said that he was liable to do anything. At that particular time she complained bitterly about his treatment towards their youngster. She said that he had slapped her on that particular day that I met her, and almost knocked her down. I asked her if that was usual. She said he had slapped her many times and that that particular time she felt as though she could kill him."

Gray sympathized, but still wondered why she couldn't divorce him.

They met at the Waldorf again in mid-January: "We went out for dinner that night and danced and had quite a few drinks, came back to the hotel around ten-thirty or eleven o'clock; started to talk about conditions. We had several drinks in the room during this time; prepared for bed."

Gray asked her how her husband was. He had the hiccoughs, Ruth Snyder said, had them the last five days. She also told him that she filed off the word POISON from the label of her bichloride of mercury bottle.

"I asked her, 'What for?'"

"She said that she had given them to her husband, telling him that it was bismuth.

"I said, 'My God, don't you know that that is deadly?'

"She said, 'I thought that it was, too, but it only made him vomit.'

"I said, 'It's a wonder that it did not kill him.'

"She said, 'It is a wonder, but he vomited about fifteen or sixteen times that night.'

"And I said, 'What was the aftereffects of this?'

"She said it apparently had cured his hiccoughs.

"I said to her that it was a hell of a way to cure hiccoughs.

"I asked her where she had gotten the bichloride from and she said that she had gotten it from a doctor for personal use. I asked her if she had any more, and she said that she did. I asked her what she was using it for. She told me for her own personal use. I asked her if she had filed any more of the poison labels off. She said that she had. I asked her where they were. She told me that they were in a Midol box. I said, 'Well, those are for headaches.' She said, 'I know it, but I have got them in the medicine chest where they will not be touched.' I asked her if she did not think this was a very dangerous thing to do. She said she did, that she had cautioned her mother not to use anything out of that box because it had a little red cross on it."

Ruth Snyder asked Gray if he would get her some chloral hydrate. "I said that I would not. She said that she was going to get some if she had to go down to the druggist and work there to get it. I told her that I did not think that this was advisable and to drop her plan. I know I had several drinks after that. The conversation later taking a turn toward sex, she told me—the substance of the conversation was that she had had nothing to do with her husband in months now, that he did not even bother her anymore. She was having great difficulty and was afraid she was having change of life. I told her that I didn't think that was possible in so young a woman. She said she was going down to see the doctor shortly for examination. The following day she left at about five o'clock, if I recall. We had lunch together. And she also asked me if I could think of any way to help her in her plan. I told her I could not."

During the latter part of February, the pressure Snyder was placing on him intensified, said Gray. They were dining out one evening at an uptown restaurant: "I do not recall the name. I had never been there before. It was a place that she suggested. We watched the cabaret, had quite a few drinks, stayed there until about midnight, came home to the room. She said she felt like getting intoxicated and fell upon the floor. I had great difficulty in getting her into bed. We were in bed, I presume, an hour and a half or so when she broached the question again of doing away with her husband. She said that she had tried all means and methods that she knew and that they had all failed, that I absolutely had to help her. I asked her how. She said she would have to think up some scheme whereby we could get rid of him, that it was either a case of she or him or all of us. I said that I knew of no way of doing such a thing. She said that it had to be done. I asked her what she had in mind. She said chloroforming him.

"I asked her if she knew anything about using chloroform. She said she did not. She asked me if I did. I said I did not. She suggested at that time of using some means while he was asleep to strike him, so that he would be insensible, and then use the chloroform. I said that was surely possible. She asked me if I would help her do this. I said I would not. She then said to me would I get the chloroform for her. I said I would.

I asked her if she was going to do this herself. She said that she would try. It was this night that the plans were born that were later carried out."

So Gray took the next step, according to his story, the step from tacit cooperation to actually helping her plan the murder and carry it out. When Ruth Snyder first told Gray that she wanted to get rid of her husband, he was adamant, "I absolutely refused to be a party to any such plan." But Ruth Snyder kept asking, and Judd Gray, like a blind man surrounded by potholes, eventually fell. He was of the firm and resolute conviction that Ruth Snyder was too strong, too remorseless, and too clever for this son of man to challenge. Gray was caught. He had, to his eyes, no options at all. The Governor's murder, and his role in it, was an accomplished fact.

Gray next saw Ruth Snyder the first week of March, in the morning, at her home. "I had two or three drinks when I came in that she gave me. We went into the living room and talked over this matter of using chloroform and an instrument of some sort. She asked me if I thought that it sounded feasible or plausible that afterwards a burglary appearance should be made. I told her that I thought that it did. She said, 'You are going to help me, are you not?' And I said, 'No, I am not going to help you, only inasmuch as getting the chloroform for you.'

"She spoke about an instrument to be used, a hammer, if I recall correctly. I think it was my suggestion about a window weight. I know I had several more drinks after lunch. We were in the living room. She asked me if I would get some colored handkerchiefs and the chloroform and the window weight and a pair of gloves, I believe, if I remember correctly.

"I was about to leave on a trip up the Hudson River and I said that I would. She asked me again if I knew anybody who would help her out this way, and I said I did not. She pressed me upon I helping her to do away with her husband. I said that I did not think that I could do such a thing, that I had never killed anybody in my life. I recall that I had several more drinks before I left, and left in a quite intoxicated condition. She came with me.

"We came over to New York in a bus, got off at Grand Central Station, she came down, said to me as I left, 'Do not forget to get the things, and you are going to help me.' I said I did not think that I could do such a thing, but I would get the things for her.

"I took the train to Albany. I got there rather late, and I went across the street and had several more drinks. I got to thinking this thing over, and thinking how terrible it was that I should become embroiled in this matter, and I swore to myself that I would have nothing to do with it."

After Albany, Gray traveled to Kingston where he purchased the window weight and chloroform. He was drinking constantly, he said. He placed the murder articles in his grip, then returned to New York, where his lover called him. "Mrs. Snyder called me up from the doctor's and said that she would meet me at Henry's Restaurant around twelve o'clock or thereabouts. I told her that I had a bottle which she had been anxious to get to make a lamp of, and a roller and the garment—I do not think I told her there was a garment or a roller there. I told her I would put the window weight in the package and the bottle, and bring it over to the restaurant with me.

"She said that that would be all right and she would meet me there within the course of an hour. I wrapped up the window weight. I wrapped up—the window weight was already wrapped in four or five papers, with the bottle, and with the roller which has been displayed here, and a garment. There was no note. And I took them over to Henry's with me. I came in, found them [Ruth Snyder was with her daughter, Lorraine] sitting at a table with this gentleman who has testified here, Walter Martin. I kissed her. She said, 'My God, what is the matter with you?' I said, 'I am frightfully nervous. I do not know what I am doing.' She asked me if I was going to have lunch and I said that I would stay for a short time, and I barely touched my food and left as soon as I could. I had had two or three drinks before I left the office and I think I had one there, if I remember correctly, and I left the package on the chair. She asked if the weight was in there. I said that it was, also the bottle and the roller and the garment. I talked with Lorraine. As a matter of fact, she wrote to me on paper so that Lorraine would not hear it, the contents of the package, and gave me the paper to tear up and throw away.

"I wrote to her on paper what was in there. Our conversation was of no great length, due to the fact of Lorraine's being there. I left after being there, I presume, maybe a half an hour or so."

The next time he heard from Ruth Snyder was over the phone: "She asked me if I could come out to the house. I told her that I did not think that I could. Asked her what she wanted to see me about. She asked me if I would meet her in Jamaica. I told her that I had had no lunch. She said that she would look up a train, and looked up one for me, if I recall correctly, and that we would meet there.

"I went back to my office and had three or four more drinks and took a small bottle with me. Went over to the Pennsylvania Station. Went out to Jamaica, and she was waiting for me on the platform.

I asked her if she had had luncheon and she said
that she had.

"It was around three o'clock, if I recall correctly.
We went downstairs, and I asked her where we could
get something to eat. I was not familiar with Jamaica.
She told me that there was a chop suey restaurant
just down from the station there. We went there, and
we went upstairs, and we sat at the last table on the
left-hand side. I asked her what she wanted to see me
about, and she said relative to doing away with her
husband. She said that she practiced with the window
weight and she lost all her strength when she tried
to swing it, and that I would have to help her. I told
her that I did not think I could help her in any way
in this respect. She then asked me again if I would
go up to this neighborhood of which she had spoken,
around 102nd Street and Second Avenue, and I said
I wouldn't. I then said, 'You will have to do this yourself.'

"I told her that I could not do it alone. If I must
do it, that she would have to help me.

"I went back to the toilet, finished the bottle that
I had brought with me, and I came back, I recall, and
spilled a cruet of juice that they had on the table,
and she said, 'My God, you are certainly nervous,
aren't you?' I said, 'I certainly am. I do not know
hardly what I am doing.' She asked me if I would
come out that night. I said that I would. She asked
me if I would bring the things out that I had purchased and also get some rope. I said that I would.
She said that if everything was all right, she would
leave the light in her mother's window lighted, and
if it was not, for me to wait. She said that she would
have her husband go to bed early that night. I went
back to the office, and I do not recall what I did do.
I know I waited around the office until about five-

thirty. When the office closed I was still there. I drank, I think—when I had come over that morning—this is going backwards, if you will bear with me, please—I had bought my sleeper for Buffalo, and when I had come over to New York I had checked my trunk to Buffalo. I was preparing to leave that night for a trip on the road.

"I will go back to the office, which was about six o'clock. As I say, I think, if I recall correctly, I drank pretty nearly a quart of whiskey in the office. I stopped over on Thirty-third Street and had a sandwich. I could not procure any rope, so I picked up some picture wire that was in the office there, and I took an old duster and started out. I don't recollect what bus I got, but I landed in Queens Village around nine—nine something. I was quite intoxicated. I walked and I walked and I walked. I think that I walked fully two hours or two hours and a half. I passed the house a number of times. There was a light in the cellar. There was no light upstairs. I knew that I would have to leave about a quarter to twelve in order to make my sleeper, from Queens Village, and I think it was about eleven-fifteen or so, as I was going by the house I heard a knock on the kitchen window and I saw Mrs. Snyder motioning to me to come in. I went up the back steps and got as far as the kitchen door. She was in her nightgown. She kissed me and had a bottle of whiskey in her hand and about half a pint in it.

"She asked me if I would have a drink. I said that I would. I think I drained the bottle, if I am not mistaken. She asked me if I would do the job that night. I said no, I could not go through with it. She said, 'Won't you stay and we'll go up together?' I said, 'No, I do not think that I can go through with it, Momie.' I asked her if she wanted to keep the things that I had brought over there. She said that she did not think that she had better, and I agreed with her. I did not see the window weight. I did not know where it was. I left with the chloroform, with a pair of rubber gloves, wire, and cheesecloth. I went down to the station. She kissed me good-bye and said that she would write me further details to Buffalo. I ran down to the station as best I could, made my train. Went over to Hoboken, took the sleeper, and went to Buffalo."

Gray testified that he remained away, traveling on business, until the following Sunday. In a letter, reaching him in Seneca, New York, Ruth Snyder asked Gray to obtain five feet of rope. Gray said, "She didn't specify the kind. She simply said rope. That if the way was clear there would be a package of cigarettes on the kitchen table; that she would leave both doors unlocked, for me to go in the side entrance. If the cigarettes were on the table, for me to wait downstairs until she came down. She did not know what time she would be back from the party, but for me to wait in there until she arrived. That under the pillow of her mother's bed would be a bottle of whiskey, a pair of pliers and the sash weight. The pliers were for me to cut the telephone wires. If anything happened to prevent my coming, she was to be notified."

Gray said he left Syracuse on Saturday afternoon, and arrived in New York, at Grand Central Station, at twenty minutes after ten that night.

12

Murder Night: "Help Me, Momie!"

"I came out of the Grand Central after buying a ticket to Syracuse and a chair as far as Albany. Came out on Forty-second Street and walked down to where the buses are supposed to come up to go over the viaduct around the Forty-second Street station, as Mrs. Snyder had told me to get a bus there.

"It started to rain," Gray continued, head down and jaw set, as though remembering the chilling storm. "I did not see any bus come along, so I walked on down to Thirty-third Street, walked over to Thirty-third Street where the buses start. I do not recall what time it was when I got there. I had a considerable wait. I landed in Queens Village shortly after midnight, I believe. I walked up to that main street, whatever it is, and some street this side—I don't know which—some street this side of the street that Mrs. Snyder lives on I walked down. I stopped and finished the balance of a half-pint bottle that I had brought with me, as it was a dark street, and I came to the end of that street and walked over towards the street that she lives upon. I don't remember whether I had to make another turn or not, but ultimately I finally reached her corner.

"I went in the side door, as I was instructed to do, and I could not recall at that time whether cigarettes on the table meant for me to go upstairs. So I stayed down in the kitchen for, I guess, ten or fifteen minutes listening for sounds and I did not hear any, so I took the cigarettes off the table and went up to her mother's room, as instructed. I took off my hat and coat and put them in the closet."

"In the closet of her mother's bedroom?" asked Millard.

"Yes, sir." Gray took a drink of water.

"Proceed."

"I kept on my buckskin gloves. I went over to the pillow and found the sash weight, the pliers, which were long nosed and nickel plated, and a bottle, I would say probably a four-ounce bottle. I drank the contents of this bottle and sat down in the chair, got terrifically hot. I could feel my head spin from this small bottle, and I sat on the floor. I sat on the floor I do not know how long, but I found a quart bottle alongside of the chiffonier, between the bed and the chiffonier. I do not know how long that I sat there on the floor. I know I took three or four drinks.

"I took this stuff out. There were two pieces of wire, a pair of rubber gloves, there was a handkerchief, a bottle of chloroform, and some cotton waste that I had picked up in Rochester. I think that is all. I do not know how long, as I say, I sat there on the floor, but I finally did get up into the chair. I took off my other coat and laid that on the bed. I can't tell you what time this is either, as it was dark in the mother's room, but I started for downstairs. I got as far as almost the ground floor on the stairs when I heard an automobile coming along and saw the lights pulling up outside of the front door. I ran back up-stairs. I stayed there for quite some time. I had probably five or six more drinks, to steady my nerves. I sat in the chair for some time. I didn't go out of the room until just prior to the arrival of Mr. Snyder, when I started downstairs again, thinking that I would leave the house.

"I was just coming down the stairs when their car drove up, and I heard them coming up the front steps. I hastily turned around and ran upstairs as quickly as I could and went back to the mother's room and sat there on the floor.

"A very short time thereafter Mrs. Snyder and her daughter I could hear coming up the stairs. I recall trying to see the time on my watch, but I could not see it. The daughter went into her room. I could not see this, but I heard it. Mrs. Snyder came along the hall, came into the room and said, 'Are you there, dear?' I said that I was. She said, 'Wait quietly, and I will be back shortly.' She left the room and went into her room. I saw her go by the door, as the light in the hall was on. She had taken off her dress and was in her slip. She went back to her child's room, and I could hear the conversation, although I did not know what they said. I think I took six or seven more drinks while I waited there. She finally came back into the room and kissed me.

"She then went into her room and was in her room when I heard her husband coming up the stairs. I could not see him, as I was down on the floor, but he went into her room and was in there for a short time when he came back to the bathroom. She wanted to know if I found the sash weight and the pliers and the whiskey. I said that I had. She said, 'You have been drinking quite a bit, haven't you?' I said, 'Plenty.' She said, 'Keep quiet and I will be back as soon as I can.' She went out and I am quite positive she went back into the bathroom. Her husband had returned to his room. She stopped at the door and whispered to me—I do not know what she said—and went right into her room. At that time she had a nightgown and a bathrobe on. I sat on the floor, the same as I had been. I took a couple of more drinks. I could not tell you how long it was. It seemed a very short time before she came back into the room again and asked me what time I had gotten there.

"I told her about midnight. I asked her to get out, go back into her room, that her husband could not be asleep. She said that he was dozing off. I can't give you the time. I don't know. I am giving it to you as best I can, as I recall. She said to me, 'Isn't it funny, somebody down at the party said tonight that if the old crab don't treat me better he was going to kill him.' She said, 'You are going through with it tonight, are you not?' I said, 'I don't know whether I can or not. I will try.' As I recall, she asked me how long we ought to wait. I think that it was then some time after—whether it was twenty minutes past two or half-past two I don't recall. She asked me how long I thought we ought to wait, and I told her I didn't know. Well, anyway, we waited there in the room. I asked her if her husband was intoxicated. She said no. I asked her if she had been drinking, and she said, 'Not a thing.' I asked her if she would have a drink, and she said no."

Gray paused and sipped from his glass of water. He continued talking with his eyes closed.

"She asked me if I found the quart bottle. I said that I had. We talked there about the length of time she thought and I thought that we ought to wait, and I think it was after three, after she had gone out of the room a couple of times to look at him and came back and said that she thought that now is the time. So I gave her my gloves, and I put on the rubber gloves. I took the sash weight, and I gave her the chloroform. I gave her the piece of wire. She carried the handkerchief with the cotton waste. The bottle of chloroform was wrapped in an Italian newspaper.

"I had my glasses off. She took me by the hand. We went out into the hall. The door of her husband's room was practically closed except on a crack. She opened the door. She entered the room, and I followed her. I don't know how many seconds I stood there trying to get my bearings, and I struck him on the head, nearly as I could see, one blow. I think I hit him another blow, because with the first blow he raised up in bed and started to holler. I went over to the bed on top of him and tried to get the bedclothes over his mouth, so as to suppress his cries."

Gray opened his eyes, grasped his water, and emptied half of it in a gulp. Ruth Snyder stared at him with narrow eyes, her lips curled in disgust.

"He was apparently full of fight. He got me by the necktie, and a struggle ensued, in which I was getting the worse, because I was being choked. I hollered, 'Momie, Momie, for God sake, help me!' I had dropped the weight. She came over, she took the weight and she hit him on the head and throwing the bottle of chloroform, the handkerchief, wire and everything onto the pillow. . . ."

Gray reached for another glass of water.

"I finally got him between my knees in some manner and had him by the throat with my left hand, I believe. My right hand was over his mouth with the covers. I did not miss her at that time. The next thing I knew his hands were tied with a towel, which she had gotten from the bathroom. I called to her to close the window on account of the outcry. The covers were pulled up over his head. If there was waste packed in his nose and mouth, I do not know, because nobody pushed them in there as far as I know. Mrs. Snyder threw the bottle, the handkerchief, she said, wire and everything, right into the pillow. The covers were heaped over his head. The next thing I remember was being upright on the floor again. I asked her for the piece of wire to tie his hands with. She said she had thrown it into the pillow with the chloroform and the handkerchief and the waste.

"I asked her what—I asked her to give me a necktie off the rack, to tie his feet with. I had a piece of wire which I tied around his hands."

Gray gulped water again. He passed his fingers over his eyes, and behind his glasses, tears glistened.

"The next thing I remember was we walked back to the bathroom. We went into the bathroom, and I washed off the blood off my hands. She took off the buckskin gloves that she had on and handed them to me. It was there that she discovered blood on my shirt and on my vest. She said, 'My God, look at me!' There was blood all over the front of her nightgown and all over the front of her bathrobe. And we walked back to her mother's room. She said, 'What will we do?' I said, 'I don't know.' She said, 'Well, blood on the front of me will be all right, because I am sick.'' I said, 'My God, not that kind of blood!'

"She said, 'Take off your shirt,' and I guess I did. I don't remember taking it off. I took the studs—or she took them out, and I waited in her mother's room, and she went out. She came back into the room with a blue shirt, which was new, and told me to put it on. She must have gone downstairs at that time.

"The first thing I remember was that she came back into the room, and I asked her to get a pair of scissors and cut the buttonhole on the shirt so as it would be smaller. This she did.

"We then went downstairs. We sat there I don't know how long. We were sitting there though—the only relative thing that I can give you as to time was when the milkman went by.

"We went back upstairs after talking about mussing up the house to make it appear like a robbery, and we did go into her mother's room. I took three or four more drinks, and we went into her front room. She asked me if he was dead. I said I did not think so. She said, 'He has got to be dead. This has got to go through or I am ruined.' I said, 'I am through with you and everything,' and I started to muss up the room. She asked me to tie some wire around his neck. I tried to and I could not. I took the wire off his hands. I tried to put it around his neck, but I could not. I went out of the room and went back in the mother's room and I finished the bottle of whiskey, and I came back into the room again, and whether there was wire around his neck or not I do not know.

"I went over to the chiffonier, started to throw things about. She came—she was in the room at the time. I told her that she had better go downstairs—no—I asked her where his pistol was, and she got it for me out of his clothespress, and she handed it to me. I took the pistol and broke it, and I think I touched his hand with the pistol and threw it on the bed. I then continued to muss up the room, and she went downstairs. I told her to muss up the room downstairs—the rooms downstairs. I know I threw everything about in her room and in her mother's room. She told me not to touch her little girl's room. So I didn't. The next thing I knew she came back upstairs, and I asked her if she had mussed up things downstairs, and she said that she had.

"She asked me if her husband was dead, and I told her I thought so, that he was cold. She went over to her bureau, and where she got them from I do not know—or out of a bag or someplace—a lot of powders, a box of what she said was bichloride of mercury tablets in a Midol box. She told me at the time that she had a capsule that had enough poison in it to kill twelve people that she was going to keep.

"We left and went downstairs. Going into her mother's room, I got my hat and coat. I think she preceded me downstairs. I guess I went into her mother's room and got my hat and coat, and she had gone downstairs, because she was downstairs when I arrived.

"I went through the dining room and through the living room, and I know I did a lot of senseless things, such as throwing cushions off, because I was intoxicated. The detectives—well, that doesn't make any difference. I went back to the kitchen and I went to the cellaret, as I was in the dining room, took out another bottle and took some drinks. I scattered things all about and came back to the living room. I do not recall whether she took the wallet out of her husband's overcoat or whether I took it out. I did ask her—she handed it to me, telling me to take the money. I asked her if she knew how much there was there. She said that she had not counted it. I asked her if she had not better keep it. She said no, for me to take it. She thought there was around seventy-odd dollars. She asked me if I would take her jewelry. I said no. She asked me how she could explain it. I said, 'Hide it somewhere, and they will not know anything about it.' It was fast getting daylight. She told

me I would have to get out, and I told her to go
upstairs—"

Judge Scudder: "You told us that, a moment ago
you said it was getting daylight."

"Well, I would like to go back, Your Honor, if possible, because we went down the cellar."

"Very good. Do not repeat, that is all."

"I see."

"Proceed."

"I asked her what she had done with my shirt, and
she told me she had taken it down to the cellar and
burned it, together with her bathrobe and nightgown. And we went downstairs and into the cellar,
and I could smell the burning cloth.

"I still had my clothes on, and I reached over into
the coal bin and picked up a lump of coal at a time
and threw it into the furnace. I asked her what she
had done with the window weight, and she told me
that she had hidden it in a box.

"She took me over and showed me where the box
was, and the window weight had been stripped of its
paper and was bare. I went back to the ashes and
took some ashes and sprinkled them on the weight.
She asked me what I did that for. I said, if I recollect,
to make it look as though it had laid there for a long
time. We went back upstairs together, and she turned
on the thermostat. It was then that we sat down and
were talking, when it was getting daylight, Your
Honor.

"I went upstairs with her. She asked me if I would
hit her on the head to make it look as though she
had been struck, too. I told her I could not. She
asked me to tie her up. She laid on her mother's
bed, and I tied up her feet with rope that she had
brought up from the cellar on her first visitation
when she burned the clothes. She told me at that

time when she had gone down to the cellar with my shirt and her bathrobe and nightgown, when she appeared to me again in a fresh nightgown, that she had taken the pillow case off her pillow. I asked her why, and she said that there was blood on it. I asked her what she had done with it and she said she had thrown it among some dirty clothes. I tied her feet and I tied her hands. I told her that it may be two months"—his voice rising—"it may be a year, and it may be never, before she would see me again. And I left her laying on her mother's bed and I went out."

That concluded Judd Gray's testimony for Wednesday, May 4.

His shoulders trembling, he lowered himself from the witness stand. When he reached his seat at the defendants' table, he began to sob convulsively, making a sound like that of a dog lapping cream. Behind him, his mother rocked backward and forward, her face covered with her hands. Sounds of sniffling and sobbing could be heard from all portions of the courtroom, except where Ruth Snyder sat, dry-eyed, staring unflinchingly at Judd Gray. Never, not even on the day that Judd Gray's confession was read to the courtroom, did she radiate so electric a fury.

13

Saint Judd

When Judd Gray was cross-examined over May 5 and 6, his story remained unshaken. Ruth Snyder's attorneys tried to make him admit that he, and not Mrs. Snyder, was the leader of the murder plot, but Gray only repeated and confirmed what he said before.

As for the D.A., he scarcely cross-examined Gray at all. Why would he need to, since Gray had already shouted his own guilt and condemnations in the crowded courtroom, and likewise the guilt of his lover, Ruth Snyder? There was nothing more to say.

Yet on Monday, May 9, the day scheduled for the defense attorneys' closing arguments, everyone was excited and electrified with anticipation. All that day the area outside the Queens County Courthouse was thronged by hundreds upon hundreds of women who were prepared to do anything to gain entrance into the already packed courtroom. All day their high-pitched voices hurled imprecations on the blond housewife famous for putting up preserves in her cellar; all day reiterations of her evil and Judd

Gray's helplessness rose from the street in a motley billow of sound.

Their excitement did not come from the question of guilt or innocence—that mystery had been solved long ago—but from the opportunity to rehearse, through Ruth Snyder and Judd Gray, their most somber sense of feminine power, to lay open to view their recognition of women's erotic ascendancy, their belief that a woman, once sexually aroused, is capable of overwhelming any man who stands in her way. After all, Judd Gray, that gentleman of impeccable conduct, had no rational motive for murdering Albert Snyder. Why, he would not have known Albert Snyder if he passed him in the street. What he did, it was now clear, was the consequence of some sort of spell; he was a prisoner in the land of the Erinyes, the Loreleis, and Sirens.

Anyway, that was what his attorney, William J. Millard, was going to try to argue in his closing speech. He stepped forward, positioned the tips of his fingers together, then looked to the corner of the defendants' table where Judd Gray sat. In that moment, Gray was the object of the saddest and most tragic look that had ever been directed at him. Millard offered Gray the faintest of smiles, his mouth twisted into an expression of tender melancholy that seemed to include everyone in the courtroom. Then, shifting his vision to the jury box, he spoke slowly and sadly, "May it please the Court and gentlemen of the jury in the dark shadows of this frightful crime, this frightful tragedy, I come to you to speak for my friend, Judd Gray. Fully realizing my responsibility, I am going to speak to you gentlemen as I would speak to members of my own family circle, solemnly and sincerely, from the depths of my soul."

Light was slanting from the windows, settling on

Millard's face, so that the illumination seemed to emanate from within him. "I am going to plead as I have never pleaded before, just as though Judd Gray were my own boy, for I believe in him. Judd Gray was born in Cortland, New York, in 1892. Shortly thereafter his parents moved to New Jersey, where he has since resided. His childhood was spent in a wonderful home; a lovely mother watched over and reared him with jealous care.

"And her care and devotion were reflected in her boy. She gave him the best religious and moral training. He was a member of the church, a member of the Sunday school, and he lived in the sunshine and happiness of a beautiful home, with a splendid environment and atmosphere surrounding his every move.

"And, gentlemen, he had a very, very fair education. He graduated from grammar school. He spent two years in high school, splendidly educated, and he was a great success in his business fields of activity, with a real bright future stretching before him. And then, in tender years, he met the young girl, the noble woman who afterwards became his faithful wife. And they lived happily together, very happily together, and a little child was born, a girl, who is now ten years of age. That was the happy life and childhood of Judd Gray from his cradle up to the year 1925.

"Not a blemish, not a move outside the normal paths of life. A wonderful boy, wonderful, not a mark, not a scratch, not a stain, not a blot, a splendid, ideal character." Millard spoke in a voice as soft and wheedling as a "nursemaid who hopes to soothe twelve unruly charges into docility—and eventually to sleep," observed a writer for the *Post*.

"Then from that very wholesome, homelike atmosphere, where the fires of the home hearth were burning continually with love and devotion, suddenly in the month of June 1925, a sinister, fascinating woman came across his path. Oh, gentlemen, what a catastrophe! Through the eye of the inscrutable mystery of human life we mortal minds cannot see the great purpose of it all, but to us it seems cruelly pathetic that those two human beings should ever have met. I would not, gentlemen, place one additional burden upon the stricken soul of a woman if I could not help it. I could not find it in my heart to do it, but the truth, the truth, gentlemen, you must have the truth. There is no other way out.

"That woman, that peculiar creature, like a poisonous snake, like a poisonous serpent, drew Judd Gray into her glistening coils, and there was no escape. That woman. Why, gentlemen, it was a peculiar, alluring seduction. I want to say here that this woman was abnormal. Just as a piece of steel jumps and clings to the powerful magnet, so Judd Gray came within the powerful compelling force of that woman, and she held him fast. She knew her man and she held him fast. I must speak plainly, gentlemen. This woman, this peculiar venomous species of humanity, was abnormal; possessed of an all-consuming, all-absorbing sexual passion, animal lust, which seemingly was never satisfied."

Why all this folderol about a "poisonous serpent"? Why wail about Ruth Snyder's "all-consuming, all-absorbing sexual passion"? Because Millard, with his apologetic manner and Shakespearean brow, knew his jurors. Because his words were an "open sesame" to one of the culture's most familiar, yet fear-inspiring, fantasies—the myth of the ruthless, amoral, stop-at-nothing woman who first saps man's vitality, then lures him out of Eden by playing the double role of Eve and snake.

"It is not for me to judge, gentlemen, how far that burning self, that flaming physical self, that volcano within, warped, distorted and changed her moral self. It is not for me to judge. I leave that to a Higher Power, but at any rate, this is the unfortunate and pathetic part of it all.

"Through excessive indulgence, that burning desire to satisfy that fire within and to satisfy it with this poor victim, Judd Gray, she sapped his strength, sapped his vitality. It was a flame that was not only consuming her, but was venting its explosive wrath upon this victim. And, gentlemen, the inevitable result followed. You are human. You have seen something of human life. You know the inevitable result."

Millard's language was stagy, operatic, artificial, even quaint, but he was making the audience feel his thought. Putting face after face on their fears, refusing to say once what he could not say twice, repeating his qualifying phrases as if they were Homeric epithets, he had the all-male jury nodding their heads. Two or three were so overcome that their tongues hung out in awe.

"With a cold, calculating, remorseless, conscienceless, inhuman planning of a human fiend, she trained Judd Gray, and with relentless determination, she kept her victim until she had him just as though one were under a hypnotic spell, just exactly. When you get into that false world, when you get into that false atmosphere, when you are living like that and under strong stimulants, and your vitality, your whole constitutional makeup is changed and warped, you look at things in a distorted way. Why, in our minds today, all things are not what they seem. Even as we rise this morning, or other mornings, we see the sun rising, and we see the setting at night, when we know in reality that the sun does not rise and set. It is only the world revolving on its axis every twenty-four hours that makes it seem that way. It makes it seem as though the sun were rising and setting. Just exactly so with Ruth Snyder. She had gotten his mental constitution so sapped, she had gotten that false atmosphere absolutely surrounding and entrapping him to the extent that the fact that she said, 'I want it so,' was enough for Judd Gray. He never stopped to think, to realize, to consider. He simply did it because Ruth Snyder wanted him to do it. That is all, and that is just as true as I live and breathe."

At this point, Millard's speech was interrupted by a smattering of applause. It was so brief and inconsequential, seeming to issue from only one or two spectators, that Judge Scudder did not think it necessary to issue any warnings, and only looked disapprovingly in the direction of the offenders. But Millard was encouraged, and spoke with renewed vigor and firmness.

"Now after that condition had gone on for a year, nearly a year and a half, gentlemen, when she had actually overcome any semblance of resistance or independent action on the part of Judd Gray, when she knew he was ripe for the act, when she knew that she had trained her mannequin so that he would go through with it, knowing that she had been unsuccessful herself in her own attempts, she finally suggested at the Waldorf-Astoria in the latter part of February that she must get rid of her husband. Well, that was the tragic part. He tried even then to rebel in his feeble way. He tried even then at the last minute to rebel. He felt, 'Well, I will try to get something that you want, but I know in my own soul I will never go through with it. I will try to do what she says. I will follow her to a certain extent.' And then they met over at the house, a meeting very shrewdly planned one morning the latter part of February or the first part of March in the Snyder home while Albert Snyder was away. Remember it. Think of it, gentlemen. Picture it. Right in that environment where the scene was to take place, she brought him."

After touching on how Ruth Snyder told Judd Gray her husband must be killed and that Gray must help her, Millard described in elaborate detail how Gray was ready to do anything Ruth Snyder asked—automatically, as if he were in a trance, "just as though a child of five years old were acting under the powerful, dominating influence of a mastermind."

"Think of it," Millard continued, "everything that Ruth Snyder suggested was reflected into action by Judd Gray. Everything. She spoke of a colored man entering the house, that that would be a good alibi. With that thought in his mind, just seeing an Italian newspaper brought it up, and he says, 'An Italian would be just as good as a colored man.' Just as good as a colored man.

"And he picks up the Italian newspaper, a very natural thing to do, just what a child would do if he had the same suggestion and thought."

Millard's assertion, strictly speaking, made no sense. It was quixotic. It was desperate. But Millard was not asking for a constitutive principle here. He was not asking jurors to think finely, but simply to think, to imagine. To imagine what was going on in Judd Gray's brain when he picked up the Italian newspaper, and to imagine how he must have responded when Ruth Snyder told him on March 7 to come to her house to help her get rid of her husband.

"And this poor blind fool, this poor dupe, this poor, broken dupe, walked around in Queens, around near the house, for two hours. She said that she would leave a signal light in the window, and he looked and looked and looked for that light, following Ruth Snyder; he couldn't even follow Gray—I mean Albert Snyder—because he didn't know him. He wasn't looking for Albert Snyder any more than he was looking for you, gentlemen of the jury. He was looking for a light, because Ruth Snyder said she would leave a light in the window. Finally, he did see a light, and finally Ruth Snyder beckoned to him through the window, rapped on the window, and up comes the poor fool, up to the house, obeying the command, obeying everything that Ruth Snyder said, and she meets him at the door, she brings him in. What is the first thing that she did that night when she brought him into the kitchen? Gave him a great big drink of whiskey. Her first act. A bottle all ready for him. Did she know her man?"

Everyone had already heard of Judd Gray's sophisticated alibi, said Millard. But think a moment, said he. How sophisticated was it, really? "Why, the little child, the little child in school will throw a putty ball at the teacher and look down at his book in perfect innocence. There is your alibi. Even animals show the power to construct an alibi. It is intuitive, it is instinctive, it is a perfectly natural mechanical thing to do. An animal will cross and recross a stream to throw off the scent. I have seen it done.

"Alibi! Well, of all alibis! Not attempting to appear anywhere so that he could account for his time, but actually conferring with another human being, telling him to put a sign on the door and to muss up his room, is that the way a criminal prepares an alibi?

"You have never heard of it in your life. He comes down on the train. He comes to Queens Village. The back door was left open by Ruth Snyder. A pack of cigarettes was on the kitchen table, as a sign to Judd Gray that all was well. He entered that back door. He saw the cigarettes on the table, and he had forgotten whether the cigarettes were to mean that Albert Snyder was home or not home, or whether anything was wrong or everything was right. So he waited for a few seconds. He had forgotten just what that signal meant. And this woman, that night, went out to a party with Albert Snyder and her little daughter, Lorraine, among friends, to show to them and to show the world that they were all together that night, happily enjoying themselves, all the while knowing, all the time planning, all the time scheming to kill that husband when he returned home with her. Isn't that the diabolical mind of a fiend?"

When Millard uttered these words, he stared at Ruth Snyder. His lips became thin and rigid, and his gray eyes bulged. "That is hardly a human mind," he resumed, turning back to the jurors.

"Now, gentlemen, now we are coming to the real scene behind the curtains. Judd Gray got there about twelve o'clock that night. He went up to the bedroom, the mother's bedroom. Mind you, her own mother's bedroom. Include that in your consideration, in your deliberation; and there under the pillow in the mother's bedroom was the sash weight, and what? A four-ounce bottle of liquid. I want you to remember that little bottle, a four-ounce bottle of liquid under the pillow with the instruments of death. Outside, not underneath the pillow, but near the dresser, was a quart bottle of whiskey. If that was whiskey in that quart bottle, what on earth was the reason for the little bottle of four ounces, when there was a quart bottle of whiskey on the dresser? You are going to think of that when you get into your jury room, and I am going to tell you why it was there.

Ruth Snyder thought that when Judd Gray went into her mother's room he would take that quart bottle of whiskey, as was his custom, and he would drink and drink and drink, and by the time she returned with Albert Snyder and Lorraine, Judd Gray would be pretty well drunk. She left it handy for him. He could not miss it. But not the little bottle. She thought that when she came home and was ready for this deed, this tragedy, that then they would go to the pillow and that he would be in such a drunken condition that he would take that little bottle without any trouble. But instead of that, gentlemen, he reached under the pillow and intuitively, a natural thing, and he finds the little bottle. He never hesitated a moment. Just imagine yourselves, gentlemen, any one of you, taking a little bottle under these circumstances and drinking its contents without a moment's hesitation. If that does not disclose the mental attitude of Judd Gray as the abject slave of this domineering power, what in the name of God's world does?

"Then he drinks, and he drinks, and he drinks, and finally, after that experience of becoming dizzy, of groping around the floor, then of drinking whiskey, a flash, a flash comes across his mind of his awful predicament.

"A flash, and he starts to leave the place. He has gotten that, we will say, just a sudden glimpse of the awful tragedy into which he is plunged. He starts down the stairs, and he gets about three quarters down when he hears an automobile horn, and just a couple of seconds later he hears steps on the front porch. He is trapped. The poor boy never even had a chance."

Sweat streamed down Millard's forehead, hung down from his eyebrows, and fell sometimes, spotting the notes in his hand. With his handkerchief, he patted the beads tenderly, as though they were somehow emblematic of Judd Gray's suffering.

In a few seconds, Millard continued, Ruth Snyder and her family would come in, and she would tell Gray that the critical moment had arrived. She would then give him the sash weight, lead him by the hand, position him beside her sleeping husband, and order him to strike. But Judd, who was now thoroughly befuddled with whiskey as well as blind—he was not wearing his glasses—was not able to direct his blows well enough to actually hit the sleeping man. All he managed to do was awaken Albert Snyder, who, before Gray knew what was going on, "was fighting and grappling and calling out and grabbed his necktie and nearly choked him. And then hear the significant words, as though Providence wanted you to hear every syllable: 'Momie, for God's sake, help.'

"Momie," Millard repeated Gray's pet name for Ruth Snyder in disbelief. Then sucking in a breath and lifting his eyes heavenward, asserted with a sarcastic chuckle, "Albert Snyder was getting the best of this poor victim." How stupid, how incompetent can anybody be? said Millard, shaking his head. Ruth Snyder had to rescue Judd Gray by leaping on top of her husband and battering him till he was unconscious. Then she threw the chloroform onto his pillow and finished him off by choking him with picture wire.

"Judd Gray was so totally ignorant of the wire around the throat that he didn't even see it there. But, gentlemen, when that wire was found tight around the throat of Albert Snyder, see what was found with it [indicating the pencil on the display table]. That wire was tightened with a gold pencil belonging to Judd Gray. And Judd Gray had not been near the scene when the wire was tightened around Albert Snyder's throat.

"Why was the pencil of Judd Gray left in the wire on the throat of Albert Snyder? Why? What good was the alibi of burglary so far as Judd Gray went, with that pencil around Albert Snyder's throat?"

Millard approached the jury box, lowered his hand to the rail, then lowered his voice to a confidential whisper. "Do you suppose that she was afraid—that she was going to take the chance of leaving a surviving witness on her crime to travel around the country?"

Resuming his normal tone: "That mind did not work that way. Not a chance in the world, not a chance. She thought that Judd Gray, the poor fool, after he drank the quart bottle of whiskey, just before the time for the perpetration of this crime, would drink from that little bottle, and that by the time the blows were delivered, the contents of that bottle would begin to do its deadly work, and she had planned to put that pencil in the wire around the neck of Albert Snyder to point to Judd Gray. And she thought that after her husband had been killed, that that poison would do its work, and that Judd Gray would also pass away, and there would be no slip, nothing wrong in that plan. She would have an absolute alibi. There would be no suspicion. He would be there, his pencil used in tightening, the sash weight there, Judd Gray there with a bottle, an empty bottle of poison near his side."

Here, Millard reminded the jurors that Ruth Snyder had given Judd Gray some mercury tablets in a Midol bottle. "Remember it? And some other poisons to take away from the house with him. And at the same time, she told him that she had a capsule of poison that would kill twelve men. Do you remember that? Why did she keep back that one tablet?

"She gave him the poison to take out of the house, but she kept that capsule. This poor, groping, blundering fool left the Snyder home. I say blundering fool and victim, for there is the living victim of this tragedy. Just then what does he do? A shrewd, calculating criminal with criminal intent? It is not in his makeup. He has not got a criminal hair in his head, and you know it. There is not a blot on his whole character, not a stain throughout his life from the cradle to the present moment. Judd Gray was all right.

"He is coming from the Snyder home, and he takes off his glasses before he leaves the house. My what a diabolical disguise that is. He took off his glasses. Isn't that terrible to think of, taking off his glasses? What a shrewd, what a wonderfully complex plan it is, taking off his glasses. And then he goes within a couple of blocks and talks to a stranger, right near the scene of the crime, with a policeman in uniform within four feet. Think of it. Is there any crime in that man's makeup? You cannot find a trace. Think of it, gentlemen, right near the scene of the crime, stands talking and waiting for a bus, without the faintest effort of disguise, his face clearly in view, with a policeman in uniform standing right by him. And then he goes to the Grand Central Station, and instead of going through the gates with the crowd, unnoticed—and he would have been unnoticed—and going into a day coach, what does he do? That wonderful criminal, that shrewd mastermind goes up to the Pullman ticket office to get a Pullman ticket. Did you ever hear of a criminal doing that in all the history of crime? Never once. Not even in fiction. He goes to the Pullman ticket window and buys a Pullman ticket for Albany, because they could not sell him one for Syracuse. Knowing that he would have to get out of the Pullman car at Albany and have his ticket taken up and be recognized by the Pullman conductor. He knew that when he bought the ticket. And he does everything in God's world to make himself conspicuous. You cannot get around it. You cannot evade it. That is absolutely the Simon-clear fact. And then he goes to Syracuse, he takes that little Pullman ticket and instead of tearing it into minute pieces and throwing it into the toilet, what does he do with it, this arch-conspirator, this distinguished criminal? He throws it into the wastepaper basket."

Yes. If you believed Millard, Judd Gray was more a victim of this murder than Albert Snyder. "Simply the blind following of a controlled, operated, human mannequin. Simply because Ruth Snyder wished it, wanted it, blindly, groping, following her."

What better example of Ruth Snyder's total dominion over Judd Gray, said Millard, than the incident in which she made him sample two sleeping powders in their room in the Waldorf-Astoria. "Without a protest, without a single moment's or second's hesitation, he took those two powders, not knowing what they contained. Just imagine any one of you taking two powders, unknown powders, at the request of a woman who time and time again had expressed a desire to kill her husband. Imagine any one of you men taking those two powders without knowing a thing about it, not knowing but what you were going to your death. If that's not absolute mental domination, what on earth in English phraseology is meant by the expression? That is absolute domination."

Millard's concluding words were said with so much sincerity that many felt that there must be something to his argument, that he must have a valid point. Millard genuinely believed in Judd Gray's innocence.

"Well, gentlemen, let those who cannot comprehend, who cannot understand the pitfalls and snares of human life, who from their self-erected pedestals of pious intolerance and scorn, cast the stones of contempt and hatred at the poor victim of tragic misfortune. Let them cast the stones, but you and I, my brothers, will go down into the mire and morass to rescue a human soul who has fallen the prey of a cruel, calculating, cunning serpent of a human being, who by her flame, passion, has become a demon in disguise. We will rescue that poor human being."

Sweat braided on his eyelids like tears. It was as though Millard's whole body was a melting, throbbing, curdling emanation of feeling for that pathetic human being, Judd Gray. "Gentlemen, I have been a public prosecutor. I know what it is to prosecute offenders against the law of the land and, fully conscious of my responsibility, I solemnly and sincerely say to you members of this jury that the ends of justice would be fully met, the laws of the state would be fully vindicated, and you would never have the pangs of regret or the reproach of conscience if you found this poor victim, this poor human being, guilty of manslaughter. That is the extreme culpability of that defendant in this case. Absolutely as a man I tell you that I would to God that you could find it in your conscience, knowing all the facts, to set him free and tell him to go home to his mother, because he fell a victim and a prey to this atrocious woman."

Wiping his brow, Millard passed to his final peroration. "There is another soul, gentlemen, of greater knowledge, of greater love than you and I can ever possess. There is another soul who sees more clearly than you or I can ever see how utterly impossible it is to reconcile any part of this act with the previous life of Judd Gray from the time his mother held him in her arms and breathed her benediction of a noble spirit into his soul.

"Gentlemen, that sweet, loving mother will be watching and waiting for you. May God help you all and guide you to view clearly the whole scene, to deliberate conscientiously and to treat Judd Gray with a Godlike spirit. I beseech you"—his voice breaking—"with all the sincerity of my soul to deal with that poor victim tenderly, for he is not to blame."

14

Fair Ruth

The jury was given barely a few moments to recover from this portrait of Judd Gray as a befuddled saint before Dana Wallace, Ruth Snyder's other attorney, was shaking his finger at him, shrieking, "This miserable filth of the earth is allowed to sit here, and before he makes his squealing appeal of mercy to you—not a defense, an appeal to mercy, and it has wrung from the minute he took and defamed that woman to the last note of his counsel's voice died away, not once a defense—a plea for mercy. . . .

Wallace's strategy was based on the theme of chivalry. Wallace, as he saw himself, was a knight pledged to free a golden-haired damsel disguised as a fleshy, steely-eyed housewife. She was being held captive on a false murder charge imposed by an evil genie who was himself wearing a disguise—that of a myopic corset salesman. Wallace's mission was to expose the corset salesman, to show the world that he was the one who committed the murder and was now trying to slither away by blaming the fair damsel. That being the case, Wallace argued, it behooved the jurors to act as honorable men. They must hold the evil genie accountable—fully accountable—and free the damsel.

His face red and lips twitching, the vein on his brow pulsing like dark lightning, he described Judd Gray as a "human anaconda," "diabolical fiend," and "mastermind of the century." The chords of his throat leaped like bow strings. "There is the most despicable man that has ever walked God's footstool as far as I have known men and as far as the pages of history recall."

Wallace reserved his most torrential burst of scorn for Judd Gray's attorney. "I think I have heard romances," shouted Wallace, "I think I have heard filth, but I think the most nonsensical attempt to throw the smoke screen before the jury and then wind up with a plea of clemency has reached its height when you are told that Judd Gray did not strike blows. He said he did. They say he did not. So his counsel wants you to believe that everything he did up to the minute where he would be personally involved, he did, and when he told you his story, it is all true, but, oh, when 'I crashed his head in,' oh, no, he could not have done that, he was drunk, he could not have hit him with the arc light on his face. Oh, no."

Abruptly shifting to a tone of benediction: "Well, thank God for the rights of Mrs. Snyder in this courtroom, in her day in court, when she asks you only justice, not pity."

Then back to scorn: "Thank God you cannot substitute for the sworn testimony of Gray the weird dream of my friend, the romancer. You cannot do it. They won't let you decide cases along that line. You may take theory and inference and apply them if it may enlighten you, but you cannot go so far as to substitute theory for the actual facts. And when that man attempts to say that he recalls everything up to the striking of that blow and, afterwards, then forgets everything that followed it, let me inform you that he has gone far afield in his attempts to fool jurors."

So Wallace battled, by bullying, bluster, name-calling, simplifications, omissions, the adoption of moral outrage, to free his Dulcinea. But the harder he fought, the angrier and more dissatisfied his audience became. His key oratorical deficiency was repetition. He not only repeated what his colleague, Hazelton, had said in his opening statement, his speech was argument for argument almost the same as Millard's closing statement for Judd Gray—only done in reverse. Where Millard cast Ruth Snyder as the seducer and Gray as the virtuous but weak man captured in a Laocoön embrace, Wallace had Judd Gray in the seducer role, and Ruth Snyder as the saintly but pathetic victim.

Poor Ruth, lovely Ruth, mother of sorrows, mother of us all—Wallace described her as nurturant, calm, a giver of life. "Do you mean to tell me," he ranted, "that a woman who in the throes of agony of child-bearing, who gave this beautiful baby to the world and to Snyder after a severe operation—which might have wrecked her health forever—do you mean to say that there lives that woman on earth that would have brought that baby to perhaps see the spectacle of the mother sending that baby's father to eternity? That woman doesn't live, and not one of you twelve men believe she does."

Ridiculing the possibility of Ruth Snyder dominating Gray, Wallace reminded the jurors that Gray was the one with the independent income, not Mrs. Snyder. He had more education than she, more money, more experience in the world, a more luxurious home and more supportive family. Consider also what Judd Gray did for a living, said Wallace. "Here was a man of influence, whose business was influence. That was his business—to talk women into things. That is why he was sent out as a good salesman, to talk them into things. When he got talking to Mrs. Snyder, he was only putting into personal effect those things he did in his daily business. It was the influence of salesmanship."

Sweat flowing from his brow, slapping at the beads as savagely as though they were mosquitoes, Wallace described how Gray lured Ruth Snyder to his office after their second meeting to "put a corset on her" and "get the cold cream to fix up the sunburn on her bare shoulders." Pulling his coat from his right shoulder to better demonstrate how this Don Juan massaged Mrs. Snyder, Wallace proved once again that Ruth Snyder's attorneys had no idea when enough was enough. As before, when they passed into the comical, they were oblivious.

The laughter which accompanied this performance was not at all friendly. Ruth Snyder noticed it, as did Wallace, who glared at the crowd and shouted, "The titterings which bespeak the vacant mind of people should never be allowed to come to court to pass judgment on a defenseless woman."

As Wallace's summation wore on—he took two hours, thirty-two minutes longer than Millard—people were continually glancing at the clock in the back of the courtroom. A hostile, impatient murmur came from every corner of the room. By the time he concluded his speech, it seemed that everything that could possibly be said in Ruth Snyder's behalf had been said, and said, and said. The crowd had enough of talk, enough of oratorical excess. Now they wanted action.

When recess was called at one-thirty, the court-

room dissolved into pandemonium. Several spectators left their seats in front, inspiring many more to
push forward, some of them climbing over the backs
of chairs to gain the coveted seats that were tempo-
rarily vacated. They jostled and elbowed, looking
grim and determined, many of them hurling insults
and denunciations on the head of the housewife who,
they believed, would be found guilty of first-degree
murder before the day was over.

Terrified, rigid, Judd Gray kept his eyes averted
during the hubbub. Twice he sighed with the depth
of someone who had been weeping for hours, but no
tears escaped and he did not move. The only other
quiet person in the courtroom, it seemed, was Judd
Gray's mother, Mrs. Margaret Gray, who kept her eyes
hidden behind her book, *When Days Seem Dark*.

15

The Verdict

Mercifully, D.A. Newcombe's closing speech was short. Leaning forward, his tone of voice almost conversational, he argued that it made no difference which one of the two defendants first suggested the murder, or which one was the dominant personality, because the fact is, they were both involved. If Judd Gray hadn't intended to murder Albert Snyder, he would not have arranged his elaborate alibi, and if Ruth Snyder hadn't been as bent on murder as her lover, she would not have unlocked her doors and let him in. It was as simple as that. Although Judd Gray claimed he was intoxicated, an intoxicated man could not have arranged such an alibi and remembered every detail in the way Judd Gray did. "That man, gentlemen of the jury, was just as clearheaded and clear thinking as you are this minute."

Newcombe reminded the jurors that the story Ruth Snyder gave on the stand was preceded by two other, radically different, stories. Her first, in which she attributed the murder to two big Italians with mustaches, was given to the police when they arrived at her home at eight o'clock, the morning of the murder. She stuck with that story for sixteen hours, until she went to Police Commissioner McLaughlin and said she couldn't keep her lies up any longer. She then told McLaughlin that she and Judd Gray had planned the murder and did it themselves, and afterward mussed the house up to make it appear like a robbery.

Newcombe's voice thickened with contempt. "Did she tell him, gentlemen, one single word as to the defense she has now? Did she tell McLaughlin that Gray took the revolver and threatened to shoot her unless she permitted him to kill her husband? Did she tell McLaughlin that she got him downstairs and got the revolver away from him and then had to go up to the bathroom to attend to some personal needs, and then Gray came up the stairs while she was in the bathroom, and while she was in the bathroom, she heard this terrific thud, and went into her room, and there was Gray on the back of her husband, and she pulled Gray off, and Gray struck her, and she fainted? Did she tell that to McLaughlin, gentlemen? And if that had been the truth, if the story she tells on the stand now and wants you to believe had been the truth, would she not have told that story to McLaughlin? What possible reason in God's name could there be for her failure to tell him that? She was not protecting her lover; she was not protecting her past indiscretions, because she told those all to McLaughlin. Gentlemen of the jury, that story she told on the witness stand is a fabric of lies. It was never conceived and never thought of until the eve of this trial and for the benefit of this trial. When she made her statement in the district attorney's office to Daly, did she say one single word how Gray had taken a gun to her and threatened to shoot her if she interfered with his plan to kill her husband? How she took him downstairs and got the gun away from him, and then the rest of that rot, about how she was in the bathroom when Gray killed her husband? Not one single word of that did she tell to Mr. Daly and, gentlemen of the jury, if that had been the truth, why in all common sense would she not have told that story to Mr. Daly? And you men by reason of your experience as men know she would have told that to Daly, but she did not tell it to Daly, because that cock-and-bull story had not been conceived or concocted at that time."

Newcombe was nearing the end of his speech, but he wanted the jurors to have one last image of the criminals, at the very moment of their crime, to remember during their deliberations. He stood close to the jury box and spoke with more intensity than he had shown at any other time during the trial.

"She, gentlemen of the jury, was like a wild beast in the jungle, crouched there and watched [her husband] sleep, waiting for the opportunity to strike with Henry Judd Gray. And when he was fast asleep, she went in and got Henry Judd Gray, and together they came in and committed cold-blooded, atrocious murder, the most vicious murder that has ever happened in the annals of Queens or the State of New York. And, gentlemen of the jury, they talk to you of sympathy. After Albert Snyder had been struck on the head, he rose up and there he saw in the act of killing him his own wife and her lover, Gray. God, gentlemen, think of that man's thoughts with a realization that he was being murdered by his own wife and her lover."

Every eye in the courtroom was now on the white-faced Ruth Snyder, who was listening attentively, one finger archly poised against her cheek. She had been holding her breath for several moments, whether from fear, anticipation, or something else, it was impossible to say.

"Gentlemen," Newcombe concluded, returning to his normal tone of voice, "our whole nation, all of our American institutions are builded and founded upon the sanctity of the American home, and if in this case there should be a failure of adequate punishment, that foundation, that cornerstone of those American institutions will totter and fall. And as men of Queens, you owe the duty to your country and to your fellow citizens, as I owe that same duty, that nothing shall swerve us in the performance of this duty, and on behalf of the people of Queens County, on behalf of the people of the State of New York, whom I represent here and now, the State of New York asks you to bring in the verdict that is warranted by the evidence, and that is murder in the first degree as against both defendants."

Newcombe half bowed to the jury and then to the judge, who called a brief recess. When they resumed ten minutes later, Judge Scudder gave his instructions to the jury. He stood up as he addressed them, and the jurors, who were mopping their faces and shifting their feet, likewise remained standing.

Reading from notes, he went over the standard legal odds and ends—the presumption of innocence, reasonable doubt, and the difference between first- and second-degree murder, how the latter lacks premeditation, and how manslaughter is a killing without either premeditation or malice. His instructions to this point seemed quite impartial, favoring neither the defenses nor the prosecution, but as he got into the issues that were peculiar to this trial, it quickly became apparent that he did not think Ruth Snyder or Judd Gray had a leg to stand on.

Judge Scudder continued reading: "The defendant Gray seeks to add strength or weight to the presumption of innocence, to which I have made reference, by testimony concerning his own good character. . . . But good character is not a defense to crime. A defendant has no right to say, 'I participated in the commission of this crime. I was part of its commission, but at the same time my character was good and therefore I should not be held to blame for it.' That is not the law."

The judge similarly demolished Judd Gray's contention that he was too drunk to be held responsible for his actions. A drunken defendant, Judge Scudder said, must be treated no differently than a sober one.

As for Ruth Snyder's claim that she only cooperated in the crime due to compulsion, Judge Scudder advised that "the compulsion which would excuse a criminal act must be present, imminent, and impending, and of such a nature as to induce a well-grounded apprehension of death or serious bodily harm if the act is not done. A threat of future injury is not enough. One who acts in concert with another, or who aids and abets another in a homicide through compulsion, having a reasonable cause to believe that his or her life would be taken or serious bodily harm would result unless he or she gave the required aid, is not responsible for the homicide committed, but the person under whose control he or she acted. But if after the immediate danger has passed, he or she continues to aid, assist, abet, or advise in such acts, he or she is as guilty as if such danger had never threatened him or her. A mere threat to take one's life, unless he or she commits homicide, does not amount to a sufficient cause for committing such homicide."

The most controversial portion of Judge Scudder's charge to the jury had to do with Ruth Snyder's and

Judd Gray's confessions. Not a word was said about the conditions under which their confessions, or any confessions, should be thrown out or ignored. Judge Scudder spoke only of the confessions' soundness, conclusiveness, and validity.

"There has been something said to the effect that the defendants were not cautioned before they made their statements, were not permitted to have counsel, and were not permitted to have friends," Judge Scudder said in a soft, melodic tone. "But I charge you as a matter of law that these things do not invalidate any confession, for the law does not hold that a statement or a confession made by a defendant is bad or illegal merely because he was not permitted to consult with a lawyer or his family or friends. Something has already been said about the defendants not having been promptly arraigned before a magistrate. Without going into the evidence in that connection, I charge you that under the law a statement made by a defendant without first being arraigned before a magistrate does not in any way invalidate such a statement, nor does the failure of a district attorney, before making a confession, to warn the accused that his statements might be used against him, invalidate the statement."

The judge ended at 5:18 P.M. and the jury withdrew to deliberate, signaling a stampede to the exits. There was pushing, shoving, threats, even screaming. Dozens of spectators, most of whom had been standing all day in the insufferable heat, pleaded with the attendants to unlock the doors and let them out. When at last the doors were opened, the crowd staggered into the corridor in the hope of finding fresh air and water, but at 6:31 P.M., when the court attendants spread the word that the jury had reached a verdict, the rush to get back in was even more desperate and frenzied.

The jury returned at 6:56, followed two minutes later by Ruth Snyder, who walked erect, her chin tilted upward. Only a few feet behind, her short, bespectacled coconspirator followed, stooping slightly, his fists clenched.

At a sign from the judge, the clerk commanded, "Gentlemen of the jury, please rise. Look at the defendants."

The court clerk called the roll of the jurors and asked, "Gentlemen of the jury, have you reached a verdict?"

The foreman nodded and the clerk intoned, "Defendants, look upon the jurors. Jurors, look upon the defendants."

Ruth Snyder and Judd Gray faced the jury in a silence so awful it seemed as if the very room would burst with the tension of it. They squirmed and blinked, and dared not look at anyone.

"How do you find?" asked the clerk.

"The jury finds the defendants, Mrs. Ruth Snyder and Henry Judd Gray, guilty of murder in the first degree."

A gust of grief blew Ruth Snyder's legs from under her. With a whispered groan, she fell into her chair, threw herself forward and buried her face in her hands. Plunged into a nameless, listless, unfathomable desolation, Judd Gray's body sagged, but stayed upright. Then, from a pocket of his dark blue coat, he pulled a small volume, *The Child's Book of Prayer,* which he read, standing.

What happened after that was a bit hard to follow. People came from all directions, from every corner of the courtroom, pressing around in an excited circle, all trying to get a better look at Ruth and Judd, all talking at once, each with his own comments, everyone debating, explaining, giving an opinion. When the judge ordered the defendants to retire, it was physically impossible to comply with his order. The court attendants had to work for ten minutes before a channel could be cut through the 1,500 persons in the courtroom to enable the defendants to be escorted to their cells.

Then, about an hour later, when Ruth was safely inside the jail, she passed Father Patrick Murphy, the prison chaplain, in the corridor. She asked him if he could give her a few moments. Why, yes, of course. She told him that she wished to become a Catholic. Why, yes, of course, he could do that. And she was converted.

Was this remarkable conversion due to the fact that the governor of New York State at that time was Alfred E. Smith, who was himself a Catholic? Had Ruth Snyder read newspaper articles in which Smith was quoted as being reluctant to consent to electrocute a woman? Did she reason that Smith would be more likely to grant a reprieve to a murderess of his own faith?

The newspapers said yes.

If that was true, she could not have made a more grievous miscalculation. Although Smith had never before consented to the execution of a woman and was on record as saying, "Just what I have feared for eight years, a woman convicted of murder, and I'll have to decide whether she is to be electrocuted or not," his political ambitions extended beyond the governorship. Alfred E. Smith was preparing to run for the Presidency of the United States. Although he could have commuted her sentence if she had remained a Protestant, a Catholic governor could not commute the sentence of a woman who had publicly covered herself with rosaries. That would have been political suicide.

The sentencing day was Monday, May 13. Once again, Ruth Snyder and Judd Gray stood before Judge Scudder, but now that there was no longer any need for her to appear in mourning, she wore lipstick and rouge, and from under the narrow brim of her black hat curled the edges of her neatly marcelled blond hair.

"Has the defendant anything to say why sentence should not be imposed?" piped the clerk.

Hazelton requested that the verdict be set aside and a new trial granted on the grounds that his client was denied her right to a separate trial, especially so because the interests of the defendants, Ruth Snyder and Judd Gray, were completely hostile to each other, and because Ruth Snyder was required to be cross-examined by both the people's and Judd Gray's attorneys.

Judge Scudder overruled them and asked the defendants if they had any further statements to make. Ruth Snyder was about to reply, but Hazelton cut in quickly. "The defendant Snyder has nothing to say as to why judgment of this Court should not be pronounced upon her."

Then Judge Scudder, who was known to be personally opposed to the death penalty, spoke directly to Ruth Snyder in a voice so low and soft, it could barely be heard.

"The judgment of this Court is that you, Ruth Snyder, for the murder in the first degree of Albert Snyder whereof you were convicted, be, and you hereby are, sentenced to the punishment of death; and it is ordered that, within ten days after this day's session of court, the sheriff of the County of Queens deliver you, together with the warrant of this Court, to the agent and warden of the State of New York at Sing Sing, where you shall be kept in solitary confinement until the week beginning Monday, the 20th day of June 1927, and, upon some day within the week so appointed, the said agent and warden of the state prison of the State of New York, is commanded to execute and to do execution upon you, Ruth Snyder, in the mode and manner prescribed by the laws of the State of New York."

During the long recital, Ruth Snyder shifted from foot to foot, and kept one black-gloved hand on the grating. A matron placed an arm around her back, ready to catch her if she fainted, but there was no need of that. She appeared quite steady and seemed, in fact, ostentatiously unconcerned. Some observers even said she smiled at the judge.

In identical words, Judge Scudder sentenced Judd Gray to die at the same time. Judd Gray stood perfectly still, his hands clasped behind his back, his eyes studying the floor. Outwardly, he looked composed and resigned, but underneath, nausea, fear, and horror overwhelmed him.

Again, the courtroom was in chaos. Spectators stood on top of their seats, on top of radiators, and on windowsills. The court attendants ran around, shouting warnings and admonishments, pulling people down, yanking arms and legs, trying to force onlookers to a more decorous level, but once removed from their perches, the unwholesome roisterers did not return to their seats, but scampered around lewdly, pressing closer and closer to the condemned, thrusting forward with brutal jubilation.

In ten minutes it was all over, and the doomed man and woman were in the court anteroom. They would be going to Sing Sing in four days, and there they would be executed, but when Ruth Snyder was asked how she felt about her sentencing, she was quite cheerful. "This is just a formality," she was quoted in the *New York Times*. "I have just as good a chance now of going free as I had before the trial started." She told her mother, "Don't worry about me. I am capable of taking care of myself." Then she asked her jail attendants if she could be allowed to stop along the way to Sing Sing. "There is a good roadhouse I know up there. I'd like to stop for a lobster dinner."

PART III

The Aftermath

16

Parade to Death House

When the tall green gates of Queens County Jail swung open at 10:25, the morning of May 16, the crowds in the streets could not be held back. They surged in great noisy waves. The sight of Ruth Snyder's and Judd Gray's cars, hers first, then his, started the surge and then nothing but a cavalry charge could stop it. Individually, the purpose might have been simply to get a look at the lovers-who-murdered, but collectively it was to trample and destroy. No, these were not harmless curiosity seekers. They were savage and bitter, especially the women, who regarded Ruth Snyder as Germans saw Jews and Romans saw Jesus, as the appropriate outlet for every injustice and frustration known to civilization.

There was another dizzy rush at Snyder's and Gray's cars. The motorcycle sirens screamed a warning. Mounted police threatened. Nightsticks were readied. Then, a squad of police reserves charged into the mob, opening a passage.

The two cars, flanked by five motorcycles, managed to escape. Eleven cars carrying reporters from each of the city's newspapers followed. As they advanced through Queens, people swarmed into the procession's path, oblivious to the danger in their desperate need to catch a glimpse of the famous prisoners. Sounding sirens continuously, the cars crossed Queensboro Bridge at forty miles an hour, but at the Manhattan end of the bridge, more people jammed the streets, forcing the procession to a walking pace.

All along the route, people knew what was coming. On roofs, crowds leaned over the parapets. They lined the boulevards, climbed packing boxes and garbage cans, filled windows and doorways, sat on fenders and running boards, ran out of shops and vaulted fences. They made catcalls, uttered jibes, pierced the air with laughter and shrieks. Even the traffic police, who were there to keep people back, craned their necks in the hope of sighting the murderers. At one point, as the procession was slowed in traffic, the occupants of streetcars deserted their seats and rushed into the roadway, shouting, "There she goes! There she goes!"

After the caravan escaped New York City, it tried to pick up speed, but three cars broke down, two almost collided, and one of the motorcycle policemen was thrown from his seat against the car in which Ruth Snyder rode. Ruth Snyder, who saw the policeman's body fly into the air and drop, screamed and covered her eyes with her hands, but the cars bearing the condemned did not pause.

Mrs. Snyder spoke only a couple of times during the trip. After the deputy asked her if her handcuffs were too tight, she replied, dejectedly, "What difference does it make how it feels?" But when she was bidding good-bye to her prison matron, Irene Wolf, who rode with her in the car, she sounded optimistic, "I hope to see you, again. If everything goes the way

I hope, I'll be back here. And maybe when I come back, I won't be going out this way again."

As for Judd Gray, when his car pulled into the Sing Sing yard, and convicts could be seen playing baseball, the deputy to whom he was cuffed, joked, "I hope you make the team."

For an instant Judd imagined he was a freshman entering college. "Well, I used to be pretty good in school," he said. "I'd like to make the team."

Little did he suspect that his would-be teammates had already rejected him. After all, ratting on a fellow criminal—particularly a woman—was not very highly esteemed among prisoners. "The prison population had little sympathy for the man," wrote Warden Lewis E. Lawes in his memoirs, *20,000 Years in Sing Sing.* "But, unlike the outside community, there was considerable feeling for the woman. The prisoners felt, rightly or wrongly, that she should not have been sent to Death House."

On May 16, the Sing Sing population was in revolt over the quality of the institutional cuisine. This was directly traceable to Ruth Snyder and Judd Gray's arrival. "The day the condemned woman came in, the menu was pork and beans," Lawes wrote. "That day the men were under a nervous tension. A woman in Death House! And all because a man talked too freely. Their peculiar sense of chivalry was touched. It did not need much to arouse them. The beans did the trick. As luck would have it, the beans were overdone and hard as marbles. The men not only refused to eat them, but commented freely in protest. And what was more, on their return to the shops from the mess hall, they continued their agitation and, under the urgings of a few ringleaders, refused to work."

Oblivious to the disturbance they provoked, the corset salesman and his lover were led to Death

House. Officially titled the "condemned cells," but often called the "slaughterhouse," Ruth Snyder's and Judd Gray's new home was located within the prison walls, but was run as a separate institution, with its own kitchen, hospital, exercise yards, and visiting room. Completed in 1922 at a cost of nearly $300,000, it was designed as the last word in scientific, humane liquidation. Substantially larger than the old Death House—a small stone structure in which the execution chamber was adjoined to the cells, and the little green door which led to it, was always in the prisoners' view—the new structure had two wings of twelve cells each for men, and a separate wing with three cells for women. There were six more cells in the infirmary section and six cells in the pre-execution chamber to which the condemned were moved the day of their execution. That section, commonly known as the "dance hall," led directly into the execution chamber and the "ice box" or morgue.

Snyder and Gray were taken to their separate wings of Death House and never saw each other again. They were strip searched and ordered to take showers. Both were given felt slippers to wear, as ordinary shoes might conceivably be used as weapons. Then Gray was given a special prison uniform designed to be unusable in suicide by hanging, although, if the truth can be told, one such suicide had already been accomplished in Death House. Because Ruth Snyder was a woman, and the only woman prisoner at Sing Sing, she was not required to wear a uniform. Warden Lawes had purchased some house dresses for her.

Among other precautionary moves, no pencils were allowed them, only a small pen, which had to be returned as soon as they were finished using it. Snyder and Gray were permitted to write as much as they wished, but all their mail, in keeping with prison rules, was censored. They were allowed to read anything they wanted, so long as the small pieces of wire used in bindings was removed. Newspapers and magazines were collected after being read and chewing gum, one of Snyder's greatest pleasures, was forbidden—all because one prisoner had made a very formidable club out of loose magazine sheets that were bound together by Juicy Fruit.

Once or twice a week, Ruth Snyder and Judd Gray put their hands out between the bars to have their fingernails pared by the attending guard, as long nails could be used to cut the arteries of the wrist. Matches were not permitted, although Gray smoked cigarettes and cigars, which were lighted upon request by the guards. Gray was shaved with a safety razor by a prison trusty under the watchful eye of a guard.

Their meals were served through a small opening in the barred door. Knives, forks, and pepper were not allowed, and instead of ceramic dishes, they ate from soft aluminum, which was collected immediately after the meal was completed. Their cells, which were illuminated by lights located outside to prevent their being broken and used for suicidal purposes, contained a table and chair, an iron cot with a straw mattress, a pillow and blankets, a tin drinking cup, and an iron slop bucket—nothing more.

According to law, the condemned had to remain in solitary confinement except for a fifteen-minute exercise break, during which they could walk or play handball in one of the three exercise enclosures. While locked in the cell, no condemned prisoner could see another, although Gray found it possible to converse with the occupants in the cells bordering his. He even managed to play checkers with them by calling out moves corresponding to the numbered squares on a checkerboard. Gray became especially friendly with a neighbor named Charles Doran, who had been convicted of murdering the proprietor of an ice cream shop during a bungled robbery. Although Doran was a career criminal who, by his own confession, went out on holdups as casually as a chauffeur goes out hacking, he and Gray had two compelling things in common: they were condemned to die on the same date, and they were both devoted to their mothers. During his trial, Doran's mother caused quite a stir when she attacked the tipster who identified her son for the police. "You sold my boy for gold," she screamed at him. "You squealer! You skunk!"

Doran thought Judd Gray "a hell of a nice fellow." "He's very polite," he told reporters via his attorney. "He always bids me 'good night' when we're ready to go to sleep, and 'good morning' when we wake up."

That sort of sociability, obviously, was denied Ruth Snyder because she was the only prisoner in the women's wing. Awful as her isolation was, though, it served as a constant reminder of how New York State disdained executing women. It reassured her to know that only two women had ever been electrocuted in New York, the first in Sing Sing on May 20, 1899, and the second, in Auburn, on May 20, 1909. As far as Ruth Snyder was concerned, those women had committed crimes far worse than any she had been accused of—all by themselves, too. One of them, Martha Place, murdered her seventeen-year-old stepdaughter in the most sadistic, brutal fashion, throwing acid in the poor girl's face, hacking her with an ax, then finishing her off by holding a pillow over her face. As if that wasn't enough, when her husband came home, she attacked him with an ax, too, fracturing his skull. The other woman to die in the electric chair, Mary Farmer, was also an ax murderer. She smashed a neighbor lady over the head with her weapon, then locked her in a trunk while she was still alive.

Ruth Snyder was obviously not in the same category. So why was she still there, she wanted to know, waiting for the same punishment as these madwomen? Because she killed her husband? Who saw her? Who?

Granted, she let Judd Gray in the night her husband was murdered. Whyever not? She wanted to talk him out of it. Of course, she neglected to warn her husband of the threat Judd Gray posed, but why warn him, risking all that disgrace, when she thought she could convince Gray to leave? Anyone would've done the same. As for returning the window weight to Judd Gray, it was his property, wasn't it?

What was particularly unnerving to Ruth Snyder was how much had been made of the fact that her husband, Albert, carried double indemnity insurance. How many times did she have to tell everyone that that's what he wanted? It was his idea. The fact that she kept his accident policy in her own safe-deposit box meant nothing. Wasn't she the beneficiary? Didn't it make sense, from her family's standpoint, that she have direct access to his insurance in the event something happened to him?

Despite these simple truths, and despite the volumes of appeals sent to the courts, and yards upon yards of names on petitions sent to the governor urging that her death sentence be commuted, no one listened. Even the public was against her, if you believed this postcard sent to each judge on the appeals court:

Court of Appeals, Queens County,

Judges:
  We will shoot you if you let that woman Snyder go
free. She must be electrocuted. The public demands it.
If she is not done away with, other women will do the
same thing. She must be made an example of. We are
watching out.

                                          The Public

We are watching out. Who were these people? And
why were they picking on her? Weren't there enough
real murderers around, real robbers, vandals, extor-
tionists, rapists, kidnappers, counterfeiters, safecrack-
ers, seducers, embezzlers, arsonists, pickpockets, con
men, skimmers, loan sharks, those who beat wives,
stole from the poor, drank and gambled, adulterated
and poisoned, forged and deceived, without having
to single out a wife and mother?

Without question, this hostility and humiliation
were taking a toll. As the months passed, as her appeals multiplied and her execution was pushed further into the year, the last remnant of her beauty
vanished. The hair which now twined around her full
throat had gone from blond to brown and then to
gray. Her heavy hips, now badly in need of one of
Judd Gray's support garments, swayed as she walked.
And her legs, which were now divided from her feet
by a single crease, appeared to land into her slippers
without benefit of ankles. She had become fat and
frowzy.

Judd Gray seemed older, too, with a suspicion of
gray at his temples and a heaviness of body which
even his bulky prison suit could not conceal, but, unlike Ruth Snyder, he appeared at peace, almost as if
he welcomed his impending execution as the only

possible atonement for his crime. Ruth Snyder and Judd Gray were responding differently to the Death House and the passage of time. What stimulated in her rebelliousness, fury, sudden fits of sorrow and, finally, something close to chaos and madness, stimulated in him spirituality and the calm acceptance of all things. Judd Gray spent his days discussing religion with the chaplain, reading the Bible, and composing letters to his daughter, his wife, and mother, in which he struggled to define himself as a Christian who had attained purification through suffering. In death, Judd Gray had become what he only might have been in life: a saved soul. "I cannot explain the mystery of being reborn in Spirit. I can only tell you of the peace that surpasses all understanding," he wrote in his prison memoirs. "Perhaps you will say: how can a murderer expect to enter Heaven—one such as I am? Just by faith I am a new creature—just born again."

Ruth Snyder, by contrast, never ceased battling and scheming. No hot flush of shame for her. No guilty look backward. No spiritual rebirth. In the midst of collapse, depression, insane restlessness, mindless fears and furies, she went on defending herself—defending, defending, defending in a kind of endless masturbatory frenzy. Defending herself may have been a symptom of whatever malady constituted Ruth Snyder, but it was also her principal, and finally, only connection with life.

That connection was severely threatened on November 22, 1927, the day the New York Supreme Court refused to grant her a new trial, commute her sentence, or in any way delay her execution, which was now set for January 12, 1928.

To Ruth Snyder, the implication was clear: Her lawyers were incompetent, so she decided to replace them with herself. Henceforth, she would take charge of everything. What could not be accomplished by legal means, she would now try journalistically, by taking her case directly to the public. The result was *My Own True Story—So Help Me God!* which was serialized in the New York *Daily Mirror* and then published as a pamphlet selling for twenty-five cents. The *Mirror* called it an "autobiography," but it had the appearance of a schizophrenic's delirium.

If poetry, in T. S. Eliot's famous phrase, "can communicate before it is understood," then Ruth Snyder's writing could communicate before it was even read. For eight days, readers of the *Mirror* not only saw her words, they saw her smudges, squiggles, underlinings, crossings-out, announcing that passion, not logic, was driving her. Excess, exaggeration, and exuberance were her peculiar metier; hyperbole her master trope; and sudden, unexplained transitions, her signature. Perhaps no author, even in the storied realm of tabloid journalism, had ever shown such a predilection for the dash. The first sentence from her January 11th entry contained no less than five:

> Judd Gray talks!—"about the big brown bug"—
> he "put out of its misery"—does (he)—J. G.—
> ever think back of RUTH BROWN'S BUG he
> "put out of his misery?"

It seemed that Ruth Snyder's editors were permitting her to give free expression to what Freud called the primary process—the primitive, nonlogical, metaphoric and metonymic precursors of mature language. The big brown bug? What was she referring to? Was this a figure of speech or something Judd said during the trial? Could it be that Albert Snyder was "RUTH BROWN'S BUG"?

I can't conceive how any intelligent man such as J. G. will permit his conscience to be cast aside and tell his infernal lies to the outside world (in HERE he's non-plus!)

I could no more do what J. G. is than fly—It is proof positive he never loved me—only for his bestialness—he's putting before the public the same lies he told on the witness stand.

Even tho he confessed to the killing of my husband, why did the WHOLE WORLD believe EVERYTHING he told as "THE TRUTH"—I admitted "the truth" in my unlawful love affair, yet—none DID believe me when I said "I DID NOT KILL MY HUSBAND"—Why was my word doubted?—Why—because—J. G.— handed the public the same suave talk that took me completely off my feet—and fed me up on the biggest lot of bunk—(as I now can see it) yet—we POOR FOOLS, love them just the same.

At first glance, one cannot imagine a prose style more thoroughly and obstinately incoherent. Always her thoughts proceeded in disconnected snippets. Always outrage, dismay, and impatience inked her pages. Always her cries were broken by conceptual silences that opened suddenly like fissures. Yet beneath her free associations, the same painted horses always rose and fell to the same tune: I am innocent, I am innocent, I am innocent. She proclaimed her innocence over and over, day after day, like a barker at a carnival.

Of course, the world Ruth Snyder's words delineated was drawn to suit her needs: an egoist's world. She felt that beyond everything, even beyond her determination to live, an almost comfortable sensation of being in the hands of something bigger than herself. She felt an overwhelming need to sermonize, preach, instruct, warn. Wives and mothers everywhere, she proclaimed, you can learn from my mistakes. No matter how dull your husband is, no matter how powerful your temptation, don't get involved in "sinning" (her word for adultery):

> I wish a lot of women who may be sinning could come here and see what I have done for myself through sinning and maybe they would do some of the thinking I have done for months and they would be satisfied with their homes and would stop wishing for things they should try to get along without when they can't have them.
>
> Maybe there are women who have nice homes (and husbands who do the best they can for them) even if they don't like their husbands and they could bear it if they would only make up their minds everything can't be just perfect.
>
> Some husbands don't make enough money to get their wives the things they wish they had and if the wives have the brains they will just take what they can get and try to make the best of it.

Ruth Snyder's messages were: (1) It's always better to live than to die; (2) Make the best of what you have; (3) GO STRAIGHT! (4) Don't think you are GETTING BY with anything; (5) What you don't pay for here, you will pay doubly for later on; (6) Do without what you cannot buy; and (7) If you can't beat 'em, join 'em.

A final strategy. Combining her campaign against Judd Gray with her special feeling for animals, her love of her daughter, and her respect for the institution of motherhood, she turned to verse. This poem, which the *Daily Mirror* published under the title "My Baby," would not only prove to the public that "sinning" does not pay, it would show that Ruth Snyder was not sad for herself, but for those she was being unfairly forced to leave behind.

So many unkind words have been spoken,
Each with a hurt in its aim,
All over the globe they keep traveling,
Causing us sorrow and pain,

These words have crushed my dear mother,
Changed happiness to despair,
Lined her dear sweet face with more wrinkles
And added more silver to her hair.

The bowed head of my only brother
To his sister brought many a tear,
For the little this world gave
Her pleasures she's truly paid dear.

My baby, God's treasure, He gave me,
Has suffered in her innocent bliss
From a wrong befallen her mother,
Who longs to have her kiss.

Only you who have scattered these words
Know well they are untrue;
Still you keep sending more along,
Not knowing when they'll return to you.

You've blackened and besmeared a mother,
Once a man's plaything—A toy—
What have you gained by all you've said,
And has it—brought you Joy?

And the hours when "Babe" needed my love,
You've seen fit to send me away—
I'm going to God's home in heaven,
Ne'er more my feet to stray.

Someday—we'll all meet together,
Happy and smiling again,
Far above this earthly span
Everlastingly in his reign.

Ruth Snyder, to be sure, had no literary future. Nothing she wrote was ever read, except as a curiosity, but if she was not privileged to make a lasting contribution to American letters, she remains a figure in its mythology. It is her reality in this sense that makes her cries from the Death House still meaningful to us. For she proved the old belief that the bad woman and the "oversexed" woman are the same, and the new one, that a woman who murders may be indistinguishable from an ordinary housewife and mother.

17

Death Watch

Sing Sing Prison was a mile from the town of Ossining, and the building nearest the main gate was a ramshackle, abandoned hot dog stand. Though the hot dog stand was scarcely larger than a hen coop, it was the nearest place to install a telegraph wire to flash the news of the execution back to the city desk.

A dignified-looking stranger, one of the reporters who had recently descended on the town, went to see the owner. "Fifty dollars for the night," was the ultimatum. The reporter argued, then refused.

That was January 9, three days before the execution.

On January 11, with one day to go, the reporter went back to the hot dog stand, inspected it gravely, exchanged a few words with the owner, then reported back to headquarters that "wire facilities had been secured."

Because a "good" electrocution could sell as many papers as a presidential election, and more than a World Series game, Ruth Snyder's and Judd Gray's "death watch" surpassed even their trial as a source of journalistic frenzy. Reporters devoured Ossining.

Phones in buildings near the prison were being leased for as much as a dollar a minute. One conveniently located saloon was appropriated as the host of several dozen telegraph wires and a detachment of operators. Impromptu news bureaus were set up in private homes, barber shops, pool halls; every hotel and ramshackle inn in the village was occupied, cellar, attic, and porch.

All the star reporters were there, all the news services in place. The only problem was the dearth of legitimate news. This was partly due to the fact that no one, save family members and attorneys, was permitted to see the condemned; journalists were even denied permission to enter the Death House. Also, Warden Lawes, being a man more concerned with the psychology of his prisoners than their publicity, refused to give the press daily briefings, unless, of course, there was some change in plans, which there wasn't. He didn't even allow members of the fourth estate to use prison phones—including the pay phone in his antechamber.

Reporters' only recourse, it seemed, was the "pipe story."

One of the tabloids scooped its rivals by publishing a story under the headline RUTH ASKS SILKEN SHROUD. According to the story, Ruth Snyder's most urgent wish was to die in silk, specifically, the black silk dress she wore so often at the house parties she attended with her husband. "She is sick of the coarse, cotton and gingham clothing that was issued to her by the state, and silk—even though a shroud—will be a welcome change." As an afterthought, the reporter noted that Ruth Snyder was also petitioning the warden for permission to wear to her death the black silk lingerie kept in her mother's cedar chest.

There was also a story that originated in an Ossining taxi cab. The driver overheard one reporter tell another, "We ought to start a rumor that Mrs. Snyder's mother is dead. She's the only one the boys haven't killed off yet." When those same reporters returned from lunch, they were informed by their jubilant peers that they had just received the "straight tip" that Ruth Snyder's mother had just died of sorrow.

Another fictional piece described how Ruth Snyder, in a desperate attempt to escape the punishment imposed by the state, tried to kill herself by banging her head against her cell's walls. Its author was responsible for a daily story datelined "Death House, Sing Sing," so labeled despite the fact that he had visited Ossining only twice in the fortnight preceding Snyder's and Gray's execution, and on the latter occasion, came no closer to the prison than a convivial saloon a half mile away.

Still another piece in the prison-suicide, cheat-the-state genre purported to uncover a plot to smuggle poison to Ruth Snyder in the Death House. The smuggling worked this way. After Mrs. Brown, Ruth Snyder's accomplice, visited her daughter, she would ask for permission to use the washroom. The unsuspecting matron, of course, would grant permission. Mrs. Brown would then secrete the contraband in the washroom, which Ruth Snyder would visit later in the day, on her way back from the exercise yard. Mrs. Snyder would then swallow the poison in the privacy of her cell.

Altogether, one might say that the newspapers managed to cook up some pretty good stories given their slender resources. Before the death knell sounded on Ruth Snyder and Judd Gray, newspaper readers were provided the most vivid descriptions of the condemned pair's prayers and dreams, fears and

forebodings, sleep patterns and digestive disturbances, their most private rituals and personal confessions—all without benefit of direct observations or
interviews.

In addition, there were countless stories about that
triumph of modern technology, the electric chair.
This was, after all, the age of the gadget, and the
electric chair was the supreme gadget. Each of its
parts was worshipfully described, from the rubber
padding that covered the seat and headrest, to the
leather straps that fastened the condemned, one at
each ankle, at the upper and lower arms, and at the
chest and waist.

The electric chair, readers learned, was a misno-
mer. No wires were attached to it. The wires connected instead onto the cathodes embedded in the
concrete floor, with the terminal at the side of the
chair.

It was true, they were told, that Ruth Snyder would
wear special apparel to the chair, but instead of silken
lingerie, she (and her lover) would don a black
leather mask extending from the forehead to just be-
low the mouth, with openings for the eyes and nos-
trils. Its purpose was not simply aesthetic; the mask
was fastened to the back of the chair to hold the head
immobile.

Readers were apprised of how the electricity would
be conducted to the prisoners' heads (through a special cap filled with steel wool and soaked in saltwater);
how the current would be applied—two jolts: first a
high voltage for a few seconds to stun, then a low
voltage for a longer period to guarantee the result;
and how death would be determined. Two attendants
would open the clothing, exposing the chest, which
they would wipe with a towel. Then the doctor would
apply the stethoscope to listen for heartbeats, and

either signal for another jolt, or turn to the witnesses and say, "I pronounce this man (or woman) dead!"

Readers were told not to expect prison lights to flicker word of the execution to the other prisoners. That was changed several years ago when the dynamo furnishing current to the death chair was dissociated from the general lighting system. Readers were also told that Ruth Snyder and Judd Gray would not suffer. Contrary to common belief, electrocution was absolutely painless. As proof, the *Daily News* interviewed a physician who claimed to have talked to a man who died of electric shock, but recovered consciousness for a few minutes, long enough for him to tell the doctor, "I was sensible from the moment I touched the wire and never suffered pain. I'm feeling a little numb now, but all right."

"The execution atmosphere is not one of horror," a reporter reassured his readers, "so much as one of solemnity. Witnesses file into the death chamber and take seats at pews—just like those in a church—in the right near corner from the entrance, facing the chair located in the middle of the room, several feet from the rear wall."

The journalistic spotlight also turned on the executioner. Dubbed the "Grim Avenger" and the "Aristocrat of the Death Room," the man scheduled to dispatch Ruth Snyder and Judd Gray, Robert Greene Elliott, was the most mythic of American executioners. Already famous for an execution he had supervised six months earlier—a double execution involving a shoe factory worker named Sacco and a fish peddler named Vanzetti—Robert Greene Elliott had at his disposal a precious asset: the physiognomy of an executioner. It was a fine physiognomy, which clearly showed all the signs of executionship: waxen complexion, cadaverous cheeks, overgrown eyebrows, gimlet eyes, all made complete by the businesslike simplicity and intelligibility of his role. Elliott was not responsible for the mechanics of the chair, nor was he supposed to do anything to or for the bodies. His duty was simply to pull the fatal switch.

There are people who think executions are ignoble news, but executions, as the coverage of Ruth Snyder and Judd Gray showed, are not news, they are spectacle, whose props, costumes, settings, and performers (the chair, the mask, the execution room, the visage of Robert Greene Elliott) converge to make everything about death exaggeratedly visible. Which explains why the men and women who ordinarily bought one morning paper got them all; why even the slightest uncertainty that they had gleaned every detail, sent them back for the evening editions and the extras. For the pleasure of Ruth Snyder's and Judd Gray's execution was not about delivering these murderers from this world to the next—it was about the perfection of iconography. More than a sadistic ritual, it was a visible one.

When January 12, execution night, finally arrived, it wasn't enough to imagine Ruth Snyder's and Judd Gray's execution, people had to view it. By eight P.M., the air was filled with the ribald shouts of curiosity seekers marching to the southern boundaries of Ossining, where the prison was, in the vague hopes of catching a glimpse of something—of anything. One might have thought they were in a parade, the way the crowd kept moving in carousel fashion around the four guards stationed at the gate. Eager to the point of frenzy, they were shouting, tussling, munching on sandwiches, conducting impromptu sparring matches, exchanging witticisms that were as coarse and mirthless as a gob of phlegm. "She'll be fricasseed chicken pretty soon," said a respectable-looking man. "Well, they pay for their fun tonight," offered a man with a kidney-shaped head and waxed mustaches. "I always say that if there was more of this sort of punishment, there'd be less goings-on," a woman added.

Some of the women brought children, despite the lateness of the hour. Dizzy, cranky, slumberous, they wailed, "Mama, I wanna see." Boys climbed on each other's shoulders to get a better view. Young men shinnied up tree trunks, strangely fascinated by whatever part of the prison they could sight.

Yet here and there, leaning against cars, sitting on running boards, were quiet figures, far less animated than the rest. They stared at the Hudson River with its floating cakes of ice, at the square yellow prison workshops that looked like inverted cardboard boxes, and at the lonely, darkened Sing Sing baseball field bordered by telegraph poles, railroad tracks, and empty bleachers. These were the reporters whose job it was to signal, by means of flares, the precise moment of Ruth Snyder's and Judd Gray's execution.

They didn't have long to wait.

18

Dead!

At eleven o'clock, the door to the execution room swung open and Ruth Snyder stood there wearing a brown smock and dark green skirt. Her hair hung wet and straight, as though she had just combed it. It was brushed back to cover a bald spot clipped by the prison barber to make a place for the electrode. Her feet were in carpet slippers and her stockings were rolled down. She looked small and disheveled.

The first thing that struck Mrs. Snyder when she entered the execution room was its brightness. The room was white, and its silver-gilt pipes and radiators glaring. Then she saw the faces. Twenty-four witnesses, packed in four church benches borrowed from the prison chapel, looked on. Physicians and attendants lined the walls. They were motionless and speechless, the only sound in the room coming from the whine and rattle of the radiators.

She stood quite still as everyone studied her face, now swollen from crying. Her eyes had taken on a wild, zealous cast. They were preternaturally alert, lynxlike, but her mouth was shuddering.

Two matrons had a hand under each of her armpits, supporting her. Her body seemed to have become limp and shrunken; but while her knees sagged, she walked until well inside the room, when she sighted the chair itself.

Then she broke. There was no other way to describe it. High, shaking shrieks came from out of her mouth. Then tearing, rasping hiccoughs caught in her throat. Her eyes rolled with wet whiteness, like the eyes of someone going into a grand mal seizure. It seemed for a moment that she would tear and run, but the matrons held firm, and she was dropped like a bundle into the broad oak seat.

The guards fastened the straps. The wire-mesh electrode was pressed against her new bald spot. Another was nestled against her right calf. It was when the buckles were being fastened that her breathing slowed, slowed, then caught abruptly as if on a hook, and finally vented itself in one more howling scream.

"Jesus, have mercy on me!"

As the black leather mask was being fitted over her face, she was sobbing steadily, panting like a dog. Her last words were barely audible. "Father, forgive them, for they know not what they do."

At that moment, a newspaper photographer readied a tiny camera specially built for the occasion. Cameras were forbidden in the execution room, but this one was smuggled in. The photographer, falsely representing himself as a reporter, had it strapped to his ankle. Seated in the front row with his trouser legs crossed, he raised his trouser cuff, aimed, and placed his finger on the plunger in his pocket.

In a voice so low that the witnesses could not hear, the priest read the prayer of consolation from the Catholic service for the dying. Then the matrons retired and the executioner stepped to his post in an alcove containing the switches.

Warden Lawes gave a slight signal and Elliott jammed up the switch. Ruth Snyder's body heaved forward, straining against the straps. One leg, the stocking rolled down to the ankle to allow for the adjustment of the electrodes, twitched convulsively and swelled.

Then the photographer snapped his forbidden picture.

Except for the clattering radiator and a slight crackle which twice came from the power feeding the chair, the room was quiet. Ages seemed to pass. The current had been on two minutes when the warden gave another signal. The switch was turned off and the body suddenly relaxed.

Attendants hurriedly unfastened the straps. Ruth Snyder's blouse was opened and a physician stepped forward, applying his stethoscope. "I pronounce this woman dead," he said, and then stepped back to his stand, opposite the warden, facing the door through which Judd Gray was to come.

Two white-coated attendants removed Ruth Snyder's body. They undid the straps, rolled a white enamel stretcher to the chair's side, and lifted Ruth Snyder's body onto it. One of her hands dangled as she was wheeled to the autopsy room, as though to say good-bye.

Then the door swung open again and Judd Gray came in between two prison attendants. He was dressed in gray trousers and a white shirt open at the neck. His body was not limp, as Ruth Snyder's had been. Instead, he stood stiffly erect, his teeth set, his lips drawn back, and his eyes wide open. Sweat literally ran down his face, and he was repeating "Blessed are they that . . . ," after the clergymen. He was afraid, deathly afraid, but fighting it.

He entered the room briskly, without the support

of his guards, but the glare of the room and the number of witnesses seemed to take him by surprise. Tears sprang to his eyes. He brushed them away quickly, shaking his head as if shaking off a memory, and looked at the witnesses. Something like diffidence or embarrassment seemed to seize him for a moment, but hearing the cool voice of the clergymen reciting the Beatitudes seemed to help him gain control. Judd Gray repeated the first line of each after the clergyman.

"Blessed are the pure in spirit," he exclaimed, as he placed himself in the chair.

"Blessed are they that mourn," said the clergyman.

"For they shall be comforted," said Gray, in a loud unnatural voice, holding himself tense and seeming to overcome his terror by an exercise of will.

Again, the guards went about their buckling. One strapped his chest, another his arms, another his legs. His left trouser leg was rolled back to apply the electrode. Another electrode was perched well back on his curly black hair, and the mask pulled over his face.

"Blessed are the merciful," he shouted after the clergyman. As he cried out, the attendants had difficulty in adjusting the black leather mask. Gray noticed it, paused and held his chin in such a way as to facilitate their work—one last display of his extraordinary obligingness.

Gray kept his eyes on the clergyman to the last. After the mask had been adjusted he continued to recite the Beatitudes. Then, as the clergyman changed to the Lord's Prayer, Gray began rapidly to repeat it.

The executioner then stepped quickly into his alcove and placed his hand on the switch. Warden Lawes nodded.

Smoke went up from the rolled trouser leg above the electrode. The current was on for nearly three minutes before a signal was given to stop. "I pronounce this man dead," said the physician.

And so he was executed.

No black flag was mounted from the turrets of the prison, no official signal came. But when a reporter leaped onto the running board of a car, screaming for the crowd to open way, crying excitedly, "They're dead!" people got the message. More reporters dashed to their cars, several photographers dusted powder in their flash guns, and laughter and shouting broke through the cold silence of the prison like a trombone in a cathedral.

Someone yelled, "It's over! It's over!" with hoarse, uninhibited abandon. The din rose and bloomed into something jagged and ugly. Then slowly it receded. People's energy faded, and the crowd broke up and went home, no doubt planning to read the newspapers the following day, to gaze with horror and fascination at the photograph of Ruth Snyder in the chair, the current surging through her body.

19

Resurrection

That should have ended Ruth Snyder's story, but three days later, the *New York Times* published details of a scheme to bring her back to life. One of her lawyers, the *Times* solemnly averred, tried to take possession of her body and revitalize it by injecting adrenaline into her heart. The prison, naturally, refused.

Whether this scheme was ever seriously contemplated seems doubtful, but Ruth Snyder and her lover, Judd Gray, were destined to have an even more surprising resurrection. Without hesitation or ambiguity, and fully mindful of the role played by such writers as James M. Cain, Raymond Chandler, and Billy Wilder, I state that Ruth Snyder and Judd Gray, dead more than a dozen years before *Double Indemnity* (director Billy Wilder, 1944) and *The Postman Always Rings Twice* (director Tay Garnett, 1946) were produced, were the most important figures in those films. *Double Indemnity* and *Postman* gave Ruth Snyder and Judd Gray new life, preserving them for all time.

Those films tell essentially the same story: a decent, ordinary-appearing male becomes fascinated with a

dominating and scheming woman. With her providing the sexual lure, and him taking care of the details,
they kill her much older, dreary husband. In both
films, the victim has an enormous insurance policy,
and in both the lovers turn against each other after
they commit murder.

In addition, what Snyder-Gray brought to these
films, through the characterization of Albert Snyder
as murderee, was the idea that sometimes a murder
victim may be seeking his own death—indeed, sometimes his right to live may be compromised by selfish,
controlling, loutish behavior.

The first Hollywood version of *Postman* showed that
what finally convinced Cora (Lana Turner) to murder
her husband was not her passion for her lover/accom-
plice, Frank Chambers (John Garfield), but her horror of her husband/father, Nick Smith. Nick pushed
Cora over the edge when he announced, apropos of
nothing, that he planned on selling her beloved diner.
They would then move in with his sister, who was completely paralyzed.

"Oh, she's going to live for a long time yet," Nick
explained. "But she needs us to take care of her, especially you, a woman."

When Cora protested the unfairness of this one-
sided decision, Nick's response was simple and to the
point. "Too bad," he said, the smile hovering about
his eyes signaling triumph and sadistic delight. He
made it clear to Cora, in that one moment, that he
intended to torture her until she murdered him.

We see the same thing in *Double Indemnity*. In the
relatively brief scene introducing Phyllis Dietrichson's husband, the murder victim (played by Tom
Powers, an actor known for playing unsympathetic,
authority figures) appeared brutal, domineering,
and gratuitously mean. Just as Mrs. Josephine Brown

depicted her son-in-law, Albert Snyder, as a murder victim for whom death represents the culmination of a strictly ordered system of poetic justice, Dietrichson appeared here as a murderee par excellence, someone begging to be slaughtered.

The scene opens with Walter Neff (Fred MacMurray) trying to convince Dietrichson of the advantages of buying accident insurance.

"I suppose you realize, Mr. Dietrichson, that not being an employee you're not covered by the State Compensation Act. . . ."

"Yeah, I know all about that," Dietrichson growls. "The next thing you'll tell me is that I need earthquake insurance, and lightning insurance, and hail insurance."

At this point his wife, Phyllis (Barbara Stanwyck), who is in the room, tries to remove any doubt that this insurance sale is on the up and up by appearing to support her husband's desire to reject the accident policy: "If we bought all the insurance they could think of," she says in her most saccharine voice, "we'd stay broke paying it, wouldn't we, honey?"

As repayment for her support, Dietrichson insults her in front of the insurance man: "What keeps us broke," he sneers, "is you going out and buying five hats at a crack."

By the end of this scene, any moral hesitancy that Neff or Phyllis or we, as spectators, have about his murder, has been removed. Dietrichson, we see, is nothing more than an egotistical loudmouth.

The scene ends with Neff attempting to have Dietrichson sign two forms, one of which is blank.

"Sign twice, huh?" says the grumpy client.

"Yes. One is the agent's copy. I need it for my files."

"Files, duplicates, triplicates," Dietrichson complains as he signs the forms, unbeknownst to himself, authorizing his own death. Till that moment he was just an obsolete killjoy; now, with his signature on the phony form, he has become a $100,000 bank account.

In Ruth Snyder's variation of this scam, she asked her husband to sign three insurance forms which she claimed were all the same—each, according to her, worth only $1,000. The second, however, was really for $5,000, and the third, for $45,000, with a double-indemnity clause that would bring Albert Snyder's net worth as a dead man to $96,000, providing he died a violent death. She had the insurance man tell the hapless Snyder that the extra copies were "for the file." The insurance man agreed to go along with her, no doubt, because she was giving him an extraordinarily large sale. As her mother told reporters, Ruth had to take $20 each week from her household budget to pay the insurance premiums. Ruth Snyder also arranged to have the mailman deliver all correspondence between herself and the insurance company directly into her hands. The policy itself was kept in a safety-deposit box under the name Ruth Brown. Albert Snyder never knew a thing.

Here are some more similarities:

Just as Ruth Snyder complained that her husband "was not companionable to me at all," that he just "liked to stick around the house," so Phyllis Dietrichson said her husband would just "sit around all evening and never say a word." Where Ruth Snyder claimed she and her husband "quarreled quite frequently about the accounting for the money he gave me," Phyllis Dietrichson whined that "every time I buy a dress or a pair of shoes, he yells his head off, he never let's me go anywhere, he keeps me shut up, he's always mean to me."

Ruth Snyder: "I was constantly being belittled by

my husband . . . he was constantly picking and nagging at me and I had gotten to the stage where I would take any means to get out of it all. I could not divorce him."

Phyllis Dietrichson: "He keeps me on a leash so tight I can't breathe. . . . I hate him, I loathe going back to him. . . . I can't stand it any longer."

In the same way that Phyllis Dietrichson told all her marital problems to her lover and partner in crime, Walter Neff, Ruth Snyder confessed that "Mr. Gray was the only one who would listen to my troubles. During the time that I have known Mr. Gray, I have told him more and more of the trouble with my husband. Things became unbearable and I was looking for a way out."

Like Judd Gray, *Double Indemnity*'s Walter Neff tried to resist, but simply couldn't refuse his lover anything. "I fought [the idea of murder], but I guess I didn't fight it hard enough." And like the police inspector, Arthur A. Carey, who questioned Ruth Snyder in real life, the investigator (Edward G. Robinson) who questioned Phyllis Dietrichson in *Double Indemnity* knew that a grieving widow who stands to gain $100,000 on her husband's death can't be on the up and up.

Even the ruse used to make Cora (Lana Turner) confess in *The Postman Always Rings Twice*—telling her that her lover had already revealed everything—came from Snyder-Gray.

But perhaps because Ruth Snyder's reality was sometimes too peculiar to be believed, the heroines she inspired did not always live up to her record of mayhem. For example, Cora in *Postman* made only one unsuccessful attempt to kill her husband—hitting him over the head while he was taking a bath—before settling on a murder method that worked.

Phyllis Dietrichson may have weighed the benefits of carbon monoxide poisoning, another one of Ruth Snyder's techniques, but her musings did not develop beyond the fantasy stage. As she told Walter Neff, "The other night we drove home from a party, he was drunk again. When we drove into the garage, he just sat there with his head on the wheel and the motor still running, and I thought what it would be like if I didn't switch it off . . . just closed the garage doors and left him there."

Another interesting difference between *The Postman Always Rings Twice* and Snyder-Gray concerned the behavior of the principals immediately following the murder. In *Postman*, after the adulterous couple kill the husband, they are overcome by raw lust. As narrated in the novel by Frank Chambers,

> I began to fool with her blouse, to bust the buttons, so that she could look banged up. She was looking at me, and her eyes didn't look blue, they looked black. I could feel her breath coming fast. Then it stopped, and she leaned real close to me.
> "Rip me! Rip me!"
> I ripped her. I shoved my hand in her blouse and jerked. She was wide open, from her throat to her belly.

Every New York City newspaper, including the *New York Times*, reported that after Ruth Snyder and Judd Gray strangled Albert Snyder, they made passionate love in her mother's room—"for more than an hour, in sight of the murdered husband's body," according to the *Herald-Tribune*. Where this story originated, and how it was disseminated, is a complete mystery. Nothing Ruth Snyder or Judd Gray said suggested they did anything of the sort. The important point, though, is that this piece of journalistic fantasy found its way into James Cain's novel. Where the actual events of Snyder-Gray failed to inspire, its mythology filled in.

Roy Hoopes, Cain's biographer, said that Cain was quite open about his debt to Snyder-Gray. According to Hoopes, when he first heard of this case, he immediately saw it as a solution to a problem he had been working on for some time. "That jells the idea I've had for just such a story," Cain exclaimed, on learning that after the murder Ruth Snyder gave Judd Gray a flask of whiskey laced with poison. "A couple of jerks who discover that a murder, though dreadful enough morally, can be a love story, too, but then wake up to discover that once they've pulled the thing off, no two people can share this terrible secret and live on the same earth. They turn on each other, as Ruth and Judd did."

The Snyder-Gray story appealed to Cain because it moves so gracefully from tension to resolution, and enfolds within its basically simple structure two most gripping themes—greed and adultery leading to their just reward. Every film noir buff is familiar with this plot structure. In these films, a femme fatale lures/tempts/seduces the hero to commit a crime (usually a murder) against a second man to whom she is unhappily or unwillingly attached (usually her husband or lover), with the final result that all three (the femme fatale, the hero, and her husband or lover) are destroyed, either literally or metaphorically. In addition to *Double Indemnity* and *The Postman Always Rings Twice*, examples include *Out of the Past* (Jacques Tourneur, 1947), *Human Desire* (Fritz Lang, 1954), *The Woman in the Window* (Lang, 1944), *Scarlet Street* (Lang, 1945), *Pitfall* (Andre de Toth, 1948), *The*

Killers (Robert Siodmak, 1946), *Criss Cross* (Siodmak, 1949), *The Locket* (John Brahm, 1946), *The Lady from Shanghai* (Orson Welles, 1948), *The File on Thelma Jordon* (Siodmak, 1949), *The Woman on Pier 13* (Robert Stevenson, 1950), *Where Danger Lives* (John Farrow, 1950), and *Angel Face* (Otto Preminger, 1953).

We should also mention the more recent remakes of *Double Indemnity* and *Postman.* The former, called *Body Heat* (Lawrence Kasdan, 1981), starred Kathleen Turner and William Hurt and the latter, still titled *The Postman Always Rings Twice* (Bob Rafelson, 1981) starred Jack Nicholson and Jessica Lange. Other recent, though somewhat more distant relatives of Snyder-Gray include *Blood Simple* (Joel Coen, 1984), *Red Rock West* (John Dahl, 1993), *The Last Seduction* (Dahl, 1994), and *To Die For* (Gus Van Sant, 1995).

In some of these films, as in *Scarlet Street,* there is a direct reference to the Snyder-Gray murder (Edward G. Robinson opens a newspaper and reads aloud to his hateful wife, as a sort of warning, the story of a spouse in Queens who was murdered with a window weight), but more frequently the incorporation of Snyder-Gray is implicitly ingrained within the atmosphere, story elements, and motivational logic of the film narrative. Instead of the incidents of a film's scenario coming directly from Ruth Snyder's and Judd Gray's lives, they revealed or suggested their personalities, conflicts, and moral struggles.

What Ruth Snyder and Judd Gray did for the movies was help them acknowledge the antiromantic possibility that nice, ordinary, God-fearing men could be adulterers and killers, too. We see this most vividly in *The Woman in the Window,* a film that had the curious distinction of having been written and produced by a journalist (Nunnally Johnson) who covered Snyder-

Gray for the *New York Post*. In this film, as in Snyder-Gray, a stalwart, law-abiding member of the middle-class—the last person in the world one would ever suspect of murder—is drawn to kill another man because of his involvement with an attractive woman. Richard Wanley (Edward G. Robinson) meets the woman, Alice Reed (Joan Bennett) while his wife and children were out of town, on vacation. She invites him up to her apartment—a fantasy come true for this middle-aged professor, but it is a dangerous fantasy, because just as Wanley and this woman are getting comfortable with each other, in walks Alice Reed's lover. He flies into a jealous rage, throws himself on Wanley, choking him furiously. At the point of being strangled to death, Wanley reaches out and grabs a pair of scissors offered by Alice Reed. He stabs his assailant again and again, killing him. Wanley then attempts to hide the body and conceal his culpability.

What is uniquely similar to Snyder-Gray, apart from the basic plot structure of murder and adultery, is the way both Gray and Wanley appeared to avoid detection at the same time that they seemed to needlessly squander their anonymity. Both wanted to efface all traces of their crime, yet both were gripped by an impulse growing more and more intense, to expose their secret before the world and free themselves from their terrible burden.

For example, as Wanley drives out of the city with the dead body in the backseat of the car, he comes to a toll booth, but instead of coming to a complete stop as he should, he hands the dime to the attendant while the car is still moving. The money drops to the road. The attendant yells, "Hold it. Come back here." Wanley stops his car and offers another dime, but, evoking Gray's nickel tip of the cab driver, the dime turns out to be a penny. By this time, of course, the attendant (who happens to be a policeman) has already had several opportunities to fix Wanley in his memory.

Wanley's compulsion to expose himself is clearest in the scenes in which he deliberately informed the D.A. and the detective in charge of the homicide investigation that he had the very sort of cut on his wrist they believed the murderer had. Wanley tells the D.A., "I'll give you an opportunity to impress the whole city." Then he holds up his wounded wrist. "Does this suggest anything?" he asks coyly. Irresistibly drawn to undermine his innocent appearance, yet, paradoxically, tireless in his efforts to construct defenses and deflect suspicion, Wanley, like Gray, appears to be two people: one who confesses and one who lies, a victim ridden with guilt and a manipulator who uses every means available to preserve his life and dignity.

Fritz Lang, the director of *The Woman in the Window*, attributed Richard Wanley's behavior to the *deus-ex-machina* dream. His adventure, viewers were told, wasn't real; the whole thing took place in his sleep. But Judd Gray's adventure was quite different. It may have felt more illusory—more baffling and grotesque—than anything Wanley experienced, but it did not allow for sudden awakenings. It took place when his eyes were open, and could not be interrupted by any alarm clock. He was trapped within that most awful prison—a consciousness in which even the possibility of self-understanding had been suspended. He was so estranged from his own feelings, that they might have belonged to another man.

How Hollywood got the idea of mining Snyder-Gray is easy enough to figure. Never before had the battle of the sexes been so noisy, so mean and empty of sense. Never before had adultery appeared so sleazily middle class. The spectacle of two lovers-turned-murderers trying to throw one another to the lions and then trying to climb out of the arena with their reputations unscathed, would sell tickets in any medium. Cheap sex, a murder, arrests, grillings, alibis, confessions, a trial, red hot details, close-ups of faces in tortured, yet silent, cries of pain—it was pre-eminently commercial.

In addition, the principals, despite all the harm they caused, possessed a certain likable, and very American, ingenuousness. Not only did Ruth Snyder and Judd Gray entertain very little esteem for meditation, they never indulged in it. They did not merely distrust ideas, they seemed incapable of having any. Their world was composed entirely of facts, external detail, bodies and things, trivia, and chitchat. At critical moments in their story, one looked for observations from them on what they were doing and what it all meant, and nothing, literally nothing, was forthcoming—no understanding of the future, no reflections on how they or others might be affected, neither insight nor the refusal of it. Everything was on the surface.

Which explains why their story was so engaging—such complete, absolute inability to think was touching. Also why their language possessed a certain crude vitality—it was so stark, so linear, so two-dimensional. Call them dumb if you like, but the world their words described was a marvelous caricature. They simplified everything. Even when they lied, as they often did, their lies had no labyrinthine passages and secret, spiral stairways; they were straight to the point, clear, American lies. As Nunnally Johnson, who wrote and produced *The Woman in the Window,* expressed it, "It was a grand show. It never failed once. It had no surprises, no theater guild stuff, no modernisms. It was good old stuff done well and fiercely. It was grim and grand. It moved slowly and inevitably, like Dreiser. And it came at last, last night, to the magnificent, the tremendous, the incomparable curtain that everybody was counting on [he is referring to their executions]. Everybody walked out with a satisfied feeling. It was regular" (*New York Post*, January 13, 1928).

But before anyone in Hollywood thought about making a movie about adultery and murder in which the lead characters are ordinary types "caught in their own schemes like ants in honey," the New York *Daily News* and *Mirror* (along with their full-size cousins, the *New York Post*, *World*, and *Herald-Tribune*) had already turned Ruth Snyder and Judd Gray into the journalistic equivalent of folk heroes. They accomplished this by making the most personal details of their lives public knowledge. Before their trial was over, everyone knew about Snyder's and Gray's favorite dishes, the names of their grandparents, the number of affairs each one had, even the hygienic and prophylactic accoutrements they used.

Journalists made the public believe that Snyder and Gray were different from other people—sexier, greedier, more tragic. Journalists selected, highlighted, and even manufactured parts of their story to demonstrate that these two belonged to a separate order of being—more real, more thrilling, more authentic. At the same time, risking contradiction, journalists showed that Ruth Snyder and Judd Gray were the sort of people everyone could understand. They showed that these stars had much the same values, attitudes, and life styles as everyone else, that they were superlatively normal, grand in their typicality.

That journalists were successful—inordinately successful—can hardly be questioned. Jumps in newspaper circulation proved it, with afternoon papers
alone selling out from five to eight editions daily. As
Hendrik Willem Van Loon quipped in *The New Yorker,*
"at least 70,000 square miles of forest had to be cut
down to make enough wood pulp for the use of the
tabloids and legitimate papers" to sustain their of
coverage of "such an orgy of killing as the world has
never seen since the days of Nero and Catherine de
Medici."

Visiting British peers, Broadway playwrights, and
Hollywood luminaries, such as D. W. Griffith and
Natacha Rambova (famous for once being married
to Rudolph Valentino), were hired as "trained seals"
by newspapers in their desperate rivalry to capture
readers. Often posing as detectives, long-lost friends,
and distant relatives, squads of reporters were recruited to expose every detail of Ruth Snyder's and
Judd Gray's amour, soliciting opinions from anyone
who might know something of the matter. In their
investigative zeal, reporters journeyed to the far corners of Queens and New Jersey, to visit the former
homes of Snyder and Gray, so that everything not
nailed down outside (and, frequently, inside) their
houses was examined or carried off. One reporter
even went to Judd Gray's daughter's school and demanded that she be delivered into his custody. Another reporter and cameraman, more zealous than
the rest, staged a twenty-four-hour vigil outside a convent school on the suspicion that Ruth Snyder's
daughter, Lorraine, was concealed there, and might
be spirited away by a rival newspaper for a photograph. As a tribute to Ruth Snyder's appeal, one

group of creative newspapermen staged a gathering, in the Sheep Meadow of Prospect Park, of forty men who claimed to have proposed marriage to Ruth while she was in prison. "I have studied the situation thoroughly," The *New York Post* quoted one of her admirers. "Ruth is a much misunderstood girl. At heart she is just a mother—a bit rough at times, but still a mother."

So hysterical was the atmosphere surrounding their trial that police reserves had to be called out to control the crowds. In the courtroom itself, one of the largest in New York State, spectators fought so violently to get in, that many were injured in the suffocating jam. As the *Daily News* reported, "Women's clothes were ripped and torn. Women's shins were bruised. Women's corns were crushed. Women's purses were stolen. . . . Ruthless Ruth was having her day and the ladies and gentlemen who had come to see her were determined to go through brick and iron and stone and police as if they were disembodied spirits."

None of this excitement was lost on moviemakers. Not only did Hollywood bigwigs such as D. W. Griffith journey to New York to see the trial of the unfaithful housewife named Snyder and the corset salesman named Gray, but several New York journalists, such as Nunnally Johnson, Ben Hecht, and Mark Hellinger, traveled in the other direction, going to Hollywood to later make movies about deceptive, but irresistible women who use men's desire first to control, and then to destroy them. Most important, no doubt, James Cain gave up his position at the New York *World* to grind out novels, and later screenplays, which showed how sexual attraction can easily lead to obsession and murder.

One can of course raise several doubts about Snyder-Gray's influence. The most obvious is the substantial time lag between Snyder-Gray and the first film noir. If the Snyder-Gray case came to the public's attention in 1927, why did *Double Indemnity* wait till 1944, and *The Postman Always Rings Twice* till 1946, before making it to the screen?

The answer is simple. They were suppressed. The movie rights to *The Postman Always Rings Twice* were purchased by M-G-M in 1934, but the Hays Commission, the agency responsible for keeping smut off the screen, ruled that the themes of murder and long-term, unrepentant adultery central to *Postman* would be inappropriate for the general public. In other words, Snyder-Gray was kept off the screen during the 1930s by an explicit system of censorship.

The big breakthrough occurred in 1943 when the Hays office finally sanctioned a treatment of *Double Indemnity*. The film created a sensation. "Never before in American film," wrote Foster Hirsch in *The Dark Side of the Screen*, "had a female character been presented so devoid of softening touches, and never before had death and sex been linked so explicitly and powerfully." For the next few years films featuring adultery and murder were literally falling off studio assembly lines, all made with the understanding that these celebrations of eros and thanatos would contain no explicit sexual or perverse sequences. This meant that the steamiest parts of Cain's *Postman*—for example, where Cora moans "Bite me! Bite me!" as Frank sinks his teeth into her lips and feels "the blood spurt into [his] mouth"—had to be left out of the movie. So the film did not have Cora telling Frank, when she is pregnant, "My breasts feel so big, and I want you to kiss them. Pretty soon my belly is going to get big, and I'll love that, and want everybody to see it." In fact, M-G-M promised the Hays commission that "all scenes of physical contact—hugging and kissing—between Frank and Cora" would be omitted. Their lust would only be suggested.

Such concessions are usually sure signs of artificial, superficial moviemaking—bad art. But in this instance, censorship had its compensations, because it forced moviemakers to be a bit more subtle. For example, Cora's "Bite me! Bite me!" was replaced with symbolic representations of desire such as the MAN WANTED sign in the opening shots and a close-up of a hamburger on the grill, the sizzling meat supposedly telegraphing sexual arousal. But more importantly, as a result of censorship, the relationship between Cora and Frank was no longer simply about raw lust. Censorship, by forcing the repression of sexuality, set the boundary conditions for a relationship that was also about fear, hostility, and obsession. There can be little doubt that the aura of doom and entrapment so closely identified with film noir, specifically its sense of hopeless, damned sexuality, would never have been articulated so convincingly and consistently in these films if it were not for working conditions which forbade overt sexual expression.

It is also important to note that although James Cain claimed that Ruth Snyder and Judd Gray inspired his novels, his novels and their stories diverged in one central way—in Cain's portrayal of uninhibited, unrepressed male desire. Judd Gray, unlike Cain's heroes, was always weak, fearful, shamefaced. He worried about everything. We don't associate this sort of anxiety with the hero of Cain's *Double Indemnity* largely because the novel unfolded in real time, progressively and chronologically. Cain's hero may have been doomed, but he didn't know it. Because his fate was kept hidden till the end of the book, his cockiness could be accepted at face value, plausible and nonironic; readers could always entertain some hope for him—they could always imagine that his story might end happily. But in the film version, no such hope was possible. Walter Neff (played by Fred MacMurray) was introduced to us as a wounded, dying man. Because the movie was told in flashback, everything was already over when the story began. Neff's narration, like Judd Gray's confession, was no more than the record of sins that had already been committed.

That the film version of *Double Indemnity* feels more like Judd Gray's story than Cain's original novel is probably not accidental. Although Billy Wilder, the director of *Double Indemnity*, was in Europe when the Snyder-Gray case broke in 1927, he was a passionate collector of stories of murderers and great criminals, and knew that the framework for Cain's *Double Indemnity* came from the real events of Ruth Snyder's and Judd Gray's lives. In this regard, we should note that the ending Wilder originally planned for *Double Indemnity* (and actually shot but never used) followed the Snyder-Gray storyline much more literally than Cain's novel. That ending was quite similar to the one used in *Postman*, where the hero was last seen in prison preparing to walk to the gas chamber. But whereas in *Postman* the gas chamber was never seen, in *Double Indemnity*, or at least in the proposed version, not only did we see the hero in the gas chamber, we saw the pellets drop and clouds of gas obscure the chamber windows.

Of course, films such as *Double Indemnity* did not become distinctive genre pictures solely because they contained certain types of scenes and plot structures. *Double Indemnity* and other film noir are famous for a range of visual elements: expressionistically harsh lighting contrasts; jarring, off-balance shot compositions; deep shadows; and tight close-ups. Here we should note one of the most obvious yet least acknowledged origins of film noir: these movies' visual style was borrowed from the art work of tabloid journalism. One has only to glance at the photographs and illustrations accompanying news accounts of Snyder-Gray to see the same deep shadows, the same tight-framing and close-ups associated with film noir.

What we see, in addition to shadows and claustrophobic spaces, is an obsessive preoccupation with the femme fatale's face. In the same way that Orson Welles studied Rita Hayworth's face in *Lady from Shanghai* and Billy Wilder studied Barbara Stanwyck's in *Double Indemnity*, tabloid journalists constituted Ruth Snyder's face as the supreme sign of truth, as the single key that could unlock the secret of her crime.

Photographs and drawings were therefore not only used to transform Ruth Snyder's face into a spectacle, into something gigantic and otherworldly, they were used to explain her, to give her depth and complexity. They were used to suggest the existence of something beneath the surface: subjectivity, motivation, guilt; to show not only the fact of the crime, but why the criminals committed it; and not only the fact of their guilt, but their awareness of it.

No denying it, the story of the young wife, the gloomy older husband, and the other, younger man, is one of the most common in literature. Which leaves us wondering what precisely Snyder-Gray offered the public. What was the source of its appeal? Where did this well-worn story get its power?

Not from its uniqueness, that much is sure. Not from the fact that it enacted the time-bound experience of individuals. Rather, its appeal came from the representation of a universal pattern. Judd Gray's pet name for Ruth Snyder—he called her "Momie"—is a dead giveaway. Consider also that Gray's nickname was "Bud," and Albert Snyder's was "The Governor." These functioned as "threshold images," signals for spectators to begin looking for a moral, and to begin thinking allegorically. The allegory of course is *Oedipus*, the story of a child destined to murder his father and marry his mother, but who could not, no matter how good a man he eventually became, free himself of his fate and understand his actions.

What Ruth Snyder and Judd Gray accomplished was to translate this allegory into everyday language. After all, these two were not glamorous, well educated, or particularly physically attractive. Apart from the fact that they committed murder, they had no distinguishing traits. They were conventional in the extreme, if such a thing is possible. And that is precisely why the public was so fascinated: that people so much like themselves could become, for a certain time, not only adulterers and murderers, but the object of an entire allegorical elaboration, in which fate overtakes free will, the incest taboo is broken and the father/husband slain. Here at last was a translatable—indeed, self-translating—version of *Oedipus*. Snyder and Gray not only performed that drama in street clothes, they narrated each movement, labeled each act, they made continual commentary on their own text.

To be sure, this murder story had very little suspense in it. Because Ruth Snyder's confession occurred almost at the precise moment her crime was made public, there was never any question of "Who done it." If in classic detective fiction, the criminal exists to be captured, then Snyder-Gray turned that formula upside down. It replaced the question of *who* with the questions of *how* and *why*. It transformed the spectator's identification as well. Instead of reading this story from the point of view of some law enforcement personnel, say the police or Sherlock Holmes, and identifying with their need to solve the crime, Snyder-Gray offered a crime that was already solved and then constructed suspense around the questions of how and why the criminals did it. Now spectators had to see the crime through the eyes of the criminals, an effect which was inescapable due to the fact that Snyder's and Gray's motives were uncovered, for the most part, not through clever detective work, not by carefully piecing together a body of evidence— fingerprints, weapons, witnesses—but through minute attention to what the guilty parties said. In other words, the truth of their crime was published in a series of protracted, voluntary unburdenings. Almost the entire Snyder-Gray story was told in flashback, with Ruth Snyder and Judd Gray as voice-over narrators.

Snyder-Gray may very well be the model for film noir, not only as a junction of major themes—the femme fatale (Ruth Snyder), the weak hero (Judd Gray), and the murdered husband/father (Albert)— but as an inspiration of the noir "confessional mode" in which the plot is driven by the protagonist's voice.

Consider the way *Double Indemnity* begins. We see a car hurtling down the street. It barely misses a collision. Then, all of a sudden, the action stops. The car parks slowly and quietly in front of an office building. A stooped, huddled figure emerges from the car and signals to the building's maintenance man to let him in. The maintenance man tries, without any luck, to engage him in friendly banter. It's obvious that Neff is not going to do any chatting. He's preoccupied.

We finally understand what the source of his preoccupation is when he gets to his desk. He wipes his brow, takes out a cigarette, lights it, draws deeply, then uncovers his dictaphone. What he needs to do, we see, is confess—or, as he prefers, set the record straight. His face dripping with sweat, he begins to speak. For the next two minutes the camera is fixed on his face. The only movement we see comes from his lips. The movie has become text.

"You want to know who killed Dietrichson? Hold tight to that cheap cigar of yours, Keyes. I killed Dietrichson. Me, Walter Neff, insurance man, thirty-five-years old, unmarried, no visible scars, till a while ago that is.

"Yes, I killed him, killed him for the money and for a woman. I didn't get the money and I didn't get the woman. Pretty, isn't it . . . ?

"It all began last May or around the end of May it was . . ."

What *Double Indemnity* owes to Snyder-Gray is not merely the insurance scam, the oedipal triangle, the ambiance of darkness, seediness, and solitude; it owes to Snyder-Gray the foregrounding of text over action. Snyder-Gray made us aware of the murderer's words. More, this case made us aware of the very process by which a murderer frames past events, signifying not only the action, but the meaning of the action. Ruth Snyder's and Judd Gray's words, and the images connected to them, provided privileged access to their consciousness, to a landscape of emotional agony and intellectual squalor far more vivid and detailed than anything that could be conveyed through classical, third-person narrative. What the confessional structure of their story offered, in other words, was a sense of direct access to the murderer's inner world.

Film scholar Christine Gledhill's description of "the plot of the typical film noir . . . as a struggle between different voices for control over the telling of the story" seems particularly appropriate for the Snyder-Gray case. For each voice—Ruth Snyder's and Judd Gray's—continuously aimed to cancel the other out. And in doing so, they forced spectators to take sides, to take an active role in deciding whose version of events was the true one. There was thus no lazy following of plot for plot's sake in Snyder-Gray. Indeed, anyone who attempted to sort out its multiple, interconnected confessions became aware of the participatory nature of this story—that it was the spectator who created the meaning of Ruth Snyder's and Judd Gray's crime.

How did Snyder-Gray manage to have such a profound influence on the movie industry in the 1940s and early 1950s? By showing how it is possible to tell stories which do not unfold from a linear, third-person or "objective" vantage. By showing how sex can lead to murder, and murder leads to sex. And by submerging the conventional question of who did what to whom in favor of these much more profound psychological questions: Can the confessors sort out, order, and locate meaning in events that have already occurred? Can we, as spectators, understand the motives and desires hidden behind their obscure and often contradictory accounts? And can we understand characters who find it excruciatingly difficult to translate memory into articulate speech, who find it almost impossible to distinguish between their thoughts and their experience—in short, characters whose ability to live and act in the world is so limited, they are in fact doomed?

The key here is that by borrowing from the Snyder-Gray story, Hollywood was doing more than learning how to push a few hot buttons for its audience. It was learning how to tell stories of extraordinary psychological complexity, in which characters appear to exist within whirlpools of subjective overdetermination, where there is no final difference between the real and imagined, and events are characterized chiefly by their want of form, direction, and idea.

How fitting that it should be a characteristically American art form that found something inspiring in Ruth Snyder and Judd Gray. Only America could have turned such outrageous and inscrutable characters into celebrities, and only film could have made us believe in their dreamlike world. Thanks to the movies, these two are still with us, forever affirming sexuality's terrible power to destroy.

HORRIFYING TRUE CRIME
FROM PINNACLE BOOKS

From the Files of
True Detective
Magazine